MW00337047

# INFRAPOLITICAL PASSAGES

# Infrapolitical Passages

**GLOBAL TURMOIL, NARCO-ACCUMULATION,
AND THE POST-SOVEREIGN STATE**

*Gareth Williams*

FORDHAM UNIVERSITY PRESS    NEW YORK 2021

Copyright © 2021 Fordham University Press

All rights reserved. No part of this publication may be reproduced, stored in a retrieval system, or transmitted in any form or by any means — electronic, mechanical, photocopy, recording, or any other — except for brief quotations in printed reviews, without the prior permission of the publisher.

Fordham University Press has no responsibility for the persistence or accuracy of URLs for external or third-party Internet websites referred to in this publication and does not guarantee that any content on such websites is, or will remain, accurate or appropriate.

Fordham University Press also publishes its books in a variety of electronic formats. Some content that appears in print may not be available in electronic books.

Visit us online at www.fordhampress.com.

Library of Congress Control Number: 2020919022.

Printed in the United States of America

23 22 21    5 4 3 2 1

First edition

*for Elena and Carlos, because we laugh*

*for Cristina, for everything since October 1986*

# Contents

And they did build vast trophies, instruments
Of murder, human bones, barbaric gold,
Skins torn from living men, and towers of skulls
With sightless holes gazing on blinder heaven,
Mitres, and crowns, and brazen chariots stained
With blood, and scrolls of mystic wickedness,
The sanguine codes of venerable crime.

— PERCY BYSSHE SHELLEY


Turning and turning in the widening gyre
The falcon cannot hear the falconer;
Things fall apart; the centre cannot hold;
Mere anarchy is loosed upon the world,
The blood-dimmed tide is loosed, and everywhere
The ceremony of innocence is drowned;
The best lack all conviction, while the worst
Are full of passionate intensity.

— W. B. YEATS


But the new barbarian is no uncouth
Desert-dweller; he does not emerge
From fir forests; factories bred him;
Corporate companies, college towns
Mothered his mind, and many journals
Backed his beliefs.

— W. H. AUDEN


To think is to linger on the conditions in which one is living, to linger
on the site where we live. Thus to think is a privilege of that epoch
which is ours, provided that the essential fragility of the sovereign
referents becomes evident to it. This assigns to philosophy, or to
whatever takes its place, the task of showing the tragic condition
beneath all principled constructions.

— REINER SCHÜRMANN


New ears for the new music. New eyes for the most distant things.

— FRIEDRICH NIETZSCHE

# Exordium
*Extinction and Everyday Infrapolitics*

> Did you hear what I just said? Is my English OK? Is the microphone
> on? Because I'm beginning to wonder.
>
> —GRETA THUNBERG, "YOU DID NOT ACT IN TIME"

This book proposes to clear a way through some of the dominant conceptual determinations and violent symptoms of globalization, to make a case for the "infrapolitical" as a thinking and acting to come. For this reason, while still at a preliminary detachment from the principal corpus of this work, I begin by offering the reader a brief illustration of the innermost relation between infrapolitics and the everyday language of contemporary turmoil, anxiety, and disquiet.[1] The Introduction that ensues from this *exordium* will then offer a more comprehensive account of recent debates around the importance and relevance of infrapolitical thinking for our times.

What follows, then, is merely one initial example among countless others, since the *infrapolitical* only ever registers and strives to account for the most quotidian of sayings and experiences, while doing so in their most uncanny proximity and estrangement. The preliminary illustration of the contemporary infrapolitical, then, is the following.

In the context of the "Extinction Rebellion," which occupied and disrupted the streets of central London for more than a week in April 2019, the then sixteen-year-old Greta Thunberg stood in public before a microphone, admonished the political classes for having failed, and wondered out loud whether she was isolated in public, speaking in the absence of all interlocution, or whether her words actually touched upon a *commonality* of some sort, thereby staging the very question of the proximity to, and of the distance from, the existence of a social bond. It was not the first time she had embraced the classical form of *parrhesia*, and it will most likely not be the last.[2]

In Thunberg's public interventions the politics of contemporary global capital is portrayed as a race to the bottom of reason itself, played out in the wake of the subordination of all thinking and living to the economized relation between means and ends, a relation that, thanks to the overall mastery of contemporary technicity, has brought humanity and the planet to the threshold of potential existential collapse. We can discern that for the young Swede political, economic, technological, and historical business as usual merely serves to conceal the underlying and ongoing question of existence and, as such, of *Being*.

In order to get the point across that what is needed is a passage toward alternative ways of thinking and acting, Thunberg renders the previously inconspicuous conspicuous by placing the routine political calculations internal to capitalism in another light, reconverting the familiarity and ordinariness of *home*, for example, into the unfamiliar ground of an existential conflagration: "I don't want your hope. . . . I want you to panic. . . . I want you to act as if the house is on fire, because it is," as she said at Davos in January 2019. The simplicity of her formulations indicates a potentially complex hermeneutic operation: She simultaneously upholds a figurative order of experience ("I want you to act as if the house is on fire") and immediately destroys the legitimacy of the figuration itself ("because it is"), thereby imploring that the political classes quit storytelling and get real for once. She overturns the apparently commonplace and the insignificant (the signifier "house") by daring to place the question of extinction — and therefore of finitude and death — at the heart of contemporary concerns. Thunberg does not address such ontological questions explicitly. Rather, they are implicit in her overall concern as part and parcel of everything she communicates at such moments. They are at the heart of the distress she voices as she unveils the political, or at least the neoliberal politics of global resource extraction extended in the name of accumulation at all costs, as the only form of life available to humanity, as the active concealment and oblivion of all fundamental existential concerns.

Of course, entire communities throughout the world have been saying exactly the same thing for decades but were never allowed access to Davos or central London. But that is a slightly different, though no less significant, question. What is noteworthy for us now is that through Thunberg's perception, language, and persona we encounter the two intertwined registers not of the political but of what precedes and underlies it, namely, the "infrapolitical." The first register is sociological and everyday (or *ontic*). But this *everyday* is also precisely the place where the second register is posited and, in its positing, breached from within, uncovering in the process an *ontological* relation to the question of *Being* (of *ek-sistence*) itself.

In his 1947 "Letter on Humanism," Martin Heidegger recuperated Aristotle's *De partibus animalium* in relation to a tale told regarding the philosopher Heraclitus: "The story is told of something Heraclitus said to some strangers who wanted to come visit him. Having arrived, they saw him warming himself at a stove. Surprised, they stood there in consternation — above all because he encouraged them, the astounded ones, and called to them to come in, with the words, 'For here too the gods are present'" (Aristotle, quoted in Heidegger, 269–70). For Heidegger Heraclitus is telling his visitors that "'even here,' at the stove, in that ordinary place where every thing and every circumstance, each deed and thought is intimate and commonplace, that is, familiar, 'even there' in the sphere of the familiar . . . it is the case that 'the gods come to presence'" (270). For Heidegger the most familiar, ordinary, and commonplace (that is, the ontic) is the very dwelling place of the question of Being. But, Heidegger asks, "can we obtain from such knowledge directives that can be readily applied to our active lives?" (272). The answer is no: Such knowledge is not necessarily conducive to any particular form of act or order of decision, since it "is neither theoretical nor practical. It comes to pass before this distinction. Such thinking is, insofar as it is, recollection of being and nothing else. . . . Such thinking has no result. It has no effect. It satisfies its essence in that it is. But it is by saying its matter. . . . For it lets being — be" (272).

Similarly, in the specific context of Greta Thunberg's concern for the question of the place of human dwelling expressed at the Extinction Rebellion of 2019 and elsewhere, we merely encounter an a-principial, infrapolitical recollection of being and nothing else, little more than a call, by saying its matter, to let being be in a way that it is not being allowed to be. This call extends itself along two simultaneous and adjoining transmissions, which together comprise the touch or trace of the infrapolitical register in thinking. Allow me to explain more explicitly.

1. Thunberg is, like me and most likely like you the reader, neither a politician nor a Philosopher and, like everybody else on a daily basis, is not political to the extent that she speaks neither entirely nor exclusively from within the calculations of the technical relation between means, ends, subjects, and specific processes of political subjectification. In other words, aside from the fact that she does not have the right to vote, she does not "do politics," and her discourse is not subordinated to any preordained ideological principle, grammar, belief system, or conceptual origin (*arche*). Neither does this mean, however, that she is or that her words are depoliticized, apolitical, postpolit-

ical, biopolitical, or merely unthoughtful. Her words, while certainly unpretentious sayings, are more than mere *doxa*, since against doxa she upholds at all times the contemporary *episteme* of climate science, which, it must be said, is not necessarily independent from the contemporary global technocracy that reigns supreme in its myriad forms of calculation, instrumentalization, and value extraction. But perhaps more significant at this point is the fact that Thunberg insists on safeguarding in her words a distance from all reigning forms of political calculation and power brokering. She does this in order to speak freely, in such a way as to tell a few home truths about the epoch that is ours and about the community of beings that dwell in it, existing fully estranged from it. If it were not for that incalculable yet most commonplace distance from political calculation, which is, however, a distance that only ever *touches upon* the ambit of every political calculation, she would be just another bureaucrat of the given, just another political "talking head," media, or university subject in search of reinstating or of finding a way to live just a little more comfortably in the shadow of a given and fully accepted master discourse. But at this point in her life Thunberg steers clear of anticipating a new master, sovereign power, reparative metaphor, unifying world picture, thetic order, or specific "way of life." She does not offer a healing or promise of any kind, merely a distance that nevertheless touches upon the political from afar. This distant yet most intimate touch is what makes her words infrapolitical rather than political per se. She is not interested in the technicalities of any particular form of belonging in contrast to others or in defining or advancing the essence of a particular form of community. Like so many who have come before her and who have been ignored or disposed of accordingly, she merely implores that we as beings lend an ear and take a decision in light of existence and in the face of an increasingly conspicuous finality of sorts. The distance that is marked so necessarily by Thunberg offers not the parameters or conditions of a specific political hegemony, counterhegemony, subjectivity, process of subjectification, or essence of community for the future but merely the democratic language of an underlying nonconformity that she extends before the practitioners of a politics that only ever administers (and with increasing force and increasing impunity) the means of global value extraction and, therefore, ultimately of devastation. For this reason, the "Extinction Rebellion," which cannot be considered to be explicitly "Marxist" in either formation or performativity, is nevertheless a street-level injunction against the translation of life into the social codes of commodification alone. In an era in which the ontology of the commodity form has saturated all recognizable forms of life and death, the "Extinction Rebellion" is an act sustained from within an infrahegemonic, or infrapolitical, register.[3] A turn toward the underlying postulation of *existence* is required, Thunberg suggests, in such a way as to concern itself with the relation between human and world. She merely asks that we let this turn come and that we do so by showing, and sustaining, a concern for the *beingness* of beings. This is a concern regarding the ruin wreaked by climate breakdown, certainly, but presumably it must also pass through the question of fundamental ontology, that is, through the question of the *Being* of human being. This would no longer be just a question of specific ways or concepts of life folded into the political, such as the conceptualization of the distinction between ordered social life and biological life, of *bios* and *zoe*, but of that which precedes both: that is, an infrapolitical thinking in light of the question of *Being*. Whether such a thing is possible is only ever an open question, dependent upon what Jean-Luc Nancy has referred to as a "decision of existence," an order of decision that is incompatible with the metaphysical principle of subjective certainty and all the common forms of politics that accompany it.

2. This leads us to the second, less explicit yet perhaps no less urgent register that underlies Greta Thunberg's words regarding the reality and politics of climate breakdown specifically but that also gives voice to the ontological concern for whether home, or human dwelling, could one day indicate something other than the brutal place for the absolutist commodification, and therefore objectification, of the living. The ontological presupposition in Thunberg's concerns — which is essentially a concern for the inheritance of technologically driven death production — leads us inevitably back in the direction of Martin Heidegger's reservations regarding Jean Beaufret's query to him in the wake of World War II: "How can we restore meaning to the word 'humanism'?" ("Letter," 241). Heidegger's response is that in the face of the technicity of reason, of what it brings to presence for thinking and the ways it goes about doing so, perhaps it is best not to restore but to learn to relinquish every facet of humanist metaphysics: "This question proceeds from your intention to retain the word 'humanism.' I wonder whether that is necessary. *Or is the damage caused by all such terms* still not sufficiently obvious?" (241). The industrialized atrocity of *world war*, in other words, was for Heidegger a humanism to the extent that it was a military *reduction* of the subjectification and objectification of humanity, of what it meant *to be* human, unleashed from within the modern telos of planetary technology. The damage Heidegger refers to is that of a "state of affairs in which language under the domination of the modern metaphysics of subjectivity almost irremediably falls out of its element. Language still denies us its essence: that it is the house of the truth of being. Instead, language surrenders itself to our mere

willing and trafficking as an instrument of domination over beings" (243). The current state of affairs shows us that while the topographies of technological domination and exploitation have shifted drastically in recent decades, little if anything has changed in the apparent limitlessness of the planetary expansion and mastery of *techne*. Like the vast majority of us, Greta Thunberg is clearly not Heideggerian. There is no reason for her to be, and Heidegger would most likely be as concerned with climate science as he was with the metaphysics and instrumentalization of *techne* in general. But for now, that is a slightly different matter. Having said that, Thunberg's words can certainly be considered an illusionless response to the subordination of all social language to the modern politics of will and subjectivity, which now, more than ever, comes to the fore as a destructive instrument of economic and existential command over beings and over the planet they inhabit. Neither is Greta Thunberg a Marxist, and she most likely cares little for the historical difference between "Left" and "Right." From within the legitimacy of her concern, however, she clearly appears to call for a transformative inception of sorts or at least for a clearing away of obstacles in current thinking and acting that might allow for such a thing. Paraphrasing Heidegger in the wake of World War II, learning to relinquish the metaphysics of humanism just might be an invitation to consider how one can perceive and think in such a way that we let *being* in its mortality, rather than in its technological reproduction as everyday humanist subjectivism and planetary destruction, *be*. If "thinking acts insofar as it thinks" and "lets itself be claimed by being so that it can say the truth of being," and if "thinking accomplishes this letting" (Heidegger, "Letter," 239), then perhaps we can conjecture that Thunberg's unannounced yet primary concern is with the potential accomplishment of a thinking and acting that *allows itself to be claimed by Being*. Such a thinking might be entirely *other than* what we have, and indeed it might be what we have never had, but if it were to come into view at the threshold that is our common lot, it might come to dwell within the language of being in the same way "clouds are the clouds of the sky" (276). Such might be the conceptual urgency that touches upon the existential finitude that has been announced with utmost clarity by this adolescent of the post–Cold War and post-9/11 world. In his prominent 1946 essay, Heidegger observes that "the talk about the house of being is not the transfer of the image 'house' onto being" (272). In other words, it is not merely a question of translating the ontic into the ontological and have done with it in the name of achieving specific and practical knowledge regarding Being and acting. Rather, it is a matter of clearing a way for thinking and for positing the question of acting via the uncanny relation of the two transmissions in question, that is, being-with as the ontological difference between, say, the turmoil of planetary extinction and the most intimate, familiar, and commonplace, such as warming oneself by the stove or the unembellished expressions of an unpolitical adolescent. But such a perception and thinking, for Heidegger at least, can only be preparatory: "One day we will, by thinking the essence of being in a way appropriate to its matter, more readily be able to think what 'house' and 'dwelling' are" (272). On numerous occasions Thunberg has told the political and economic powers that be that they did not act in time, that it is too late, that the Enlightenment *ratio* by which they have existed and by which they still insist on existing—that is, the willful assertion of the positing power of subjectivity—is catastrophic, since therein *ending* is fashioned and manufactured internally to the technocratic calculations of domination rather than being what merely comes to pass to the living in their being. In the wake of the events of 1968, Jacques Lacan said something strikingly similar regarding the destructive force of what he called *the capitalist discourse*. It is too late, he said. Herein lies the urgency of demarcating an infrapolitical passage to let *being* say its matter, in such a way as to let the ontological difference (or *ek-sistence*) be, at a distance from the forms of life generated and determined by the political.

These two intertwined transmissions of the infrapolitical register in thinking and saying—the everyday *ontic*, or sociological, *distance from* the modern metaphysics of subjectivity and the technical calculations of sovereignty, in conjunction with that distance's simultaneous *touch upon* a *thinking of being* uncaptured by the ontology of commodity fetishism—are the point of departure for *Infrapolitical Passages*.

This is not, however, a work about climate collapse or the Anthropocene specifically. It is, rather, a modest invitation to consider just some of the sociohistorical consequences and conceptual passages that might yet remain, as "inconspicuous furrows in language" (276), after having passed a historical and conceptual limit or point of no return (that is, global capital as the "total subsumption" [Balibar, "Towards a New Critique of Political Economy"] of all forms of human and planetary life). It is this passing that concerns us now in the form of capital opened up fully to the extinction that it has always carried within itself.

My insistence on referencing Martin Heidegger writing, responding to, and essentially using Jean Beaufret in the wake of World War II, and this in the context of Greta Thunberg's speech on climate breakdown and the threshold of existential collapse at the Extinction Rebellion in April 2019, is not happenstance. After all, the point of mediation between the two instances is what Jacques Derrida referred to in 2005 as the concept "of the 'world' or of the end of a world (in globalization [*mondialisation*] and in *world war*), and especially that of 'war,' a wholly other end of war that we are perhaps living at this very moment, an end of war, the end of the very concept of war, of the European concept, the juridical concept, of war (of every war: war between nation-states, civil war, and even what [Carl] Schmitt calls 'partisan war'" (*Rogues*, 123). In the 1930s Heidegger had already referenced the dilemma in question as "the disappearance of the distinction between war and peace," adding that as a result "nothing remains any longer in which the hitherto accustomed world of humankind could be salvaged; nothing of what has gone before offers itself as something that could still be erected as a goal for the accustomed self-securing of human beings" (*The History of Beyng*, 154).

This leads us to the second point of mediation between the two instances and languages in question, namely, the question of intellectual responsibility in the face of globalization as a tumultuous *world of war*, as much as in *world war*. It is, of course, well documented how despicably Heidegger fared in this regard.[4] On the other hand, it is precisely the end of the juridical concept of war that upholds the relation between the end of *world war*, the planetary devastation of the present under the auspices of a *world of endemic war*, infrapolitical actions such as those of the Extinction Rebellion, and the everyday language of Greta Thunberg and of millions of others.

For Derrida, in his incessant distancing from Heidegger's Nazi commitment, the stakes and responsibility unveiled by the end of the concept of war "appear inseparable, in fact, from the future of reason, that is, of philosophy, everywhere that the concepts of international law, nation-state sovereignty, or sovereignty in general, tremble from this tremor that is so confusedly called "globalization" [*mondialisation*])" (*Rogues*, 124).[5] Likewise, *Infrapolitical Passages* is an attempt to contribute, from within the neoliberal university, which is as deficient in this regard as it was in the 1930s, to the question of the inseparable relation between existence, responsibility, and the future of reason. The extent to which this endeavor fails or succeeds is an entirely different matter.

# Introduction

The horse of thought . . . that imagines itself for a while to be the one that pulls the stagecoach of history, all of a sudden rears up, runs wild, then falls down.

— JACQUES LACAN, *Anxiety*

Here too corruption spreads its peculiar and emphatic odours
And Life lurks, evil, out of its epoch.

— W. H. AUDEN AND CHRISTOPHER ISHERWOOD,
*The Dog Beneath the Skin*

Every designation is already a step toward interpretation. Perhaps we need to retrace this step again.

— MARTIN HEIDEGGER, *Nietzsche*, VOL. 4

All scientific and commonsense indicators suggest that for some time now we have been taking leave of, or bidding farewell in somnambulistic fashion to, the conceptual and institutional legacies of the modern. Faith in the relation between the modern production of wealth in the form of commodity fetishism, capitalist development, human progress, the freedom of the subject, and the philosophy of history that has anchored all of them since the Enlightenment is succumbing before a generalized sense of expiration and of growing stupefaction. It is becoming patently clear that people of all political and nonpolitical persuasions now have to confront the fact that progress "can no longer serve as the standard by which to evaluate the disastrously rapid change-processes we have let loose," as Hannah Arendt put it back in 1972 (*Crises of the Republic*, 132).

Almost half a century later Alain Badiou has echoed Arendt's concerns. In *The True Life* (2017), the philosopher of the *communist hypothesis* observes that "everybody talks about 'the crisis' today. People sometimes think it's the crisis of modern finance capitalism. But it's not. Not at all! Capitalism is expanding rapidly all over the world" (30). For Badiou the current predicament is the direct consequence of the contemporary world having accomplished the full consummation of modernity's "abandonment of tradition." This definitive relinquishment, he says, is provoking a gigantic and irresistible collapse in humanity's symbolic organization, in which the mandate to "Live with this Idea and no other" of traditional society has been overrun by that of the contemporary mandate to "Live without any Ideas" (86). This immediate diagnosis is worthy of further consideration, for here an invisible historical limit has been passed, and in the face of constant variation and flux, rather than in the movement of a specific orientation, Badiou laments the fact that "we don't know what the positive side of this destruction or negation is" (28).

This reference to the positive side of our times is where our questioning begins. Badiou suggests that our only legitimate task is to struggle against the finitude and perplexity — against the uneasy sense of a *perishing* — that the crossing of a certain limit appears to have brought into full view but that remains beyond any definitive meaningfulness, representation, and therefore understanding. Contrary to every attendant understanding of finitude, Badiou proposes the extension and application of a new directive principle — the *true life*, communist militancy, the subjectivation of a new subjectivity — which he strives to bolster and legitimize as the definitive Platonic solution to the current historical and social predicament. Something strikingly similar occurs in his book *The Rebirth of History: Times of Riots and Uprisings* (2012), in which he seeks to attend to the significance of the so-called Arab Spring of 2011. Here Badiou opens his reflection by giving voice to an inaugural sense of anxiety:

> What is going on? Of what are we the half-fascinated, half-devastated witnesses? The continuation, at all costs, of a weary world? A salutary crisis of that world, racked by its victorious expansion? The end of that world? The advent of a different world? What is happening to us in the early years of the century — something that would appear not to have any clear name in any accepted language? (1)

What is at stake in the opening lines of *The Rebirth of History* is the determination of a question for the meaningfulness of contemporary social upheaval. This leads to the question of how to conceptualize collective action in a "weary world" in which any transitional time appears to have succumbed in the face of a relation of utter indeterminacy between "end," "continuation," and "advent," a phenomenon that indicates that our age, which is no longer that of modern Revolution, is characterized by an increasing inability to distinguish clearly between eschatology and the entire planetary infrastructure of capitalist development, or value extraction.

Having said that, the title of Badiou's 2012 work indicates that he seeks nothing less than the definitive closure of the exhaustion of significations and the subordination of all thinking to the expediency of that closure, the conditions and determinations of which the author has already decided upon. Just for a minute, Badiou invites us to linger on the tragic condition of the contemporary as an incommensurable theoretical and practical experience of expropriation and abandonment. However, his point of departure is also that we get over that condition immediately and move in the direction of the commencement of a *new* political story, toward the manufacturing of a *new* epochality, of a *new* empowerment and uniformity of value guided by "the urgency of a reformulated ideological principle, a powerful idea, a pivotal hypothesis . . . a new figure of organization and hence of politics. So that the political day which follows the reawakening of History is likewise a new day. So that tomorrow is genuinely different from today" (42). For this reason, *rebirth* and the *closure* of the "weary world" are not only synonyms in Badiou's questions regarding "what is going on" but appear to be absolutely necessary preconditions for pulling the shutters down definitively over the anxiety that had produced the question regarding contemporary turmoil in the first place. "This is the state of historical, political, and existential disarray in which we find ourselves; *now get over it!*" Badiou seems to want to say in *The Rebirth of History*. What the book uncovers, therefore, is the fact that *anxiety* — "What is going on? Of what are we the half-fascinated, half-devastated witnesses?" — should be actively concealed when considering contemporary patterns of political action and social turmoil. Badiou seeks to inhibit the movement of disarray, demise, and collapse via the rediscovery and extension of doctrinal militancy.[1]

There is certainly much with which to concur in Badiou's political analysis of the contemporary, which is for the most part resolute and incisive. However, his categorization of the prepolitical forms of contemporary *riot* and *uprising* (immediate riot, latent riot, and historical riot) are entirely predetermined in terms of their relation to a transitional understanding of history and to the current absence of a countercapitalist Idea (21).[2] His gestures toward the (in)existence of those who find themselves *in* but not *of* the fallen world of globalization are fundamental to our understanding of the question of *riot* now, though these gestures remain essentially anthropological in their deployment because they are grounded largely in *doxa*.[3]

But it is in relation to the question of epochality and to the absolute suture of the contemporary phenomenon of riot not only to the demand for a process of subjectification grounded in doctrinal fidelity to the "Idea" — the "communist hypothesis" — but also to an unmovable principle of historical predetermination that *The Rebirth of History* raises questions. Indeed, this is the case to such a degree that the self-confident pronouncement that *"riot is the guardian of the history of emancipation in intervallic periods"* (41) ends up resonating like an article of faith manufactured to guarantee the closure of the anxiety that had opened up the question of the contemporary in the first place, while in the process also grounding the subjectification of the subject as the sole placeholder of meaningfulness and sense-making throughout modern and contemporary history.

How, then, does Badiou reckon with time in such a way as to go about manufacturing the rebirth of history? In this endeavor, the question of the "intervallic period" becomes central. The "intervallic period" is a specific locus in time akin to the transitional time and experience of the *interregnum*. However, it applies not to the death of a certain form of sovereignty but to a latent protosovereign form for the future:

> What is an intervallic period? It is what comes *after* a period in which the revolutionary conception of political action has been sufficiently clarified that, notwithstanding the ferocious internal struggles punctuating its development, it is explicitly presented as an alternative to the dominant world, and on this basis has secured massive, disciplined support. In an intervallic period, by contrast, the revolutionary idea of the preceding period . . . is dormant. (38–39)

The "intervallic" is a moment of latency in the history of modern representational consciousness, and, as a period of latency (rather than as negativity), it is a moment imbued with a pregnant *now* that exists solely in function of, and is therefore subordinated to, that which is inevitably yet to come, which is another selfsame "now." The primacy of the future is anchored by the intervallic period. As such, what is at stake in the passage from "now" to "now" is the closure, via a humanist historicism that places time within a "real" space of empirical existence, of each and any indeterminacy that might underlie the conceptual or historical relation between "continuation," "end," and "advent." For this reason, the communist Idea is also the name — the assigned locale or "thereness" — of a supposedly new sovereign Age, of a new name and onto-theological ground of Being.

When the "intervallic," or the interregnal, is applied retroactively to time there is no need for the recognition of a state of collapse and equally no need for anxiety. All that is needed is the reaffirmation of the *cogito* and its will to orient thinking and action back in the direction of a future transcendence.[4] "The Idea," in the form of the subjective decision for it (for *Idea* in Badiou refers to the *visibilization* of the militant will in its being, in its essence as will to power, and therefore as the thinking of everything as value, valuation, and representedness) returns in the form of a historical negation of historical negation. In this sense, thanks to the intervallic as a period of historical latency, *cogito* and subjective will alone offer the tools for the rebirth of history, or for the *Spirit* of a new Age. Moreover, by maintaining the validity of the "intervallic period" as the conceptual point of departure for the consideration and guarantee of a potential *rebirth of history*, Badiou also posits his thinking — and, of course, the communist "Idea," the "True Life" — firmly within the ongoing unfolding, from Plato to Nietzsche, of the history of metaphysics. The rebirth (or reactualization) of history is also the rebirth of idealism and metaphysics, the most intimate presupposition of which is the value and will to power of *subjectivity*.

One could say that the "intervallic period" in Badiou provides history with a messianic principle of exclusion or with an experience of dormancy (though not necessarily of a *negativity* or of an abyss). This principle is anchored necessarily to the most intimate subjective decision for a metaphysical *surmounting* and transcending of the prior moment. It is therefore internal to the unfolding and extension of the modern, revolutionary *spirit* as the dialectical elevation and preservation of things past. For this reason, despite the seismic shifts in the scope and scale of capital's "spatial fix" (Harvey), forms of war (from "total" to "global"), and technological domination on a planetary scale, Badiou can draw a relation of absolute equivalence, of infinite selfsameness, between for example the "now" of the capital-labor relation in the Paris of 1848 and the myriad manifestations of that same relation on the planetary scale of the twenty-first century (12–14). The system of elevation and preservation is still the same for Badiou. Historical shifts in the biopolitical arrangements of commodity fetishism, for example, appear to be of little concern to Badiou because the visibleness of the decision of the subject is still, and only ever, the primary and necessary subordination of existence to a normative genealogy and to the understanding of an invariant subjectivist will to power traversing universal history. Neither is there reason to contemplate negativity, the void, the abyss, the inhabitual, or the uncanny within the intervallic period or in its relation to the nonintervallic, for the *surmounting*, and therefore the *transcending*, of latency — or of any a priori — is always determined, a posteriori, as a locus internal to the understanding of history as a succession, that is, as a flowing torrent of nows. Furthermore, to the extent that the "intervallic period" is essentially a spatialization of time (the extension of a locus of ideological dormancy), we can see that it appears to be of little concern to Badiou that the forms of modern political space from out of which a counter-Idea could rise up against contemporary capitalism are in an increasing state of collapse. What is perhaps not so uniquely at stake in Badiou is the safeguarding of the primacy of subjectivity above all else, which then absorbs and subordinates modern and contemporary political space, its relation to shifting means and forms of war, and the myriad forms of the capital-labor relation throughout time.

Perhaps Badiou and his adherents will say that such is the critical assessment of "a dupe of the dominant ideology" (10). A fitting response would be to indicate that while his thinking is certainly more noteworthy than the vast majority of the demagogic protofascist and biopolitical rot currently on display as conceptual thinking or "politics," there is an underlying thoughtlessness that comes to light in Badiou's devotion to a Hegelian dialectic that remains the sole metaphysical site for the synthesis of consciousness of all that comes and becomes before it. In other words, for Badiou's prophetic, transcendental "Idea" it is only the unconcealment of a synthesis of consciousness (the experience and expression of a disciplined and fully unified We) that can coerce thinking and acting in the direction of the realization of what is essentially an absolutely ordinary and average understanding of history. It is the upholding of an infinite transitional time between one "now" and another — a humanist historicism, in other words — in which the reproduction of the will of the subject offers the only guaranteed overcoming of any given past, and it is therefore ultimately the dominant figure and metaphorization of the Enlightenment ideology of progress in its "communist" variation.

And yet, all indicators now suggest that precisely this absolute metaphorization of the humanist suture of the *cogito*, will, subjectivity, history, and progress has entered its definitive *terminal* phase in the age of total biopolitical subsumption, or "globalization." In Badiou's evaluation of the historical relation between riot and history, the phenomenon and experience of *turmoil* itself is immediately brought to closure in such a way as to privilege the Enlightenment-based subjectification of a political subject that is, in fact, not just wanting but, by the author's own admission, lacking in contemporary forms of social upheaval. The subject is asked to *dispose* of the Idea in all its potential metaphysical representedness, but the Idea itself is actually absent. Quite the quandary . . .

Perhaps a shift of a certain kind might be beneficial in our approach to the question of the relation between the contemporary and the turmoil it produces. In the same year Hannah Arendt published *Crises of the Republic* (that is, 1972), Jacques Lacan also signaled the unmarked passing of a historical limit, the sense of perishing that accompanies it, the impending absolute self-realization of capital, and a fundamental limitation in our way of thinking, which to this day stands as an obstacle to transformative thinking: "It is already too late," Lacan omened, "for the crisis not of the discourse of the master but of the capitalist discourse which has substituted it has opened up. . . . [Capitalism] runs on casters, it couldn't run better, but for that very reason it runs too fast, it consumes itself, it consumes itself so well that it is consumed" ("Discours de Jacques Lacan," 10). Half a century ago Lacan had already envisioned the problem that Badiou is now signposting for the present and future of mass action via *The Rebirth of History* and *The True Life*.

But we are faced, Lacan noted in the wake of the events of 1968, with a constitutive limitation, which is the self-certainty of Cartesian mental representation: "It is an effect of history that we are handed over to questioning ourselves not regarding being but existence: I think 'therefore I am' in quotation marks: *Therefore I am* being that from which existence is born; the there that we are. It is the fact 'of what is said'—the saying that is behind everything said—, which is, in the contemporary, that something that comes to the fore" (14). Despite the somewhat imprecise relation between signifiers such as "being" and "existence" in these phrases, Lacan indicates that the question of Being precedes and is occluded in the Cartesian certainty of the "therefore" that situates logos and the subject as coextensive and coterminous, together and complimentary in the everyday (ontic) experience of subjectivity and its representations.[5]

Lacan announced in these formulations that a fundamental historical limit—a limit inaugurating the full planetary accomplishment of the ontology of the commodity—had been crossed. It is too late, he said in reference to the *capitalist discourse*, thereby implying that the history of the modern can no longer be salvaged. From now on, he seems to indicate, thinking can only ever position itself on the side of a mourning for, and of a ceaseless commemoration of, what Martin Heidegger referred to as "the *a priori*, the prior in its ordinary temporal significance [meaning] an older being, one that emerged previously and came to be, and was, and now no longer comes to presence" (*Nietzsche*, 4:157).

Lacan was indicating in 1972 that a prior understanding of the ontological difference between being and beings—an understanding crystallized in the infamous and foundational *therefore* of René Descartes—had already run its course. From now on, conceptual attentiveness should orient itself not toward the primacy of the future — for example, toward the will to power and rebirth of the history of Western metaphysics — but toward care for the possibility of a departure from the value-thinking of that history. However, as Badiou's formulations in recent years demonstrate, in the wake of 1968 thinking remained, and for the most part still remains, firmly entrenched in the Enlightenment tradition of the logic of the master discourse and therefore in the domain of subjectivity, empiricity, logical commonsense storytelling, and the metaphors of subjective proximity and gathering. With this fundamental limit and problem in mind perhaps it could be suggested that, from Lacan's perspective, unflinching Platonic fidelity to 1968 under the auspices of the "communist hypothesis" would place Badiou's thinking within the frame of a fundamental unwillingness to address — to mourn — the historical shift signaled by Lacan in 1972, in the wake of Nietzsche and Heidegger. In contrast, Badiou's position would always be something akin to an announcement of the glad tidings that "there was 1968 and 'therefore I am' and 'therefore' there always has been, there is still, and there always will be a 'communist hypothesis.'" "History" can always be salvaged and transcended through recourse to subjective will in Badiou. In contrast, for Lacan this would be both unsustainable and undesirable because, rather than marking the emergence of a new relation of the subject to its desire, it would merely reinstate a traditional relation of the subject to its masterful desire in an epoch that is no longer that of modern ethics but, rather, that of its expiration. While Kierkegaard posited in an oblique reference to Kant that ethics is an "'ideal' science" striving "to bring ideality into actuality . . . the more ideal ethics is, the better" (*Anxiety*, 21–22), now it is increasingly apparent that Ideality itself — that of metaphysical humanism, for example — is crumbling, as Lacan pointed out over half a century ago.[6]

It is with the crumbling of Ideality in mind that Alberto Moreiras has speculated recently that the true legacy of 1968 is perhaps that of an existential experience that has since been concealed under a mountain of subjectivism designed, against all possible forms of deconstruction, to guarantee the coextensiveness of the political with life itself. In this light, Moreiras points to the secret possibility of an overturning, or of a turn in thinking:

> The true legacy of May 1968 could in fact be the dissolution — the
> cut — of the link between the notion of the political and that of life,
> between politics and life, in favor of the reformulation of the notion of
> existence. But we say this without knowing: Wasn't 1968 the effective
> end of the old politics in favor of a new existential, though not for that
> reason any less anti-political, experience? This has, I fear, been forgotten. (*Infrapolítica: La diferencia absoluta*, 20)

Something has withdrawn from the field of perception and thinking, Moreiras notes. We are living in, and paying the hermeneutic and existential price for, a labor of historical concealment in which what is obscured via the ceaseless elevation of subjectivism is the facticity of the closure of metaphysics. From this perspective the ongoing legacy of Badiou's thinking in relation to the events and political inheritance of 1968 or of the so-called Arab Spring of 2011 would certainly appear to forge a question regarding the termination of progress, the end of modern understandings of freedom, the ongoing will to power of the subject, and the demise of a certain philosophy of historical development. But it also points in the direction of an occluded analytic in which the possibility of a new existential thinking of experience is folded back into the historical coordinates of Enlightenment subjectivation in such a way as to guarantee militant faith in the will to power of revolutionary subjectivity, and that alone and above all else.

Having said that, this is not a work about *la pensée 1968*. My interest at this initial point lies in highlighting that, deep down, Arendt, Lacan, Badiou, and Moreiras are all signaling the fact that while the modern, and to a large extent world-defining, faith in progress and development provided the basis for much of the historical-materialist conceptual apparatus in the wake of Marx, that essentially constitutive faith is now revealed to have been hollowed out entirely: not only unfilled but perhaps even vacuous. In this regard Badiou's *true life* and *rebirth* would stand as flawed monuments to a largely unexamined will to close over any potential abyss in thinking the political, via the language of a metaphysical doctrine of political subjectivism in an age in which the history of that metaphysics has already run its course.

Hannah Arendt pointed out in the early 1970s that the nineteenth-century doctrine of progress had united liberalism, socialism, and communism into the "Left" (*Crises of the Republic*, 126): "The notion that there is such a thing as progress of mankind as a whole was unknown prior to the seventeenth century, developed into a rather common opinion among the eighteenth-century *hommes de lettres*, and became an almost universally accepted dogma in the nineteenth" (127). She continues this insight in the following terms: "Marx's idea, borrowed from Hegel, that every old society harbors the seeds of its successor in the same way every living organism harbors the seeds of its offspring is indeed not only the most ingenious but also the only possible conceptual guarantee for the sempiternal continuity of progress in history" (127). But, she adds, such a metaphor is not a solid basis upon which to erect a doctrine of continuous progress (128). Progress, she says, is, and always was, an article of faith "offered at the superstition fair of our times" (130–31).

Let us take up briefly the example of Antonio Gramsci's recuperation of

Engels's understanding of "historical materialism" as the supposed discovery of a *law* of historical processes capable of orienting thought and action toward freedom. This recuperation bears witness to the way that much of the modern tradition of emancipation has been predicated on a superstition, on something other than Marx's fundamental thinking of value and of the ontological function of the commodity in the movement of modern society. Gramsci defined the transitional temporality of historical materialism — the time of progress — in the following terms:

> That historical materialism conceives of itself as a transitory phase in philosophical thought should be clear from Engels's assertion that historical development will, at a certain point, be characterized by the transition from the realm of necessity to the realm of freedom. . . . Every philosopher is, and cannot but be, convinced that he expresses the unity of the human spirit, that is, the unity of history and nature. Otherwise, men would not act, they would not create new history. (*Prison Notebooks*, 2:194).

Badiou is certainly not Gramscian in his thinking, but what they share remains striking. This is the case even though their conception of the law of the movement of modern society and of intellectual life, in which the dominant ontology of the commodity form leads to the subjective realm of transcendental freedom from necessity and in which the proletarian spirit (or militant subject) is posited in such a way that it *is* to the future what the bourgeois spirit *is* to the present, is increasingly, if not entirely, unconvincing now. In contrast, Felipe Martínez Marzoa's words stand as a welcome and necessary antidote: "Engels's works . . . present such a lack of rigor that it makes no sense to address them in a work of philosophy," for it was Engels's positivism, rather than Marx's thinking of value and of the commodity form, that produced the entire pseudoscientific apparatus generally referred to as "historical materialism" and "dialectical materialism" (*La filosofía de El Capital*, 26).[7]

Potentially this leaves a good part of the tradition of Marxism beyond Marx without one of its primary articles of faith. There is probably nothing new or unknown in any of this. But if, as Alain Badiou puts it, we are currently undergoing the apotheosis of the modern abandonment of tradition (the hollowing out of a certain suturing relation between conceptual inheritance and world), then it appears that the full consequences of the definitive and ongoing demise of the ideas of the nineteenth century are only coming to light in full force in the first decades of the twenty-first century, despite all attempts to safeguard against that conundrum. But as Lacan put it, it is already too late.

Following a path that echoes but steps back from the overall area of con-

cern portended by Badiou — for what follows neither obeys nor seeks to rein-
stall a directive principle of subjectivation for present and future thinking and
acting — *Infrapolitical Passages* implies neither nostalgia for the nineteenth-
century teleology of progress (of both the historical Left and Right) nor an
endorsement of Francis Fukuyama's famously misguided prophecy from the
early 1990s that following the fall of the Berlin Wall and the collapse of world
communism, humanity would undergo an "end of history" characterized by
the utopic conditions of the classical political economy of the nineteenth
century.[8]

In an echo of Arendt and Badiou's overall sense of unease, the pages that
follow suggest that a certain approach to and understanding of *ending*, of what
it means to reach and even pass a certain threshold, or an existential extremity
of sorts, remains incumbent upon us. It does so understanding full well that
every concept carries within itself the conditions of its own decontainment
to the extent that what delimits the concept is precisely, and only ever, what
precedes and exceeds it. If we can only arrive too late to a crisis that already
runs smoothly and rapidly, then what happens when inherited concepts that
already depended for their existence on a preconceptual frontier that framed
them — such as the historical reality of the Westphalian-Enlightenment world
and its imperial peripheries — succumb before the crumbling of the topographical and temporal conditions of that world and, therefore, before the
historical twilight now commonly referred to as "globalization"? Certainly, a
peculiar form of wakefulness — of perception and understanding — is at stake
in this approach to tardiness, topographic collapse, and penumbral reborder-
ing in the face of planetary *techne* and the full-on quest for the extraction of
surplus value at all cost.

Within the context of an enigmatic yet fully shared *perishing* — a mortality, however, about which we can claim no specific experience, since contemporary consciousness cannot provide it with a given moment, with the
appearance of a single object or representation, and therefore with no definitive "before" and "after" — the generalized sense of expiration and mortality
we should have confronted a long time ago (but when precisely?) is denied
(though for different reasons) by both the acolytes of the communist hypothesis and the active pursuers of capitalist surplus value, is reconverted into
administrative prowess or into a problem of the exclusion and inclusion of
certain identity formations by liberals and conservatives of all persuasions, or
is staged as an increasing demand for morality by the eschatologically minded
devotees of Christian metaphysics.

The question emerges, however, as to what language to give to a leave-
taking that fell to us as an inheritance at some point more or less recently

(or maybe not so recently, since ultimately we are only ever referring to the problem of thinking from within the closure of metaphysics) but that did so without allowing us to recognize the point at which a border, perhaps even a point of no return, was passed and remains for the time being in its passing as an ongoing question of ever-shifting limits and ends and, ultimately, therefore of finitude, death, and mourning.

## Toward an Infrapolitical (Non) Passage

From where, and in what direction, to proceed? In Alberto Moreiras's 2006 work *Línea de sombra: El no sujeto de lo político* (Line of shadow: the nonsubject of the political) — a book that radicalized some of the conceptual propositions developed in the 1990s around the experience of the Latin American Subaltern Studies Group — the author provides a formidable critical response to *Empire*, Michael Hardt and Antonio Negri's influential and widely commented-upon tome of 2000.[9] It is in this critical reading of Hardt and Negri's *Empire* that the infrapolitical begins to take shape not as a new or alternative philosophical or political concept, system, plan, school, or method hell-bent on *overcoming* other concepts from before. There is no dialectical or bureaucratic interest herein. Rather, it is a movement toward a quasi-conceptual attunement in thinking formulated in order to inquire into the determining power of our given conceptual systems and to propose the contours for an alternative (for example, nonsubjectivist, nontranscendental, noutopian, postmessianic) relation to the political in the age of total (that is, of planetary) subsumption.[10]

The reading in question is extended in particular reference to *Empire*'s primary libidinal principle, which is the figuration of emancipation even from within the fact that, according to the authors, Empire not only contains counter-Empire but *is* the container. In other words, global capitalism, or Empire, is the achievement of capital's own outer limit, while sovereignty remains the antagonistic container of the multitude and also its boundary (Moreiras, *Línea de sombra*, 206–7). It is from within this historical and conceptual conundrum that Moreiras begins to address the problem of the metaphysics of counter-Empire as a promised *overcoming* from within Empire's fulfillment of Empire itself. This is the question that dwells at the heart of Hardt and Negri's work, yet it remains largely un(re)marked, to the extent that it is presented merely as a transcendent given or as the logical and inevitable outcome of Empire in much the same way the communist "Idea," or the *True Life*, is in Badiou's recent writings.

While *Empire*'s presentation of the totalization of subsumption is laudable (and is perhaps consonant with the overall diagnosis also contained here in *Infrapolitical Passages*, though always with a divergent vocabulary, differential prognoses, and contrary hermeneutic responses), questions begin to emerge around Hardt and Negri's figuration of the biopolitics of *the multitude* as the always immanent, and therefore always potentially transcendent, *counter-empire* to the biopolitics of global capital.[11] How, asks Moreiras, can the conditions of a transcendent counterbiopower — the multitude — be thought from within the total subsumption that is Empire, when the latter is already biopower at its absolute planetary limit? How could such a thing — the primacy of an immanent and future *counter-Empire* — bring an end to subalternity when "in *Empire* the end of subalternity is willfully and messianically affirmed while remaining theoretically unfounded" (213)? In other words, what price does thinking pay in the wake of Hardt and Negri's "frankly optimistic intellectual position" regarding *counterempire* as the subjectivist precondition for the surmounting and overcoming of Empire (215)?

Echoing Badiou's *The True Life* and *The Rebirth of History*, in which the will of the militant subject is both the truth of "the Idea" and the dialectical rebirth of history simultaneously, what remains at stake in the relation between Empire and the book's onto-theological prophesy of an emergent *counterempire* of the poor (205) is the specter of the Hegelian dialectic — and therefore the determination of philosophy as *the* science or absolute knowledge — as the unmarked and therefore overlooked and unexplained instrument of subjective consciousness and common sense that lies at the heart of the modern history of the political Left in the wake of the French Revolution.

In contrast, Moreiras advances in the direction of the infrapolitical by turning back, that is, by advancing backward for the purpose of clearing a way across and out of the imperial ground of modern metaphysics.[12] His reading achieves this in such a way as to emphasize (or, rather, to actively unconceal) the Spanish Inquisition as the underlying Latin-Romanic onto-theological ground, or "infrapower" (prior, that is, to Foucault's modern determination of the biopolitical), upon which all subsequent ontological forms of modern Western imperial and nation-state sovereignty, including that of the onto-theological biopower that Hardt and Negri recuperate in their political understanding of both Empire and *counter-Empire*, are construed and understood.

Moreiras's calling into question (or destruction) of Hardt and Negri's excessively expedient dialectical overcoming of Empire prompts us to consider the extent to which, when thinking from within the modern politics of emancipation, we are in fact thinking from within (and in our quest for a positive politics merely reaffirming) the unexamined onto-theological determinations of the historical processes by which emancipation entered the modern history of Western metaphysics as both biopower and counterbiopower, *beneath* the visibleness of the Christian imperial and national histories of state sovereignty.

It is important at this point that the *infrapolitical* not be confused with the extension of the *infrapower* of the Inquisition in the imperial history of modern metaphysics. They are not the same, for the latter is a reference to the working of biopolitics as the everyday naturalization of domination, while the former strives to move in a different direction. Any confusion here would lead us to embrace (as in fact Hardt and Negri do) the nihilism that dictates that one can fight the biopower of Empire by mobilizing the biopower of counterempire, which is akin to fighting the metaphysics of subjectivity (*cogitatio*), in the age of the closure of metaphysics, with the will to power of a supposedly better metaphysics of subjectivity (the *cogitatio* of the multitude).

This is the fulfilled nihilism that overlooks its own onto-theological foundation in the name of political militancy and expediency, which is then consequently overlooked by the vast majority of modern and contemporary thinking on both the Left and Right. It is here, however, that the infrapolitical register in thinking assumes responsibility for the conceptual conditions of an exodus from the biopolitical itself. This is proposed by Moreiras not in order to fantasize about the possibility of freeing oneself from nihilism but to confront the consequences of actively skimming over nihilism in the name of a transcendent, messianic counterpolitics. Such a fulfilled nihilism is, after all, what Badiou and Hardt and Negri have in common in their figurations of *counter-Empire*, the *True Life*, and the *Idea*.[13]

In 2006, the possibility of an alternative to a thinking fully determined by fulfilled nihilism was registered in the chapter's concluding expression: "Infrapolitics is but the search for a non-biopolitical exodus" (Moreiras, *Línea de sombra*, 238). Almost a decade later, in 2015, the possibility of an exodus from thinking in the shadow of fulfilled nihilism came to be delineated as "an exodus with regard to the subjective prison that constitutes an ethico-political relation ideologically imposed on us as a consequence of metaphysical humanism" (Moreiras, "Conversation," 152).[14]

The question of the distance between infrapolitical thinking and fulfilled nihilism was recuperated and extended in 2017 by Jaime Rodríguez-Matos in *Writing of the Formless: José Lezama Lima and the End of Time*.[15] In this work the author grapples actively with the realization that any step back now from the onto-theological affirmations of metaphysical humanism — such as those of so-called revolutionary thinking — requires an entanglement with nihilism attuned to the possibility of doing something other than treating "the problem of nihilism as a mere pitfall or as an obstacle that can be simply surpassed" (100). In this work, Rodríguez-Matos addresses the demand for an instrumentalization of, and within, contemporary political thinking (for instance, via the revamping of Lenin's programmatic question from the turn of the twentieth century, "What is to be done?") in particular reference to two of the most prominent modes of political thought today, namely, postfoundational thinking (as evidenced, for example, in the writings of Marchart and Laclau, in their mutual relation to Schmitt) and communist horizonal thinking (as extended in the work of Badiou and others).[16]

Herein Rodríguez-Matos points out astutely that so-called postfoundational thinking stakes a claim on the nonexistence of an ultimate ontological ground for thinking (politics, for example) yet addresses the absence of foundation by actively forgetting about being, or the beingness of beings, which is the originary void itself (104). *So how postfoundational is postfoundational thinking?* Rodríguez-Matos seems to ask. The answer, he suggests, is not very postfoundational at all, for the "absence of *arché* ends up being the very legitimating mechanism for the multiplication of finite foundations, which will take on the form of a decision — as was also the case in Schmitt" (103).[17] Postfoundational thinking is therefore founded on the essential occlusion of the originary ontological question regarding the difference that (un)grounds political thinking in the first place. For this reason, postfoundational thinking is "a rehabilitated form of modern thought as a whole" (104), to the extent that it is a revamped metaphysical humanism couched in the vagaries of contingency and the metaphysical oblivion of the question of Being (that is, of fundamental ontology, or the thinking of existence itself).[18] The problem stems from an ideologically determined unwillingness in both forms of political thinking to grapple with the legacies of so-called Left Heideggerianism.[19] It is this unwillingness that, in the case of both postfoundational and communist horizonal thinking, flattens out the problem of the ontological difference, thereby preparing "the way for the accusation of nihilism to be leveled at whoever does not forget what is essentially at issue in thinking the difference between being and beings as difference and not as a stratification of 'ontic' and 'ontological' levels. . . . The fight against nihilism continues, but it is now a fight against those who think the problem" (104). For Rodríguez-Matos, however, thinking the political in the name of an instrumentalization, and this in the absence of an essential attunement to the nothing, that is, to the void, produces both the compensatory domination of dogmatic certainty and the glorification of what is essentially a poorly occluded yet fully fulfilled nihilism. Against the dogmas of occlusion, Rodríguez-Matos reminds us that

> the void is not an aesthetic or imagined supplement; it is the first
> evidence of modern political experience, particularly after the great
> political revolutions of the era. . . . But the void does not pick sides;
> the day after the revolution that void is also there already gnawing at
> whatever new institutions are put in place. The paradox of historical
> materialism is that it is unable to come to terms with the materiality of
> this emptiness. (110)

For this reason, the failure or refusal to reckon with the void, and this in the name of a politics of emancipation against which nihilism is measured, "does not make choosing between evil and a lesser evil anything other than a forced choice for evil" (Rodríguez-Matos, "Nihilism," 46–47). It is with the banal optionlessness of the political in mind that Rodríguez-Matos suggests a differential pathway for thinking, as he conjectures that "perhaps it is time to reconsider the problem of foundations from the perspective of the ex nihilo without any further qualifications, that is, from the perspective of a thoroughly a-principial thought" (*Writing of the Formless*, 121). In a companion text ("After the Ruin of Thinking"), Rodríguez-Matos clarifies what a-principial thought might imply for certain understandings of political action today:

> What does infrapolitics say when a militant asks what bearing can
> thinking the absence of foundations, the ontological difference, the
> structure of the question, the vigilance against the temporality of the
> present and of presence, what can any of this possibly have to offer to
> the group marching down the street protesting the real and massive
> injustices being carried out today at every level of existence? (4)

The answer is twofold: (1) "The focus on politics runs the risk of blinding you to the problem of politics. . . . What if the problem of politics is that politics always entails an instrumentalization, an illegitimate appropriation that is presented as legitimate? And further, what if this problem is only exacerbated by confronting it only politically?" (4); and (2) "Infrapolitical thought/action begins by affirming that what goes under the heading of politics can be contested as such, and also that what the standard meaning of politics excludes from its own reduced sphere of 'action' is more important in its politicity — even as this entails a retreat from politics in the business-as-usual sense of the term" (5).[20] It is for these reasons that infrapolitics is "not a politics otherwise" (5–6). Rather, it is the "deconstruction of politics or politics in deconstruction" (Moreiras, "A Conversation," 144). It is a proposal for the deconstruction of every illegitimate appropriation and expropriation that is presented as legitimate, including, but not limited to, the sociological, the anthropological, and the cultural.

As illustrated in the opening Exordium, infrapolitics can be understood as a significant withdrawal or retreat from the political field that touches never-theless upon the political "to the extent [that] it seeks to glimpse and reflect upon a certain outside of politics" (Moreiras, "Infrapolitics: The Project and Its Politics," 9–11).[21] The notion of withdrawal, or of difference from the politi-cal, has also been extended by Sergio Villalobos-Ruminott, who observes that infrapolitics "points toward a dimension of existence that has not dropped into the will of will . . . it supposes a relation of withdrawal [*desistencia*] from the political itself" ("¿En qué se reconoce el pensamiento?," 52). In the same vein, infrapolitics has been approached as "the non-place from which the place of politics is radically interrogated . . . infrapolitical questions are not *strictu sensu* political questions; they are neither questions that could be answered from within the political realm nor are they questions that interrogate politics exclusively for the sake of establishing *another* politics . . . infrapolitical ques-tions lie and die as *questioned* questions that are *incapable* of mastering ~~their own~~ questioning" (Mendoza de Jesús, "Sovereignty," 53–60). It is precisely for this reason that infrapolitics marks "the experience of the impossibility of the total conceptualization of experience. Therefore, infrapolitics is a form of negative realism that . . . prevents the onto-theological from taking hold of the various regimes of representation, identity and the totalizing power of communitarian politics" (Álvarez Solís, "On a Newly Arisen Infrapolitical Tone," 139). It therefore exists at a distance from "what was understood as pol-itics throughout modernity, that is, since the foundation of political theory, as a so-called science" (Álvarez Yágüez, "Crisis," 23). In specific reference to the Heideggerian legacy, infrapolitics "insofar as it is *an-archic* thinking . . . occurs in the form of a kind of Heideggerian 'backtracking,' specifically concerned with retrieving traces of the previous heralding of the infrapolitical dimen-sion. This is the hermeneutical effort of dialoguing with a certain 'tradition' of thinking involved in dealing with the end of onto-theological thought" (Cerrato, "Infrapolitics and Shibumi," 98). For this reason, infrapolitics resists becoming a paradigm or world image, since its "questioning cannot be orga-nized easily into the conventional history of paradigms, schools or structuring principles for the history of being or knowledge. On the contrary, conceived as infinite and irrevocable inquiry, infrapolitics is the question regarding the end, or the finality, of an epoch" (Villalobos-Ruminott, "El poema," 107). Finally, for Ángel Octavio Álvarez Solís infrapolitics inaugurs a modification in tone and, as such, "a change in the orientation of thought, a change in the fragile conceptual structure of theory, a change in the way in which discursive practices admit new horizons of experience. . . . The politics of tone indicate a dispute regarding open ears" (124–27). The author then continues, "Infrapolitics is part of the history of deconstruction, but not of the American history of deconstruction" (131). It is, in this sense, a return to and a renewal of the legacies of deconstruction.[22]

From all of this, one can discern that infrapolitics inaugurates a diagnosis of the epochal collapse of modern thought. However, rather than apocalyptic thinking, infrapolitics thinks from within ~~the end~~, for it is extended in conjunction with the attempt to elucidate a turn in our inherited metaphysical legacies. It comes with a particular attunement to the ontological difference between beings and the *beingness* of beings and moves in such a way as to give language to the ontological difference's relation to "the active infra-excess of the political" (Moreiras, "Infrapolítica y política," 56). This infra-excess of the political is the excess to the ontology of the subject, or the opening to *existence* itself. As Martin Heidegger named it, it is *ek-sistence*, or being-*toward-death*. It is the unconditional nonplace of *politics in retreat*, which is understood as the potential uncovering of what cannot be captured and remobilized from within the Hegelian metaphysics of absolute knowledge, political consciousness, subjective will, and the dialectic of experience.

In retreat, infrapolitics strives to clear a way toward a thinking uncaptured by the modern history of subjectivity, ethics, and politics. The act of clearing is therefore carried out in the name of freedom.[23] In this regard, Maddalena Cerrato ("Infrapolitics and Shibumi," 2015) has addressed the importance of the question of *passage* in the age of the end of metaphysics, which in *Infrapolitical Passages* I take up in conjunction with what Ángel Octavio Álvarez Solís has referenced as a modification in tone and as a change in the orientation of thought. In her reading of Heidegger, Schürmann, Malabou, and Derrida, Cerrato frames the question of the *passage* in the following terms: "The affirmation of the end of the hegemony of epochal principles, insofar as it is an-archical, also marks the end of epochality itself, but it is, at the same time, the beginning of a passage, of the time of the transition from the passing of ontotheology to a new historicity" (84). *Passage* voids the demand for a new topology from which to think: "An-archic thought loses its mooring, it is displaced, dislocated into *tropologies* without return. This is the condition of the passage. In the passage, thinking can just expose itself to singular tropes, singular displacements without any expectations of stability neither as return to an originary birthplace nor as relocation elsewhere . . . what is passing away in the passage is philosophy itself" (89–97). For this reason, infrapolitics, as a denarrativizing activity, "dwells in the passage" (98).

*Infrapolitical Passages: Global Turmoil, Narco-Accumulation, and the Post-Sovereign State* is, in this regard, an extension of two tropologies without return that attempt to give an orientation to the task of denarrativizing the contemporary inheritance of the political. In 1931 Walter Benjamin denoted something analogous and referred to it as the work of the "destructive character":

> Some people pass down things to posterity, by making them untouchable and thus conserving them; others pass on situations, by making them practicable and thus liquidating them. The latter are called the destructive. . . . The destructive character sees nothing permanent. But for this very reason he sees ways everywhere. Where others encounter walls or mountains, there, too, he sees a way. But because he sees a way everywhere, he has to clear things from it everywhere. Not always by brute force; sometimes by the most refined. Because he sees ways everywhere, he always stands at a crossroads. No moment can know what the next will bring. What exists he reduces to rubble — not for the sake of rubble, but for that of the way leading through it. (542)

Both Benjamin's destructive character and infrapolitics seek to situate themselves in the passage toward another beginning, though not in the onto-theological terms of surmounting, overcoming, or transcending, since they both spurn the dialectical movement of *Spirit*. However, this does not mean that Benjamin's destructive character and infrapolitics are entirely coincident, for in Benjamin the destructive character still derives from "the consciousness of historical man" (542). In the wake of the economic collapse of 1929, consciousness remains the ultimate *arché* of both subject and experience, and there is still present in Benjamin a residual romanticism in the delineation of the destructive character as the exercise and affirmation of the *ego cogito*. As a result, both the rubble and the possible beyond are established by and for consciousness, with destruction as the self-conscious experience and consequence of knowledge and understanding. Herein experience can only be understood as the experience of (self-)consciousness, without anything cast off. In the "destructive character," then, we remain in the land of the self-certainty of mental representation, or of the "I think, *therefore*, I am" that was unmoored by Lacan throughout his intellectual trajectory and, as already referenced, in his brief exposition of the *capitalist discourse* in 1972.

In a slightly different tone to that of Benjamin's destructive character, as we now come to the end of the second decade of the twenty-first century we can but strive to desist from romanticism, since we can no longer place faith in the determination of a way through the rubble or accede to an "other side" via the Enlightenment "consciousness of historical man." Now the struggle is to delineate a way to backtrack from the Hegelian metaphysics of consciousness — from the humanist metaphysics of the ontology of the subject — that helped accumulate the underlying rubble of modernity in the first place. This backtracking is the basis for the infrapolitical exodus from all the metaphysical legacies of the dialectic of consciousness and the politics of intersubjective recognition that we have inherited since the Enlightenment. Now our only task is to think in a relation of mourning to a world of humanist promise now essentially obsolete. Infrapolitics in this regard is neither melancholic nor apocalyptic. Rather, it is a thinking that dwells in the closure of the metaphysical humanism that previously anchored our faith in "the consciousness of historical man." Such is the negative realism of the infrapolitical register in thinking.

Within this context, the passage is not handed down as a given. Rather, it can only be given an orientation via thinking and writing. For this reason, *Infrapolitical Passages: Global Turmoil, Narco-Accumulation, and the Post-Sovereign State* comprises two *passages across* the normative horizons of the political, the sociological, the historical, and the cultural. These passages are formulated in the name of elucidating the necessity of the infrapolitical, of explaining what attunement to the infrapolitical might imply, and of thematizing the possibility of wresting experience from the age of planetary subsumption, that is, from the contemporary ontology of commodity fetishism, or globalization.

## Infrapolitical Passages: Global Turmoil, Narco-Accumulation, and the Post-Sovereign State

It is as a result of all of the above that I have opted to structure this work not via chapters with specific thematic differences or dissimilar forms of development between them, or with a historicist sense of metaphysical closure orienting and accommodating the work in the story it tells from start to finish, but as the problem of the *experience* of a border, of a boundary, and therefore of a (non)crossing between two intertwined *infrapolitical passages*. My purpose in configuring this work thusly is fourfold:

(1) to register and formalize the specifically historical question of whether in the tremor we call globalization we are "going through a time that can in fact be gone through, hoping to go through it so as one day to get beyond it" (Derrida, *Rogues*, 124);

(2) to register and demarcate the interrelated spatiotemporal question of whether in globalization there is in fact a traversing to be experienced, or simply no passage, "not yet or . . . no longer a border to cross, no opposition between two sides . . . no longer a home and a not-home . . . no more movement or trajectory, no more *trans-*

(transport, transposition, transgression, translation, and even transcendence)" (Derrida, *Aporias*, 20–21);

(3) to register and orient the conceptual question of inheritance in view of the necessity, similarly registered by Giacomo Marramao in *The Passage West* and Alberto Moreiras in *The Exhaustion of Difference*, that "from now on the demand for meaning has to go through the exhaustion of significations" (Nancy, *Gravity*, 48);

(4) to register and demarcate, or strive to clear a path for, the possibility of a *decision of existence* (which cannot be fully coincident with a subjective decision *for* existence) from within the endemic violence of a *world of war*.[24]

Therefore, this is a book that makes no progress, and intentionally so. Rather, it circles around these four problems internal to the question of a certain indiscernibility between *passage* and *nonpassage* — time, space, concept, and decision — striving to provide orientation nevertheless to the existential, infrapolitical register that comes to pass prior to the distinction between the theoretical and the practical and that haunts the demise of the modern ideologies of progress and development, the total subsumption of life to capital, or (and this is the same thing, though in inverted form) the planetary extension of the "necropolitical."[25]

Some might feel that this offers in fact the formalization of very little, since herein there is no implementation of a specific political agenda, program, or solution. Perhaps it could be countered that in the same way "by definition, one always makes *very little* of a border" (Derrida, *Aporias*, 21), by definition one also makes very little of the infrapolitical register of the ontological difference. Having said that, the *very little* in question in both cases just might be what is most worth the risk in terms of the demarcation and formalization of a thinking to come. Moreover, the experience of attempting to *clear a way* is, to my mind at least, as sizeable as conforming officiously to preassigned conduits for so-called responsible (which some will doubtlessly opt to understand as historically recognizable, representable, and therefore readily translatable forms of) thinking and acting in the name of a program or of a specific political conscientiousness.

In light of this formalization of *very little*, that is, of the *intimate distance* that exists prior to and in conjunction with every infrapolitical *touching upon*, what specifically is the work advanced in the movements comprising *Infrapolitical Passages: Global Turmoil, Narco-Accumulation, and the Post-Sovereign State*?

The first passage, on the figure of *decontainment* as the origin of contemporary turmoil, is titled "Posthegemonic Epochality, or Why Bother with the Infrapolitical?" and passes through four essential and intimately connected conceptual configurations related to the problem of the meaningfulness, and therefore to the factic life, of the contemporary turmoil we refer to as post–Cold War globalization. The latter is understood here as the master discourse of the ontology of the commodity, unleashed and enforced planetarily. The first two sections ("Prometheus Kicks the Bucket" and "Katechon, Postkatechon, Decontainment") examine the contemporary as the topographical reconfiguration of political space, as the hollowing out and expiration of the political-theological imagination of Paulist restraint, and as the collapse of the subjectivist Promethean forms of historical and political understanding that have bolstered and perpetuated modern notions of *nomos* and that have now, perhaps conclusively, run their course. The third section of this opening passage ("From Hegemony to Posthegemony") analyzes the consequences of Promethean expiration for the concept of hegemony, which throughout the twentieth century has sat at the core of Marxist political thinking from Vladimir Lenin and Antonio Gramsci to Ernesto Laclau and Chantal Mouffe and beyond. In this reading it comes to light that our times are no longer marked by the historical cycle of the bourgeois revolutions that made hegemony and hegemony thinking hegemonic in the twentieth century. In the era not of the governmental separation of state and market but in the post-sovereign rule of the market-state duopoly on a global scale, there is an overabundance of consent to domination, and the Right is increasingly capturing spaces and conceptual genealogies previously developed by the Left (hegemony being a case in point), thereby leaving the Left increasingly little room to think or to imagine alternatives to the given.[26]

But our times — the times of endemic turmoil, narco-accumulation, and the post-sovereign market-state duopoly — are in fact posthegemonic. For this reason, posthegemony is not interested in propagating representative fables of closure and containment designed to suture subjectivity once again to the political. Rather, it is interested in opening up both — subjectivity and the political — to a sustained questioning of their ontological ground, material conditions, and political potentialities for both past and present. In a work devoid of a specific political agenda, program, or solution, the final section of this passage ("Why Bother with the Infrapolitical?") can be read, ironically, as an a-principial manifesto for the dismantling of the ontology of subjectivity via the thinking of the most distant and the most intimate (that is, *ek-sistence* as being toward death). It is an a-principial proposal in the name of freedom, and in the wake of the teleology of progress and development, for a thinking that remains at a distance from subjectivity and its representations via state and market thinking, received notions of the political, and every homeland we are told to strive to belong to or to reject.

The second passage on *narco-accumulation*, titled "Of Contemporary Force and Facticity," passes through eight closely connected conceptual, historical, cultural, and sociological configurations related to the problem of the meaningfulness of post–Cold War globalization — or the market-state duopoly of the post-sovereign state — as a fully decontained and endemic *world of war*. The first four sections of this passage ("Toward Narco-Accumulation," "Toward Facticity," "Facticity, or the Question of the Right Name for War," and "Decontainment and *Stasis*") examine narco-accumulation as a name for the transnational illicit movement and turmoil of the commodity form — drugs, guns, bodies — now unconfined by the legal restrictions of the modern state form. It is the active decontainment of the constitutional form itself: the turmoil in movement of the post-sovereign market-state duopoly. This is the case in large part because it is the market-state duopoly itself that *depolices* its own legal restrictions on unlawful economic activity while simultaneously performing the *militarization* of the *depolicing* in order to maintain the enactment of a law and order that is extremely profitable and, indeed, politically and socially necessary (for domination) because without it the entire national and global economy would collapse.

Building on and moving beyond Giorgio Agamben's notion of globalization as *global civil war*, these sections address the question of endemic force in the context of the narco-wars of the last decades in Mexico, Central America, and the United States, in such a way as to highlight the fact that "meaning-making — our very way of staying alive — is possible only because we are mortal; and our mortality is the groundless ground for why we have to make sense" (Sheehan, "Facticity and Ereignis," 47). The following two sections ("Theater of Conflict I: 'Here There Is No Choosing'" and "Theater of Conflict II: *2666*, or the Novel of Force") explore questions of mortality, rape, murder, meaning-making, and the socialized death sentence in the specific context of the writings of Cormac McCarthy (*The Counselor*) and Roberto Bolaño (*2666*).

Finally, this *passage* on narco-accumulation shifts, via the section titled "Toward the Void," in the direction of the militarized deterritorialization of Mexican sovereignty (*nomos*) and the transformation of Mexican territory into the post-sovereign place of execution of US homeland security by essentially converting national territory into a buffer zone, a military architectural network for mass arrest and deportation.

It is in this context that *Infrapolitical Passages* can turn in its final section (titled "The Migrant's Hand, or the Infrapolitical Turn to Existence") toward the question and possibility of a *decision of existence* — at an infrapolitical distance from turmoil, narco-accumulation, and the post-sovereign state — in specific reference to Diego Quemada Díez's film addressing Central American migration to the United States, *La jaula de oro* (The golden cage [2013], which was distributed in the United States as *The Golden Dream*).

As the book's closing sentence indicates, the aspiration upon writing this work is quite simply that, despite all evidence to the contrary, it might not be too late to clear a way through contemporary turmoil, narco-accumulation, and the post-sovereign market-state duopoly, in the name of the infrapolitical *decision of existence*, of the ontological difference as the trace of a possible inception in thinking and acting.

This is, like a border, the formalization of very little, and it could very well lead to absolutely or virtually nothing. However, the question of the infrapolitical register in thinking just might be worth contemplating further, for there might be absolutely everything at stake therein.

# Passage I: Contemporary Turmoil
## Posthegemonic Epochality, or Why Bother with the Infrapolitical?

Monarch of Gods and Daemons, and all Spirits
But One, who throng those bright and rolling worlds
Which Thou and I alone of living things
Behold with sleepless eyes! Regard this Earth
Made multitudinous with thy slaves, whom thou
Requitest for knee-worship, prayer, and praise,
And toil, and hecatombs of broken hearts,
With fear and self-contempt and barren hope . . .
Ah me! Alas, pain, pain ever, for ever!
No change, no pause, no hope! Yet I endure.

—PERCY BYSSHE SHELLEY, *Prometheus Unbound*

This is the limit of an era, which was the era of the representation of
a meaning. . . . We have exhausted the schemas of progress and of the
progressive unveiling of truth. In this sense, History is indeed finished,
or finite, and "finitude" opens another history . . .

—JEAN-LUC NANCY, *The Gravity of Thought*

I have no *Weltanschauung*.

—JACQUES LACAN, "DISCOURS DE JACQUES LACAN
À L'UNIVERSITÉ DE MILAN LE 12 MAI 1972"

# Prometheus Kicks the Bucket

This Passage is a work of grieving for the increasingly clear coexistence of two terminations: one is ongoing and ceaseless (the closure of metaphysics); the other appears increasingly as a potential terminus that can take us immediately and without any apparent mediation of any kind from what Badiou calls "the end of the old world of castes" (*The True Life*, 29) into the stark realities of potentially catastrophic upheaval, turmoil, and violence. Grief lies heavily at the heart of the decision for thinking. If grief uncovers the singularly passive and inoperative experience of staring mortality in the face, of keeping silent watch over that of which nothing can be said (death), then grief is the originary and unspeakable other of language that carries itself not only in advance of mourning, as the toil for a certain understanding, but also in advance of every action's possibility. Grief is the other of language, the affective passivity that carries itself in advance of every responsible act of thinking and writing. As such, grief per se can never be political. Rather, it is only ever an erstwhile infrapolitical caring for the depths of the abyss of being-toward-death, or for the painful assumption of a certain responsibility toward the limit and possibility of existence. For this reason, the work of mourning, the laborious pursuit of an assignable place for death, or for the death of the other, traverses the prepolitical passage from grief to an attunement in thinking and writing (and therefore in acting) that strives to account for the possibility of freedom and existence. As Jacques Derrida put it in *The Gift of Death*: "Concern for death, this awakening that keeps vigil over death, this conscience that looks death in the face is another name for freedom" (15).[1]

It is not just *as a result of* globalization, or of the contemporary order of planetary technology, that modernity's teleology of progress — the time of the movement of wealth production understood as economic and societal development and freedom — is on the way out (even though it is increasingly clear that it is). It is, rather, that globalization is the very name of modernity's ongoing *perishing* as a continual immanence of mortality, as an ontological challenge that, thanks to the rationalizations of contemporary techno-capitalism, comes *at* us and *to* us as the living demise of the Enlightenment justifications of an entire system of guarantees and representation, freedom, rights, citizenship, subjectivity, economic and human development, the legitimacy of the Westphalian interstate system, etc. The list is endless.

The awareness that "postmodernity" signals the "end of the metanarratives of modernity" (Lyotard) is now almost quaint when contemplating contemporary patterns of wealth accumulation, impunity, ecological destruction, technological domination, and the ideology of the survival of the fittest converted on a global scale into the quest for economic growth and resource extraction at all cost. Politics has become and will continue to be the administration of the violence of historical expiration and of our traversal of it, if there is such a thing. There is probably no political party old or new that can change this reality of expiration, only its forms of rhetoric and representation. The reality of the extension of, and of the ever-changing limits created by, ongoing expiration and our relation to it, however, remain and endure.

At this point, conservatives might wave their flags of anti-intellectual moral outrage and say that this is just jargon. More than a few on the academic Left, most likely without the flags but perhaps with the conviction etched silently in their hearts that militancy is closest to saintliness, might agree. Some will insinuate a certain whiff of "Eurocentrism," as if their own postcolonial certainties were not themselves Eurocentric in nature.[2] Some populist illuminati will cast aspersions because the last few pages have not been written in the journalese of contemporary cultural studies in such a way that "the People" can understand it without having to think too much. Others will respond with the word "Revolution" as an affirmation of a proletarian will to power in the belief that the quest for a new epochal destiny is still the only true path for transformative participation and guidance, as if the desire for a new representational order (of subjectivity, for example, or of a *ratio* capable of anchoring and reproducing a less brutal organization of abstract labor) could inaugurate something more than, or something different from, the maximization of a thetic reality (that is, the laying down of a "new" principle by which to live and dominate, entailing once again the active subsumption of the everyday under a new law of comportment or morality).[3]

While rioting and upheaval appear everywhere, either in reality or *in potentia*, "Revolution," understood as the definitive finitude of the history of capital inaugurated by the emergence of proletarian consciousness, is not, it appears, on the horizon anywhere. It is, after all, only capital, rather than an external proletarian subjectivity or "ideology," which produces in the first place the conditions of its own potential consummation and demise. For there is nothing more bourgeois in its origins and extension than proletarian consciousness, to the extent that the latter can never exist *in and of itself* but only as a determinate negation of a previously given political, economic, and ideological form.[4]

For the purposes of this particular work, in which a different understanding of and ground for finitude from that of "Revolution" is pursued, what is at stake is to begin to understand a sense of ending, certainly, but in the absence of both eschatology and apocalypse, as well as in the absence of any claim to the representation of a new epochal destiny or thetic reality. In 2003 Fredric Jameson referenced his 1994 book *Seeds of Time*, in which he affirmed that "it is easier to imagine the end of the world than to imagine the end of capitalism." He returned to this comment in the following terms: "Someone once said that it is easier to imagine the end of the world than to imagine the end of capitalism. We can now revise that and witness the attempt to imagine capitalism by way of imagining the end of the world" ("Future City," 76). In 2005 Slavoj Žižek seemed to echo these observations in the documentary *Žižek!*: "It's much easier to imagine the end of all life on earth than a much more modest radical change in capitalism." Both Jameson and Žižek, in other words, have addressed the question of ends. However, they both remain firmly anchored within the ontology of the commodity form. They occlude the possibility that what might actually be at stake now is the uncovering of a thinking of *existence* and *world* that has remained for the most part concealed within the dominant tradition of political thinking from the late 1960s onward. Žižek's and Jameson's insights are immediately graspable as gestures toward the contemporary predicament of the subject in capital. However, without recognizing the question of *existence* as the exploration of "everything in the human condition that is not susceptible to being integrated into the movement of the commodity" (Alemán, *En la frontera*, 50), neither of their formulations can move in an alternative direction to (I will not say "beyond") the modern orthodoxies of received political thinking and their inherited forms of representation. Both Žižek and Jameson remain firmly anchored within the commonsense politics of the Left that has accompanied the ontological ground of the epoch of commodity fetishism and its subjective ends, circulating persistently around the ontic (sociological) question of ontology formulated by Marx in the opening paragraph of volume 1 of *Capital*. Since now it is clear that there is no "form of 'life' as agency, activity and passivity, even suffering, even dying" that can be "lived outside a commodity form and a value form that is in fact a moment in the valorization process of capital" (Balibar, "Towards a New Critique of Political Economy," 56), the initial approach to *existence*, as the extension of an "absolute difference between life and politics, and between being and thinking" (Moreiras, *La diferencia absoluta*, 2), becomes paramount.

But first, what can be understood by the "ontological ground of the epoch of commodity fetishism and its ends"? What is the problem that lies therein? Obviously, it is still a question of technological reification, of the absolutization of the human as commodity form, and therefore of relation *as such*. It is by now well documented that the 1970s saw the beginning of a shift to "neoliberal" economic policies, a utopian regurgitation of classic political economy that was later consolidated in the 1980s under the tutelage of Thatcherite and Reaganite anti-Keynesian monetarism and financialization. In his *Brief Introduction to Neoliberalism* David Harvey refers to neoliberalism as an expansive transformation in the modern forms of "accumulation by dispossession." Due to this transformation in form, the subordination of the modern state form to global capital, that is, the establishment not of the end of the state but of the new post-sovereign form of a *market-state duopoly* (Levinson, *Market and Thought*), transformed the general recessive tendency of the early 1970s into a fully deterritorialized tendency for the expansive pursuit of surplus value and of value extraction beyond the onto-topological frontiers of the Nation and its legal structures.

While the Cold War had provided the era of petroleum extraction, atomic energy, and fossil fuels with a combination of territorial-military containment and previously unseen technological advancement, the *globalization* of commodity fetishism that has extended itself in the wake of the collapse of the Soviet Union has instigated the death throes of that previous era of development.[5] Globalization, in other words, is a planetary quest for the extraction of absolute surplus value (the limitless increase in the amount of work provided by labor power) and simultaneously for the limitless (deterritorialized) extension of the *production of relative surplus value* (the decrease in the time of socially necessary labor). Within the world of the disarrangement of "socially necessary" labor, the deterritorialized commodity form reigns supreme, and the role of the post-sovereign market-state duopoly becomes to manage and foment an entire life of consumption and debt from birth to death, while guaranteeing resource and value extraction on a global scale at any cost.[6]

As already briefly referenced, the Spanish philosopher Felipe Martínez Marzoa delivered in a book published in the early 1980s a reading of Marx's first volume of *Capital*, examining the ontological ground of "the elemental form of existence of 'wealth' in modern society" (*La filosofía de El Capital*, 33). For Martínez Marzoa the commodity is the content of the ontology that refers to the mode of being of modern society. Marx, he says, "begins with the confirmation that things are commodities, *they are* to the extent that they are commodities. He investigates what that specific mode of *being* consists of, and the path of that ontology ends up being the construction of a model, a structure, which we call 'the structure of modern society' or the 'capitalist mode of production'" (45).[7] Martínez Marzoa effects a potentially major shift in the reading of Marx by emphasizing the "productive dialogue" between Marx and Heidegger that was first suggested in the latter's 1947 essay "Letter on Humanism."[8] In other words, Martínez Marzoa strives to establish the ground for a conversation that Heidegger gestured toward but never fully extended. The immediate effect of the communication between Marx and Heidegger, via Martínez Marzoa, is the realization that the ontology of the commodity conceals the essence of *techne*, which Marx refers to as the capitalist mode of production. The true subject of *Capital*, says Martínez Marzoa (132), is *techne*, with *value* as the ground through which Marx approaches the complexity of the question of what *being* means in the modern epoch of the commodity. Under these conditions, terms such as the *bourgeoisie* and *proletariat* become predicates of that primary subject. In order to come to terms with this insight, the author begins to open up Marx's ontology of the commodity to the question of the difference between *beings* (or "particular ontology") and *Being*, understood as the *beingness* of beings (or "fundamental ontology").[9] In this regard Martínez Marzoa thinks Marx in light of the *ontological difference*. He echoes Marx's groundbreaking realization that the "fact that things are commodities determines the being of things in that world" (149), thereby indicating that the fetishism of the commodity form as a modern metaphysics is also defined by what it conceals. In this formulation fundamental ontology is what capital, together with *Capital*, camouflages and what the commodity form obscures. The result is that the exploration of the essence of metaphysics is what grapples best with the question that *Capital* points toward but does not address:

> The ontology of *Capital* is not particular, since it does not delimit a field for beings in the face of others. It refers to the entirety of being. But at the same time, it falls short of being a fundamental ontology.

Marx apprehends what mode of presence for being belongs to modern society as a destiny, but he does not know how or why that destiny takes root in being itself. In order to get to know this, in order to root Marxism in fundamental ontology and thereby enter into what Heidegger called "a productive dialogue with Marxism," one would have to provide the Marxian analysis of the "modern mode of production" with a ground that could not be found in any so-called "Marxist philosophy," "Historical Materialism," or conceptual application to the entirety of history of "economic law" and "mode of production." . . . In the light of *Capital* so-called "historical materialism" (and therefore, *a fortiori*, so-called "dialectical materialism") can be discarded. (141–42)

It is precisely with this awareness in mind — that is, that the time has come to provide the Marxian analysis of the "modern mode of production" with a ground that could not be found in any so-called Marxist philosophy or historical materialism — that I embark on this Passage with an echo of Jacques Derrida's fundamental discussion in *Aporias* of Martin Heidegger's existential analytic, in particular reference to the question of *perishing* that comes to the fore in *Being and Time* and later in his 1941–1942 lectures on Hölderlin (*Hölderlin's Hymn "Remembrance"*). I propose this path since, despite the obvious difference between the ontological and the ontic, the question of finitude is particularly pertinent to the contemporary understanding (as well as to the problem of how to account for the understanding) of the ongoing collapse not only of the modern teleology of progress but of the modern political space that has grounded it at least since the inauguration of the imperial age and the Westphalian order from 1648 onward.

In *Aporias* Derrida observes the following regarding our approach to and understanding of *perishing*:

Heidegger says that he has called the ending of the living (*das Enden von Lebendem*) "perishing," *Verenden*. . . . This *Verenden* is the ending, the way of ending or coming to the end that all living things share. They all eventually kick the bucket. In everyday German, *verenden* also means to die, to succumb, to kick the bucket, but since that is clearly not what Heidegger means by properly dying (*eigentlich sterben*), by the dying proper to *Dasein*, *verenden* must not be translated by "dying" in order to respect what Heidegger intends to convey. . . . I prefer "perishing." Why? . . . Because the verb "to perish" retains something of *per*, of the passage of the limit, of the traversal marked in Latin by the *pereo*, *perire* (which means exactly: to leave, disappear, pass — on the other side of life, *transire*). (30–31)

In *Aporias* Derrida emphasizes the place of *verenden* not only within the overall movement of the existential analytic in *Being and Time* but also in relation to the passing of a limit in the historical unveiling of truth. Thus, Derrida traverses and echoes in Heidegger's thinking from the 1920s to World War II the relation between the existential analytic and the critique of empire. By the early 1940s, Heidegger was addressing *verenden*, via his readings of Hölderlin, in a critique of the history of the West as the time of neo-Roman imperialism.[10] In her recent book on the cultural imaginary of European imperial thinking, Julia Hell observes that in the early 1940s Heidegger was making a fundamental distinction between *decline* and *perishing* and therefore between different kinds of ending. As Hell notes, *perishing* is a "clinging fast to the ordinary," a desire for "the continuation of the same" (*The Conquest of Ruins*, 438). Within this context, Heidegger considered "the future of the American world empire," for example, to be a "form of perishing, not decline," or *Untergehen*, which was a term reserved exclusively for the greatness of the Greeks (437). *Verenden*, on the other hand, was essentially "linked to a meaningless life" (437), in contrast to the possibility of historical *inception*, which implied "thinking of endings as modernity's originary difference that returns throughout history but always in a different form" (438). Hell observes that Heidegger's turn toward inception, against *perishing*, was both "an attack on the Nazis' imitation of Rome" and "an implicit critique of [Carl] Schmitt's version of the Paulist *katechon* who, while residing in the danger zone, acted in order to postpone the end as long as possible" (438).

I telegraph this path toward the relation (and toward the possibility of thinking at a distance from the relation) between *perishing* and the restraining force of the Paulist-Schmittian katechon as a reference to be recalled in the pages to come. For it is here, in the heart of the contemporary perishing of an American planetary empire, which was already a perishing of the territorial forms it superseded through the course of the twentieth century, that we intuit that the necessity of an inception in thinking probably haunts us more today than ever.

Against, for example, Francis Fukuyama's vulgar "end of history" announced in the wake of the fall of the Berlin Wall in 1989, by bringing Heidegger's question of ontology and *being* to bear on recent social history we confront the uncovering of the contemporary as an ongoing and intensifying perishing, as the continuing passage of an ending to the ideological and historical movement of modernity. Therein it comes to light finally that an end is in fact ending or, as Derrida also says, is "demising," which of course is not the same as death. Since the aporia of *perishing* "can never be endured as such; the ultimate aporia is the impossibility of the aporia *as such*" (*Aporias*, 21), the ontological problematic signaled via globalization points to the impossibility of an experience of passage *through* or *beyond* the contemporary, which *is*, one can perhaps speculate, the intensification of a second-order (duopolistic American-Chinese post-territorial, technological, post-sovereign) perishing from within perishing itself. It is capitalism running on canters, consuming itself meaninglessly yet so well that it is consumed, as Lacan noted four decades ago. It is already too late.

It is with this (im)possibility of an experience of passage in mind that, in the following, the reader will encounter three perhaps unfamiliar terms: *decontainment*, *posthegemony*, and *infrapolitics*. Indeed, the first term, *decontainment*, is a way of referencing another perhaps unfamiliar term, the already signposted Paulist-Schmittian katechon or, even more specifically for our current purposes, the post-katechontic. This is a planetary configuration of force extended along the breakdown of the limits between the state, the economy, and private existence, between what could be called governing, exchanging, and living (Harcourt, *Exposed*, 26).[11] In what follows, contemporary turmoil is essentially the actuality of ongoing unconcealed and bottomless political-theological perishing experienced as the perplexity caused by the continuation of the closure of metaphysics and of the globalization of the ontology of the commodity.

The reader will have noticed, however, that I have chosen to begin this Passage with three epigraphs penned by Percy Bysshe Shelley, Jean-Luc Nancy, and Jacques Lacan, respectively. Therefore, I will begin by addressing briefly their inclusion as a collective point of departure and movement toward the question of contemporary epochality, posthegemony, and the infrapolitical.

I have begun with these epigraphs because their combination illustrates that the sphere of questioning I propose to pursue in this work is multiple. Allow me to explain. In his seminal reading of Nietzsche's words "God is dead," Martin Heidegger observed that "at the beginning of modernity, the question dawned anew how man amidst the entirety of beings, which means before the beingmost ground of all beings (God), can become and be certain of its own continuing duration, i.e., of his own salvation. This question of the certainty of salvation is the question of justification, i.e., of justice (*iustitia*)" ("The Word of Nietzsche," 183). In the modern age of mass uprising and rebellion in the wake of the French Revolution, such a dawning can be located in the recuperation and secular extension of the Promethean tradition. For example, writing in 1820 at the dawning of the age of the steam engine, the poet Shelley, in his proposed overturning of Aeschylus's *Prometheus Bound*, explored and extended the legacy of Platonic dialecticism — that is, the very heart of Western metaphysics — by representing a decision for freedom from tyranny via an act of *parrhesia* inaugurated against Jupiter by the proto-Satanic spirit,

Prometheus, thereby indicating that the only theme available for consciousness, understanding, and judgment in the wake of the French Revolution, and of course at the dawning of the Industrial Revolution, was that of the relation between Master and Slave. Clearly Shelley was not alone in this thematization in the wake of the French Revolution.[12]

Prometheus's decision and act of freedom in *Prometheus Unbound*, this modern desire for the exercise of free thinking grounded in voluntary and conscious action against the Gods and their unjust world order, consisted in the reduction of the mastery and will of the highest being as a result of the recognition that the earthly order of the One and his acolytes ("Monarch of Gods and Daemons, and all Spirits") was that of an originary, inexplicable, and groundless hostility caused by the mere act of placing humans as the object and slave of divine will ("Regard this Earth/Made multitudinous with thy slaves").

In the wake of Prometheus's ardor, perennial suffering, and the recall of a curse he had placed previously on his tormentor Jupiter, the latter declares omnipotence upon his throne, immediately, however, appearing to fall victim to his own will to power and descending into the abyss, aided by Demogorgon, the tyrant of the shadow world who arrives on the chariot of the hour. In light of this apparently spontaneous emergence from the shadow world of a new restraining order against tyranny, Prometheus is immediately and inexplicably released from all punishment and suffering, and "veil by veil, evil and error fall" (285, l. 62), the world envelops its children in love (286, ll. 90–91), earth and heaven unite, and a new world order comes into being in which Man is declared to be "sceptreless, free, uncircumscribed . . . equal, unclassed, tribeless, and nationless . . . Passionless? — no, yet free from guilt or pain" (293–94, ll. 194–98). Prometheus's very name evokes foresight, of course, and it is in the context of the privileging of the imminent and present over the past that a Chorus of Spirits sings to the future, announcing victory even over death, chaos, and night: "We will take our plan/From the new world of man,/And our task shall be called the/Promethean" (300, ll. 156–58). Earth celebrates its newfound boundlessness as a "vaporous exultation not to be confined!" while Man is said to become "one harmonious soul of many a/soul/Whose nature is its own divine control" (307, ll. 400–1).

The final words, the concluding ethicopolitical *ethos* of *Prometheus Unbound*, belong to the orator Demogorgon, who eschews the idea of freedom as lawlessness and circumscribes Promethean emancipation by subsuming it under a thetic reality based in the values of hope, goodness, life, love, and empire. As such, the final gesture of the poetic drama is to illustrate and extend a rhetoric of freedom as a political relation to a specific moral and therefore to a specifically regulative comportment: "To defy Power, which seems/ omnipotent;/To love, and bear; to hope till Hope/creates/ . . . This, like thy glory, Titan, is to be/Good, great and joyous, beautiful and/free;/This is alone Life, Joy, Empire and/Victory!" (313, ll. 572–78). Demogorgon offers the world instruction by anchoring Promethean *parrhesia* to the principle of a norm for all future action; "to defy Power which seems omnipotent . . . is to be Good . . . This is alone Life, Joy, Empire and/Victory!"

In Shelley's poetic rendering of the mythical origins of modern-day demagoguery, the tyrant of the shadows preemptively vindicates all future acts of contestation or rebellion against tyranny as fully justified and good, emphasizing that it is not only the action that is good but that to defy power is *to be good*; in other words, for Demogorgon the subject that carries it out *is*, in its very being, the living embodiment of virtue. Demogorgon's order upholds the principle of virtue and therefore of value itself. At the end of *Prometheus Unbound*, Demogorgon the orator converts an individual complaint into a hegemonic phenomenon for the understanding of all future decisions for action against injustice. He thereby presents the Earth with the value of the conditions and significance of the new Age of freedom and justice (*iustitia*), in which the restraining of omnipotent power extends toward the future, deferring the end of the history of the Earth in the name of value (the Good).

Within this hegemony, the mere possibility of freedom requires defying and deactivating, that is, detotalizing, the tyrannical totalization of power. But as can be seen in the relation between Prometheus's personal suffering — "Ah me! Alas, pain, pain ever, for ever! No change, no pause, no hope! Yet I endure" — and Demogorgon's ode to speaking truth to power as a decision for a hegemonic notion of subjective freedom, Shelley's recognition of the sovereign will to omnipotence as an onto-theological act of placing the human as mere object also belies an implicit correspondence with the emergence of the agonistic order of the subject and, indeed, with the very idea that the objection to injustice in the name of freedom should become in the future the sole enduring *solution* for the common suffering of the multitudes.

In the name of an egological "But One" ("Monarch of Gods and Daemons, and all Spirits But One") and presumably of a future time that is the active negation of both the present and past, the spirit Prometheus takes the decision to question the legitimacy of an earthly order dominated by a common relation of inferiority to the One — to the onto-theological realm ordained and ruled by the Monarch Jupiter — in which equality and co-belonging, or in what would later be called "general equivalence" in the economic law of the modern materialist order of capital, have never been disentangled from the tribulations of subordination: "Behold . . . Regard this Earth/Made multitudinous with thy slaves, whom thou/Requitest for knee-worship, prayer, and praise,/And toil, and hecatombs of broken hearts,/With fear and self-contempt and barren hope." For Shelley's Prometheus, the human and the Earth exist to the extent that they are reduced to the status of means alone.

Prometheus's reproach to the divine Monarch rests on a moment of vision ("Behold . . . Regard this Earth"), the positing of an all-seeing perspective, and therefore of a perception that fleetingly binds the transcendental, the human world of slaves, and the morality of improvement that Prometheus advocates. This scopic moment is the metaphysical focal point at which the gathering of an image — of a "world picture," as Heidegger puts it — translates the a priori of the kingdom of the divine into the fallen realm of the human and vice versa, mediated by the sight of the individualist "I" that sees.[13] In this moment, earthly existence is captured and contained within the *subiectum* of representation — Prometheus himself — and the only shadow internal to that representation is that of a human life overwhelmed by "hecatombs of broken hearts,/With fear and self-contempt and barren hope," prior to the unveiling of an earthly utopia grounded in the combined *hegemon* of subjectivity and morality in the knowledge and rejection of tyranny. But the incalculable distance that inevitably joins and separates the transcendental to and from the human remains unaccounted for and, as such, remains concealed in Shelley's poem, rendered oblivious in, and thanks to, the recuperation of Prometheus's subjective vision and placing of the human in its unjust relation to "the being-most ground of all beings (God)" (Heidegger, "The Word of Nietzsche's," 183).

For Shelley there can be no loosening of the metaphors and demagoguery of the will to power, which covers over the abyss between beings and what is represented as the theological foundation of freedom; the divine Monarch and, later, "Man," as the divine Monarch's impossible replacement (impossible because man as such can never occupy the place of God; he can only enter the realm of *subjectity*).

In his taking on of Aeschylus via the legacy of Platonic dialecticism, Shelley's Prometheus strives to reproach the entirety of Western ontology as the perennial drama of the might and theological power of the Sovereign. The poet proposes Prometheus's act of *parrhesia* as the inauguration of a new epoch of willful accusation — the commencement of a subjective order of confrontation grounded in the decision and of the new epoch it unveils — but it is clear that there is still no distinction to be made in *Prometheus Unbound* between earthly existence and the sovereign power of divine force, which are coextensive to each other throughout, even when divine omnipotence is undermined and man becomes "one harmonious soul of many/a soul/Whose nature is its own divine control" (307, ll. 400–1).

The God Jupiter is denied as omnipotent but is replaced by the representation of the omnipotence of utopian humanism, that is, Man as his own divine control, as the revaluation of the divine Monarch as highest value. If at one point it is clear that emancipation is predicated on the detotalization of totalization, that is, on *parrhesia* as a subjective decision for a restraining force against the tyranny of omnipotence, by the end of the lyric drama we see that freedom actually comes to be predicated on the absolute retotalization — the reunification, the becoming One via the representation of "Man" — of the detotalization of totalization and, as such, on the reconversion of all prior negativity (such as the abyss underlying the relation between Jupiter's slaves and the supersensory sovereign) into a positivity beyond mediation. In this process man and Earth unite in undetermined immediacy, the underlying shadow world is cast into oblivion, and, in classic Platonic poetic form, metaphorization — representation — erases the morbid inequity of life on Earth.

In Shelley's proposed confrontation with the entire history of Western onto-theology (from the conformism of Aeschylus's Prometheus to the legacy of contestation opened up by the French Revolution), we come face to face with the unquestioned persistence of the ontology of the human as a relation of subordination to the persistent onto-theological order of the Idols (first God and then Man). We come face to face, in other words, with *humanism* as a fundamental and constitutive feature of the onto-theological constitution of both metaphysics and of the modern concepts of subjectivity, representation, and emancipation. For this reason, Shelley's apparent renunciation of the metaphysical inheritance of tyranny guarantees nevertheless the persistence of that very same inheritance. Herein, no distinction can be made between beings and the heavens, in the process indicating that for the poet of 1820, in Prometheus's decision for freedom the humanist validation of a theological instinct endures in the form of a romantic decision for, and act of, emancipation devoid of negativity, since by the end the dialectical line between restraint and boundlessness is rendered indistinguishable via the language of the orator Demogorgon.

As already suggested, at the drama's close Demogorgon orients the entire Earth toward the hegemonic comportment of the good decision, subject, and act, as he initiates a closing language of value, and of values, by which all future comportment should be willed into existence, determined, judged, represented, and repeated in a world that is now posited implicitly as an object of subjective positing.

While the utopian order of Man in *Prometheus Unbound* is rendered possible by Prometheus *deciding* to admonish the divine *nomos* from a position of *anomos* (from the rock upon which he is crucified), and while he does so

acting in an attitude of direct rejection of divine law and will over the multitude of abject living beings, by the end of the lyric drama emancipation is fully
consonant with the emergence of Man as the *nomos* of a new epoch-making
empire of humanity grounded in tyrannicide and perennial conflict over the
mastery of the world. Henceforth defiance to, and the overthrow of, tyrannical
power is the sole technique for a destinal awakening of humanity understood
as the modern epochal truth of Spirit. In this formulation humanism is by
definition an originary form of populism, and there is no politics without the
representation and containment of tyranny.

But thanks to the emancipation of Prometheus, we also see that the new
world order is devoid of all *anomie*, or *anomos*. This is where Shelley's political delusion comes to the fore, for there can be no empire without anomie or
in the absence of a distinction from eschatology, and what we have at the end
of Shelley's *Prometheus Unbound* is a rendering of emancipation as absolute
temporal, spatial, and human arrest, that is, the new epoch of Earth as both
object of representation and as placelessness, as Utopia, and as the new epoch
of Man, indeed, of the New Man as the embodiment of Heaven on Earth, as
the spontaneous coming into itself of Absolute Spirit.

In Shelley, the Hegelian dialectic of consciousness begins with Prometheus's initial individual *parrhesia*. From there the dialectical schema of thesis, antithesis, and sublation continues through the poet's overall vision of
world transformation via *parrhesia*, *tyrannicide*, and humanist *resurrection*.

At the dawn of the Industrial Revolution, Shelley provides us with an enduring neo-Hegelian metaphor for political emancipation as the end of history that, over a century later, Alexandre Kojève would express in his introduc-
tory lectures on Hegel in the following terms: "History stops at the moment
when the difference, the opposition between Master and Slave disappears: at
the moment when the Master will cease to be the Master, because he will no
longer have a Slave; and the Slave will cease to be because he will no longer
have a Master" (43–44). In other words, both history and politics are rendered
mute in Shelley's metaphysics of emancipation, that is, enslavement to the
heavenly life on earth of the new "Man," or *subiectum*. If, as Martin Heidegger
observes, "each historical age is not only great in a distinctive way in contrast
to others; it also has, in each instance, its own concept of greatness" ("The Age
of the World Picture," 135), then perhaps it can be suggested that in Shelley's
*Prometheus Unbound* the concept of greatness of the Revolutionary age is to
be found in the relation between foresight (tyrannicide, futurity, the ontology
of moral improvement, the "becoming-One" of humanity, or the teleology of
secular progress decades before Marx), the *subiectum* of representation (Man,
humanism), and the regulative hegemony announced by Demogorgon re-

garding what constitutes in the present, and for the future, a good subject, a good act, and a good value.

But the metaphysical idealism of *Prometheus Unbound* is utterly delusional, since the unrestrained power of Man (humanism) cannot restrain the unrestrained omnipotence of the tyrants, since they are both part and parcel of an indistinct will to power, or sovereign political theology, of Good versus Bad. Quite simply, what *Prometheus Unbound* presents in the end is the fact that the hegemony of the Good, of the virtuous, is the impossible humanist transvaluation of God, now with Man as the highest value predicated on the metaphysical maximization of a shared moral value, or world picture. In this order of representation, the freedom of hegemony proportions a doctrine of mediated subordination to the humanist moralism of the Good, constituted by the subjective decision as the first step toward the retotalization — or re-unification, the becoming One again — of the detotalization of totalization. This retotalization is the recommencement of the omnipotence of the order of the One ("Man"), in its becoming. It is the spiritualization of value and the secularization of the divine simultaneously, whether it recognizes it as such or not.[14]

For this reason alone, hegemony is the actualization of a modern nihilism — an eternal recurrence of the self-willing of the *subiectum* — that, to this day, saturates the political world of both Left and Right via the never-ending representation and subjectification of life as will to power, with power as the production of the dispensations of value, truth, and therefore of nontruth, or even of the claim to fakeness as a manic expression of doubt cast on the nature of truth and on the virtue, and therefore value, of the other (human, gathering, genus, race, gender, person, sexuality, profession, group, nation, etc.). The claim to *fake news* is only ever the will to power of the *subiectum* orienting individual and public anxiety in the direction of the certainty of, and of acquiescence to, domination.

Hegemony, like domination — indeed, hegemony as a form of sanctioned domination — is the exercise of consciousness as self-certainty, the active positing of the "I think, therefore I am," and of faith in the representation of both self and other as good or bad, that is, as value at war with itself as the actuality of the political, via the never-ending positing and securing of representation and law. The highest value is transvalued and becomes a political humanism in which *justice* remains at an incommensurable distance from, or proximity to, *logos*.

Reading Shelley's poetic analysis of modern freedom retroactively through Heidegger's seminal reading of Nietzsche's words "God is dead," we see that, in *Prometheus Unbound*, "unexpectedly and above all unprepared, man finds himself placed, on the basis of the being of beings, before the task of undertaking mastery of the earth" (Heidegger, "The Word of Nietzsche," 188). Demogorgon's closing soliloquy discloses the beginning of a movement away from theological thinking toward ontological thinking, that is, from the demise of onto-theological metaphysics to the birth of humanist subjectivist metaphysics, in the name of the demise of tyranny. Jupiter occupies the onto-theological; Prometheus's *parrhesia* the Cartesian *cogito sum*, and Demogorgon their reconversion into the moral order of all future decisions and acts.

By the end of Shelley's lyric drama, life can no longer be sustained from within the reign of Jupiter while, in Demogorgon's words, value-thinking is elevated into *the* principle of everything that will carry through into the future. To the extent that Jupiter has been cast into the abyss he has been killed. The abyss, however, continues to exist, as does the closure of the onto-theological metaphysics of Jupiter's sovereign reign. As such, via Demogorgon we begin to see that "if God and the gods are dead in the sense of the metaphysical sense . . . then mastery over beings as such in the shape of mastery over the earth passes over to the new human willing" (Heidegger, "The Word of Nietzsche," 190). It passes over, in other words, to the reign of the subject as the *impossible* highest order.[15] This is a highest order that can endure only as long as it can hold in restraint — or purport to cast into oblivion — the question of the ontological difference between Being (as the *wherefrom*, or fundamental ontology, concealed within the metaphysics of subjectivity) and beings (the meaningful, or particular, ontology): "Ah me! Alas, pain, pain ever, for ever! No change, no pause, no hope! Yet I endure."

But the question is not only how long can the order of the "I endure" endure. Perhaps more importantly in the context of contemporary *perishing* and planetary mortality, another question persists: Is the order of the "I endure" as it has been bequeathed via Enlightenment history and its political and cultural forms — that is, as the order of the *subiectum*, of the representation of the subject, and of the will to power of political subjectification — still worth fighting for in a context in which it has been overtaken by the problem and reality of perishing? After all, the subjectivism of the *I* of the order of the *I endure* is nothing more than the affirmation of nihilism as concealment in motion. What is really at stake for the approach to existence is the clearing of a way through the perishing that underlies the *I* of the *I endure*. What follows is an attempt to demarcate such a clearing.

The Italian philosopher Massimo Cacciari in a recent work observes that "it was Promethean power that made possible belief in the synthesis of time and concept, and made possible the 'projecting' of history by organizing-containing energies and subjects" (*The Withholding Power*, 109). "The *kate-*

*chon*," Cacciari continues in reference to the political theology of restraint and containment that lies at the heart of secular Promethean thinking, "in its highest and strongest dimension belongs to this family of titans" (109). However, the author concludes, in the contemporary world of globalized capital "Prometheus has withdrawn — or has once again been crucified on his rock, and Epimetheus is at large and in our world opening ever newer Pandora's boxes." In other words, for Cacciari the Promethean order of the "I endure" is collapsing, along with the onto-theological humanism that grounds it, which might explain in metaphorical terms why subjectivism is becoming increasingly rampant and increasingly forceful, or reactionary, in nature.

In the wake of Nietzsche's word, Cacciari points to the ongoing eclipse of the Promethean perspective and the modern political theology it inaugurated because, he says, global capital reduces "all conflict to calculation, and so make[s] possible the end of the struggle for hegemony between the powers." It does this, he continues, "in the eschatological sense of inaugurating the space of permanent crises, of passing seamlessly from crisis to crisis with no armistice, let alone peace." Cacciari points (quite fundamentally, we should say) to the fact that the contemporary order of permanent crises that we refer to as globalization is no longer the consequence of hegemony. On the contrary, it is the thematization of the exhaustion of hegemony and of the seemingly infinite indetermination and turmoil that extends as a consequence. It is the basis of *posthegemony* in action, a fact that we will return to shortly.

Meanwhile, for Cacciari the dominant question for our times involves determining how to assess the order of representation (the onto-theological metaphors of the subjective will to power) in the service of an alternative power, while still in the wake of the ongoing eclipse of a prior metaphysical order, which is modern Promethean power itself. While unlike Cacciari I have no investment in breathing new life into the ancient and modern political onto-theology — or humanist populism — of the Promethean perspective, I would suggest that it is indeed here that we can begin to determine with greater clarity the further determination of our path toward the contemporary work and significance of post-sovereign turmoil (or *decontainment*), *posthegemony*, and the *infrapolitical*, all of which establish for thinking a distance from the modern onto-theological metaphors of the subjective will to power — that is, from inherited political form — not by striving to breathe new life into Promethean metaphysics but by remaining attuned to, precisely, the consequences for thinking and acting politically in the twilight, and consequently in relation to the perishing, of their modern history.

Herein lies the timbre of my second and third complementary epigraphs penned by Jean-Luc Nancy and Jacques Lacan, respectively: "This is the limit of an era, which was the era of the representation of a meaning. . . . We have exhausted the schemas of progress and of the progressive unveiling of truth. In this sense, History is indeed finished, or finite, and 'finitude' opens another history" (Nancy, *Gravity*), and Jacques Lacan's announcement in the wake of the events of 1968: "I have no *Weltanschauung*" (cosmovision, worldview, or directive principle). What is at stake herein is that while Shelley's reincarnation of Prometheus in the wake of the French Revolution belongs clearly to the era of the Christian metaphysics of the One, of the sovereign God of all (that is, of onto-theology, in which every subjective decision is by definition an a priori extension of the Final Judgment), and while Cacciari *laments* the ongoing collapse of this metaphysics and the history it has engendered, Nancy attests to the collapse of the era of the Final Judgment — to the ongoing closure of (and since ongoing, not entirely closed) Christian metaphysics — and Lacan to the exhaustion of the "world picture" as a fundamental means of rethinking the history of metaphysics.

The contemporary is in these terms the eclipse and potential demise of a notion of political authority grounded previously in the representation of the "mortal God" of Hobbesian sovereignty. The contemporary is also, however, its permanent reactionary regurgitation in the form of political demagoguery, brute force, and biopolitical absolutism. This explains Cacciari's approach to the contemporary as the uncovering of a space of "permanent crises, of [a world] passing seamlessly from crisis to crisis with no armistice." "The figure of the 'mortal God,'" he observes, "which contained all individuals equally within itself is exploded and the power of representation, through which the one who represents really thinks he can contain within himself those represented, is weakened — but from this crisis there emerges neither the absolute and simple absence of law and command, nor anarchy, nor the prospect of a new Age" (69). My contention is that what emerges is the postsovereign market-state duopoly, contemporary turmoil, narco-accumulation, and the need for an infrapolitical exodus from the biopolitical, in the name of existence.

At the end of *The Withholding Power* Cacciari characterizes the challenge to contemporary thinking as the need to traverse the obscurity produced by the exhaustion of the schemas of progress and the demise of the progressive unveiling of truth. He does this by suggesting that the perpetual reassessment of the Promethean conditions of belief in the synthesis of time and concept, and the "projecting" of history by organizing-containing energies and subjects, is still the only path toward the reorientation and transformation of a world devoid of armistice: perhaps thereby leading to a new sense of epochality capable of once again casting anxiety (the poet Shelley's "hecatombs of broken hearts / With fear and self-contempt and barren hope") into oblivion in the name of a "new politics."

What is at stake for Cacciari in *The Withholding Power* is contemporary thought's engagement with the possibility of a not-so-obscure recommence-ment of a *katechontic energy*, of a metaphysics of restraint, and therefore of representation, against turmoil and catastrophe. Having said that, he remains very much aware that "all that the permanent crises can today allow us reason-ably to claim is that they will not give rise to new catechontic powers" (117). The question Cacciari brings us to confront is whether there is an alternative in the wake of the tradition of Promethean thinking. Cacciari, of course, is all in favor of a revamped alternative politics, and he is not alone in the realiza-tion and identification of this fundamental problem. Neither is he alone in lamenting the collapse of that Promethean tradition.

In contrast, what is at stake in my own particular intervention is not an al-ternative politics — a revamped metaphysics of the subject, for example — but the possibility of an alternative place from which to think the limits of the political and the possibility of a turn away from the ontology of the subject.[16]

What is at stake, in other words, is what to do with the ongoing *perishing* of the Aristotelian-modern political tradition itself. Obviously, this is too weighty a task to address here in its entirety. But I would like to provide a few pointers before proceeding. Before advancing in a different direction from Cacciari, who proposes the reinvention of the metaphysics of political subjectivity from scratch, we should clarify first what can be understood by the exhaustion of Aristotelian politics in the era of globalization, in order to then address the problem of the katechon, its political-theological energies, and its relation to contemporary global capital. This will allow us to move in the direction of a possible turn toward *posthegemony* and *infrapolitics* not as an alternative politics but as a differential relation to the political, as a distance-taking in the name of freedom from the everyday turmoil of the ontology of the commodity form and the subjectivity it determines.

In a recent essay, Jorge Álvarez Yágüez ("La forma 'política' y el popu-lismo," 202–5) highlights the Aristotelian origins of classical and modern political form in which (1) politics takes place between *free* beings, rather than slaves; participants should be free from coercion and protected by the imperium of the law; *nomos* is opposed to tyranny and *physis* [nature]; (2) the *equality* between beings of the same nature, the possessors of *logos*, guarantees movement in a space of symmetrical positions, that is, in a homogeneous geo-metrical space in which all subjects are positioned equally and equidistantly in relation to the *arche*, or power, that cannot be occupied definitively. This subsequently produces the metaphor of the *polis* at the moment at which the *agora*, the gathering place or assembly, supersedes the acropolis; (3) equality is exercised actively, rather than being passively received, and citizenship is not defined in terms of blood ties; (4) deliberation rather than expertise or paternalism is an index of political quality, and, as such, in freedom and equality there can be no figure of despotism; (5) instrumentalization and violence — the reduction of the *other* to a mere object — are both excluded, since they would represent an act of despotism and a violation of the equal sharing of *logos*. Therein lies political and ethical virtue and the possibility of a political "reason without appetites"; (6) plurality and difference, rather than unity (which is antipolitical), guarantee freedom and equality in, and as, the constant confrontation with the *logoi*; and (7) this constant confrontation is the guarantee of a *justice* protected by the imperium of the law, without which there can be no political form.

What Álvarez Yágüez highlights is a republican political form defined in Aristotle by spatial symmetry, the equidistance to power, the essential ground of the *polis*, the exclusion of violence, and the spatial guarantee and containment of equality and freedom. Republican politics, in other words, is the spatially coordinated political form for the containment of and safeguarding against despotism. In contemporary political philosophy Jacques Rancière is perhaps the most Aristotelian of thinkers, since his point of departure is that there can be no "democratic State." Álvarez Yágüez points this out when he observes that Rancière considers democracy to be not a political regime but the egalitarian principle as such (205).

For our purposes, however, there is a fundamental problem herein, since globalization signifies the explosion of the spatial metaphors — the representability — of political form itself. Rancière, in other words, still thinks from within the modern nineteenth-century Aristotelian republican tradition, when what is currently experienced is actually the ongoing *perishing* of that tradition. In neoliberal globalization we can still speak in terms of the egalitarian principle, certainly. The problem is that it can no longer be operational in the real or metaphorical geometrical space of representation in which all subjects are positioned equally and equidistantly in relation to *arche*. By definition, in globalization the metaphor of the *polis* or of the *agora*, the gathering place or assembly, has been deterritorialized by the despotism of capital in its planetary technological mode, which, it would appear, cannot itself be mastered.

What is at stake, in other words, is the late-neoliberal decontainment of political form in a world that already supersedes the republican principle of containment, since in the nonfinite system that is globalization — a nonfinite that forces us to confront the finitude, or the infinitely finite, of all prior forms, modes of representation, and ways of thinking — nothing definitive can be produced by "negation." What we find ourselves immersed in is a violently open indetermination—the metonymic *continuum* of the circulating signifiers of the post-sovereign market-state duopoly—that extends immanently through and beyond itself, but without access to general subjectivation or a universal signifier (Bazzicalupo, "Populismo y liberalismo," 369). This raises the question of how to begin to think in the register of the coming to presence of the dissolution of every modern project, form, and representation.

## Katechon, Postkatechon, Decontainment

It is well known and widely commented on that for early Christianity from Saint Paul up to the Reformation the katechon provided the Christian tradition with the metaphor of the restrainer, or of that which guarded against the coming of the Anti-Christ, which was generally understood to be the negation of all Christ-like attributes. The idea of the katechon (derived from *katechein*: to detain, to contain, to withhold, to gain possession of, to be master of, to slow down; also, that which, or he who, slows down or defers) echoes apotropaic magic but originates in the Second Epistle of the apostle Paul to the Thessalonians. It provides us therefore with the expression of one of the originary metaphors of political theology that is still producing its effects today (Szendy), for it is through the figure of the katechon that the specifically Christian onto-theological understanding of Being translates temporally and spatially into the sociopolitical world of beings. In this sense, the katechon is an originary and constitutive onto-theological metaphor of Being that is designed to install the heterogenesis of ends (that is, the ends of Good or Evil, or of the Master and Slave) as the projection of historical knowledge, understanding, and action.[17]

Presumably, when the Apostle penned the Epistle he did so in the knowledge that the Thessalonians had a number of lingering questions about the appearance, absence, or inexistence of the ultimate meaning of Christian dogma. One can imagine the Thessalonians wondering in what form Christianity might make itself intelligible and in what way Christian meaning-giving could be produced in order to anchor an understanding of the relation between their existence, their history, and death. What, in other words, might the gift of Christianity actually give? In his response, the Apostle sought to clarify the meaning of the coming to presence of the Messiah in the face of ongoing absence. In the process he provided the Thessalonians with the metaphor of an originary and specifically Christian *fort-Da*: the metaphysics of a Christian history of revelation and postponement presumably designed to neutralize and conceal all prior non-Christian understandings and meanings of the relation between history and being. Via this metaphor Paul reassures the

Thessalonians that there can be no accidents in the Christian gift of death and salvation, for there can be no genuine, undetermined repetition or freedom. Absolutely everything, he insinuates, is always already folded into the energy of the preordained katechontic *fort-Da*. In fact, in the Paulist formulation it is precisely this folding (represented and therefore fully determined, law-giving, in its "indeterminacies") that consolidates the projection of Christian metaphysics.

It is in the Second Epistle to the Thessalonians that the apostle Paul explains why the Lord has not come yet. Here he installs a Christian relation between history and being in the context of a conflict between law and lawlessness, in the specific interest of the moral judgment of the relation between Good and Evil. As Michael Hoelzl observes:

> Among biblical scholars, it has been agreed that verses 6–7 are the central part of the letter. These two verses, in their wider context, read as follows: "5) Do you not remember that I told you these things when I was still with you? 6) And you know what is now restraining him, so that he may be revealed when his time comes. 7) For the mystery of lawlessness is already at work, but only until the one who now restrains it is removed. 8) And then the lawless one will be revealed, whom the Lord Jesus will destroy with the breath of his mouth, annihilating him by the manifestation of his coming." What precedes the second coming of the Lord? According to the apostle Paul, the "lawless one," ὁ ἄνομος, has to be revealed and this is the precondition for the second coming of the Lord. ("Before the Anti-Christ Is Revealed," 99–100)

The Lord's absence is the precondition of his appearance as the invisible restrainer of the lawless one, and his coming to presence leads to simultaneous devastation and deliverance. In order for full presence to come into being, the Christian *imperium* perpetuates lawlessness and the threat of eschatological annihilation. Herein Paul establishes a thetic standpoint from which to understand the relation between power and history in the age of Christian metaphysics, framing human existence as the effect of the onto-theological restraining force against chaos.

The katechon is the specifically Christian instantiation of the onto-theological within the ontic and vice versa, as the point at which power, morality, time, history, and human life each become coextensive to the others. In the name of Christian understanding, the katechon obscures and conceals the finitude of existence — mere death — by sublimating it into the metaphysics of Christian eternity, just as Hegel's dialectic of consciousness would do, millennia later, in the name of Spirit.[18] The Apostle tells the Thessalonians a story — a translation of the word of the Christian God — in which the kate-chon is the metaphor of the passage of absence into presence and vice versa, of finitude into eternity and vice versa, of the improper into the proper and vice versa, of death into eternal life and vice versa, and of time into tempo-ralization, or Christian history, as the placeholder, the restraining force, in which anxiety is overcome by self-certainty (faith) and the "I endure" endures eternally in its relation to the absence and will of God. Here there is no onti-co-ontological difference, merely its concealment in a struggle against anxiety in the face of mortality, in a postponement of catastrophe, or death, that con-ceals the question of an understanding other than that offered by the Apostle.

This storytelling allows the Apostle to make something of time. It provides time with the value of the postponement and perpetuation of catastrophe, with prophetic futurity as the fully predetermined temporalizing hetero-genesis of destruction and salvation, of mastery and subordination. Within this metaphor, power — indeed, any notion of selfhood, of the subject, of a "People," of a politics — becomes fully determined by the energy, grammar, and perpetuation of the Christian katechontic extension of, and restraint against, lawlessness.

It is thanks to this specifically Christian political theology, in which es-chatological representation and Christian postponement are so intimately intertwined, that "empire has to do with *katechein* just as any form of earthly power does. Any law, any jurisdiction expresses a *catechontic* subjectivity," even though "it is not the power of the empire that restrains but rather the prayers of Christians," for, as Massimo Cacciari puts it, "the true catechontic power is the Christian seed" (*Europe and Empire*, 146–48).[19] In other words, katechontic power is the temporalizing mediation of a Christian metaphysics that is sedimented fully into the ontic world of beings as heritage, tradition, in-stitutionality, governance, morality, chaos, anarchy, consciousness, decision, power, war, etc.

To this day, the figure of the katechon — the figure of restraint against, and the containment of, mundane evils — is evoked in relation to the con-ceptualization of both the *nomic* and the political. In *Multitude: Between Innovation and Negation* Paolo Virno maintains that the ancient concept of katechon — the "force that restrains" — "resists the pressure of chaos by adher-ing to chaos" in such a way that it remains "in no way absolutely tied to the vicissitudes of State sovereignty" (56). He then goes on to refer to the katechon as the institution of *the Multitude*, as that which "surpasses and exceeds the concept of state sovereignty." Virno is not necessarily wrong in this strictly Paulist formulation of the katechon, but the problem is that by detaching the concept from the specific history of empire he overlooks the history of imperial land appropriation and spiritual conquest in order to affirm the multitude as the privileged agent for a renewed theology of politics for the present. His suggestion that the katechon "is in no way absolutely tied to the vicissitudes of State Sovereignty" upholds the religiosity of the power of Christian metaphysics, certainly, but it elides the history of Christian empire in which the discussions on the just cause for war, that is, on the nature of the *juris hostis* and the emergence of the *jus publicum Europaeum*, are absolutely central to the establishment of modern sovereignty and to the imperial order born from the creation of the Christian grand-space from the sixteenth century onward.[20]

For this reason, it is hardly by chance that the Vatican has recently recuperated the figure of katechontic restraining force precisely in order to counter the contemporary turmoil of the post-sovereign market-state duopoly. For example, in his first speech addressing the global economy, delivered on May 16, 2013, Pope Francis provided a strikingly secular interpretation of the katechon, in which the restraining force and structuring principle of the modern nonsacred world—the secular, integral nation-state—no longer does its work, thereby leading to economic lawlessness and tyranny on a global scale.[21] Restraining force for the contemporary Vatican should be essentially Westphalian in nature, and no doubt many on the Left (other than the thinkers of the *Multitude*, perhaps) might be in agreement with Pope Francis regarding his defense of what Gramsci called the "integral nation state."[22] Clearly, the pope's concerns are intimately related to the figure and *imperium* of the sovereign to the extent that the *nomos* is the order created by the restraining effect of sovereign law in the modern interstate system. Neither is it by chance that in *Leviathan* Thomas Hobbes referred to the Sovereign as a mortal God with the right to decide over the life and death of his subjects. In contrast to Virno's reading, then, and as Pope Francis appears to be fully aware, any contemporary dissolution of restraint is ultimately the result of the breakdown of the restraining force of the imperial *nomos* that originated in the sixteenth century, in its often cruel and inhuman simulation of Roman humanism.[23]

Having said that, it was the Catholic jurist Carl Schmitt who bequeathed the concept of the katechon to contemporary political theory by reconverting the time of redemption into the history of the spatial-political form of the modern Nation. Like Thomas Hobbes—who considered that for a Christian sovereign "there can be no contradiction between the Laws of God and the Laws of a Christian Commonwealth"—Schmitt was a thinker of the ancient Paulist katechon.[24] Schmitt's apocalyptic imaginary, with the idea of the *jus publicum Europaeum* as the world restrainer against all *mundane* evils, is rooted clearly in the imperial legacies of Roman law and its translation into the theological language of the Christian *imperium*. It is in this context that Julia Hell questions the tendency in her scholarly field to consider Schmitt a thinker of the German Reich alone. Hell is right to observe, in contrast, that Schmitt is a thinker "of the imperial imaginaries of Europe's (post) Roman empires, haunted by the knowledge that all empires end in ruins" (2009, 284). As she notes in *The Conquest of Ruins* (2019), for the Schmitt of *The Nomos of the Earth* the katechon was a bridge between eschatology, historical thinking, and the political form of Empire: "The belief that a restrainer holds back the end of the world provides the only bridge between the eschatological paralysis of all human events and the tremendous historical power of the Christian empire of the Germanic kings" (410). The katechon, then, guarded against the coming of the Anti-Christ and translated the theology of history into the spatialized times of empires. In her analysis of Schmitt's katechon, Hell somewhat hastily conflates the distinctive histories, institutional configurations, and structural characteristics of the Spanish (territorial) and Portuguese (maritime) empires. However, she is correct to point out that in *Nomos* "Schmitt did not glorify the Spanish-Portuguese Empire because it was a Catholic empire but because he thought that this empire's *katechontic* political theology produced the most effective form of imperial mimesis. . . . The *katechon* is a function of imperial logic, or more precisely, it is the effect of Schmitt's engagement with the trope of imperial rise and decline and with the scopic scenario that is part of all imperial mimesis" (411).

Julia Hell's approach to the Schmittian legacy echoes Massimo Cacciari's observation that in the wake of the twentieth century's two world-scale European civil wars, it is particularly significant that it was Carl Schmitt's *The Nomos of the Earth* that put the political energy of the katechon at the center of debate regarding the grounds of political theology in the modern secular period. Schmitt did so by moving away from the idea that the katechon is essentially the *imperium* and redemptive time of the church alone. Building on the figure of the Hobbesian "mortal God," for Schmitt the katechon stood for the organizing principle of a metaphysical matrix occupied by different mundane factors, such as the power of the sovereign exercising its anti-adversarial, anti-*anomic* energy in the name of the *Nomos*. For this reason the political and legal territorialization of the Euro-Atlantic imperial order initiated in the sixteenth century by the empire of Spain was for Schmitt the Latin-Romanic *nomos* that restrained the coming of the Anti-Christ up until the emergence of Britain's maritime empire and the consequent liberal Americocentrism that emerged toward the end of the nineteenth century.[25] Through Schmitt, then, it becomes clear that "the basic, restraining function of the *katechon* remains the same, but it changes according to the changing nature of its object, that is, the particular Anti-Christ at a certain time. Every epoch, one might say, has its Anti-Christ and generates its appropriate *katechon*. The old antagonism of Christ and Anti-Christ has been replaced by the antagonism of the Anti-Christ and the *katechon*" (Hoelzl, "Before the Anti-Christ Is Revealed," 108). If anomie, in Carl Schmitt, is measured by *nomos*, and if it remains always subject to it, then anomie is mediated and mitigated by modern legislative restraint, which is clearly thematized, for example, in his *Theory of the Partisan*. Sovereign decisionism — the sovereign's ability to decide on the state of exception — is what mediates the relation between *nomos* (law) and anomie (lawlessness). Anomie is internal to the sovereign's ability to suspend the law in the name of the sovereign order and is therefore internal to the *imperium* of sovereign territorial authority. It is the basis for the state's monopoly of the legitimate and exceptional implementation of force.

It is for this reason that Massimo Cacciari observes that the idea that conservative energies can hold back, if not stop, anomie "is the result of two errors" (*Europe and Empire*, 154): "The first consists in not being able to grasp the internal dialectic of anomy (and in not distinguishing the *stasis*, the 'civil war' between the political and the spiritual dimensions). The second consists in believing the sign of the Antichrist to be simply anarchic" (154–55). The katechon clearly partakes fully of anomie, which is the very principle it strives to contain, postpone, and even halt: "It is impossible not to *retain* what you seek to *contain*. Every catechontic power must constitute itself from within the dimension . . . of the principle of *anomie* that is destined to triumph" (Cacciari, 2018, 51).

Within the katechontic structure of the deferral of the end of history, anomie bridges the divide between catastrophe and empire. The only thing that changes is its form in relation to the figuration of the Anti-Christ, or public enemy, and in relation to the dominant extension of political space (Empire, Nation, etc). Restraining force is intimately related to the figure and *imperium* of the sovereign to the extent that the *nomos* is the order created by the restraining effect of sovereign law in the imperial interstate system.

In contrast to Paolo Virno's reading, then, any contemporary loosening or dissolution of restraint is ultimately the result of the breakdown of the restraining force of the imperial *nomos* that originated in the sixteenth century, that consolidated the bourgeois revolutions internal to the European imperial state system of the nineteenth century, that provided a grammar of unification for the emergence and extension of the modern nation-state, and that achieved its apotheosis at the beginning of the twentieth century. The spatial and institutional effects of its dissolution were subsumed by the realities of two imperial European civil wars waged on a global scale, as well as by a combination of Keynesian welfare economics and the Cold War restraining division of the planet into First, Second, and Third Worlds, which, in agreement with Hannah Arendt (*Crises of the Republic*, 123), were an ideological projection rather than a reality.[26]

Neil Davidson has traced the increasing tensions in the relation between bourgeois revolution at the national level and a world structured around imperialist power at the end of the nineteenth century (*How Revolutionary Were the Bourgeois Revolutions?*, 618). In this analysis he describes the territorial logic of command in relation to the restraining function of the era of the integral bourgeois state as it strived to (a) suture internal social order to the interests of capital in the nineteenth and twentieth centuries, (b) administrate a common "we" via the *fictive ethnicities* of cultural nationalism, and (c) maintain the competitive edge of the nation in an international system of accumulation coordinated between sovereign imperial territorialities (578). This then allows the author to characterize the definitive apotheosis and closure of the national bourgeois era — that is, the exhaustion of the imperial interstate system in its specifically territorialized capitalist forms — in the following terms:

> The Russian Revolution should have signaled the end of the bourgeois revolution and the opening of its proletarian successor. Given that it did not, the era finally came to an end in 1973–75, when the feudal-absolutist regime of Ethiopia was overthrown, the Portuguese colonies of Guinea-Bissau, Angola, and Mozambique were liberated, and the United States was defeated in Indochina with the fall of its client states in Cambodia, Laos, and South Vietnam. The climax of the bourgeois revolutionary era coincided with the retreat from, and in the case of Eastern Europe and the Soviet Union, the collapse of the state capitalism model that had been the characteristic outcome of its last phase. It was in China, home of the greatest of these revolutions, that one important entry point to the neoliberal era was first opened, when Deng announced the Four Modernizations to the Third Plenum of the Eleventh Central Committee Congress of the Chinese Communist Party in December 1978. When Deng looked back from 1992 on the transformation he had initiated in China he used the slogan "to get rich is glorious"; the echo of Guizot advising disenfranchised French citizens to "enrich themselves" if they wanted to be able to vote was unlikely to be accidental. And perhaps this is appropriate. Regardless of the vast differences between them in most respects, what the Frenchman and his Chinese successor had in common was

that they represented not counterrevolution, but the consolidation of the bourgeois revolution that brought them to power and that is now over. (621)[27]

The restraining order of the bourgeois nation-state, that is, the modern katechon of the territorialization of capital within specific geometries of regional, national, and imperial containment of relative values, that is, the Cold War, was a history of relative containment between state and non-state capitalisms and therefore between counterfeit enemies who in fact were fighting for the extension of the same system of competitive accumulation but in two different forms.[28] The definitive deterritorialization of capital — this crisis of limitations, which has been more than a century in the making — has initiated the breakdown of the received measures and subjection of normlessness, or of anomic exceptionality, to the nomic world of the law. If anomie in Schmitt is measured by *nomos*, and if it remains always subject to it, then anomie, as already stated, is mediated by legislative restraint. What we now refer to as globalization, however, shows something far more intense, profound, and problematic. As already suggested, we are now experiencing the demise of inherited historical and spatial forms of mediation between territory, authority, culture, and economy and perhaps even the radical modification of the *nomos*-anomie relation itself, which is central to the organized sovereign monopoly on violence. Globalization — in which capital transgresses the territorial and legal boundaries of the state and extends across borders — inaugurates the dissolution of modern geometries and grammars of restraint and containment; the exhaustion of the legal norms of land appropriation, division, and distribution; and the socialization of that exhaustion via the multiplication and corporatization of sovereign force(s). Sovereign decisionism becomes generalized, socialized, corporatized, franchised, often as if the contemporary were a regurgitation of the forms of piracy and enslavement that characterized the sixteenth century. The state wages war in order to regain the monopoly on violence and to resuture the *nomos*-anomie relation internal to the exercise of sovereign force: for example, through the War on Terror or the War on Drugs or, in the evangelical era of Donald Trump and Jair Bolsonaro, by fueling the flames of social war on absolutely anyone who does not agree or who is not white. But the state does not do this anymore in the name of hegemony and the territorialization of capital. It does so in the name of domination passing itself off as morality and security ("Law and Order").[29]

The profitability of illicit deterritorialized capital demonstrates with utmost clarity that the restraining mediation of the state — the state's ability to suture national territory to the law — has been overcome by the immediate mediation of corporate profit in either legal or illicit ("offshore") forms. The ability to decide on the relation between peace and war is purely cosmetic. The decision itself has become deterritorialized and, as a result, infinitely more arbitrary, violent, and widespread. The strong political decisionism of the era of katechontic restraint has evolved into the terror of ubiquitous corporate and paramilitary decisionism on a global scale. In his reading of Carl Schmitt, Carlo Galli observes that "all the important spatial axes on the basis of which the State constructed itself — internal/external, public/social/private, particular/universal, center/periphery, order/disorder — have become obsolete" (*Political Spaces and Global War*, 157). For Galli, globalization is the force that "de-spatializes both politics and war, removing them from the logic of the friend and enemy and the categories of 'the partisan'" (182). This means, he continues, that "the logical frontier of Schmittian thought, which surpassed itself in the moment it was reached, has become everyday life. The extreme has become normal, and the unthinkable, unplaceable in political space or modern political categories, is today the new figure of politics and war" (182). As a result, "the political thought of Schmitt is dead," for "Global War commences only where Schmittian political theory is exhausted" (182).[30] Galli observes that the "global war" that characterizes the post–Cold War period and the post-9/11 period in particular carries to fruition the spatially nihilistic dynamics of the doctrine of Total Mobilization of the 1930s (Ernst Jünger). This "mobilization" was, he continues, "temporarily halted during the Cold War. The (then) much condemned bipolarity between the United States and the U.S.S.R. was truly, as we know now, the last *katechon* — the last 'restraining force' holding back the coming of a new age" (161). As a result of the eclipse of the Cold War katechon, Galli affirms, "*globalization is itself a world of war*" (162).[31]

There is no specific territorial anomie of the earth. What we face is the privatization and extension of the anomie of sovereign exceptionality applied to an earth and a humanity positioned increasingly by *techne* as a standing reserve for labor/resource extraction and surplus value.[32] The modern nexus between hegemony, culture, and the subject is no longer of consequence. It is precisely in the hollowing out of this nexus that we begin to confront the contemporary question of post-sovereign decontainment and therefore of *perishing*.

The sociopolitical reaction against this tendency is notorious. For example, Wendy Brown examines the contemporary proliferation of supposedly post-ideological border walls designed and erected with a view to closing off territories and controlling migrant population flows. These constructions signal the projection onto the contemporary of a classic modern prosthesis of Hobbesian force, designed to represent and contain a sense of home and shelter. On the other side of the same divide, they are designed to represent and shield against "invasion." This "post-Westphalian" and therefore post-sovereign political architecture is iconographic of the predicament of contemporary state power, since constructions such as the US-Mexico border wall and, we might add, the increasing securitization of Mexico's southern border, alongside many more possible examples around the world (such as the Mediterranean Sea), denote a "theatricalized and spectacularized performance of sovereign power . . . a wish that recalls the theological dimensions of political sovereignty" (*Walled States*, 26). The post-Westphalian order in Brown is predicated on the attempt, and failure, to contain the effects and symptoms of contemporary unfettered capital and the perishing of modern political theology. They are simply administrative and often militarized architectural reactions against the demographic and racial realities of the contemporary world's territorial, economic, and cultural post-sovereign "decontainment."[33]

Brown points to the ongoing eclipse of modern political space — the institutionalized metaphysics of the nation-state — understood as a force of restraint or geometry of social containment. Contemporary demands for the construction of more and larger border walls mark the political expediency of a regressive desire for a specifically modern (by this I mean specifically "Hobbesian") katechon. In the emergence of new technological forms of immediate mediation between territory and the vagaries of the quest for surplus value — forms for which the Left has no stable or fully trustworthy vocabulary, for which there appears to be no affirmative biopolitics, immunization, or theory of an alternative political actuality but which the international Right has managed to capture in the apocalyptic tone of white nativist "antiglobalism" ("Build that Wall!") and imperial reformation ("Make America Great Again!"; "Make Spain Great Again!"; "Take Back Control. Vote Leave!") — the conceptual legacy of Carl Schmitt certainly comes to mind, though we might also intuit that in Brown's work, as in Galli's before her, Schmitt's relevance seems to be that he is irrelevant for explaining, despite all political reactions to the contrary, the effective truths of a present dominated by the waning sovereignty of the post-Westphalian redistribution of space and jurisdiction under the auspices of the late-neoliberal market-state duopoly.[34]

Taking into consideration all of the above, we can begin to specify that the contemporary lack of distinction between war and peace is *post-katechontic*, indicating the twilight or *perishing* of the political form of the modern nation-state understood as the restraining force against uncontrolled civil conflict within and across borders. However, we should also note that the post-katechontic can only ever be *simultaneously neo-katechontic*, indicating that the post-sovereign market-state duopoly, the force that *globalizes* as the very perpetuation of the dissolution of the modern nation-state, is *the* katechontic principle of our times, but without signposting the contours of a *passage* or *transition* to a new sovereign form or epoch. Contemporary techno-capitalism is a never-ending battle (via the fully integrated TV, mobile phone, computer, and tablet screen) for the measurement, extraction, and valorization of adrenaline, dopamine, and serotonin — that is, for the increasingly shortened attention span and distracted awareness — of the species.[35] Meanwhile exclusion — a basic tenet of representation — is replaced by a generalized biopoliticization in which humanity in general is included, though the selection process for inclusion remains an absolute mystery, which might explain why the trash entertainment of reality TV is obsessed with restaging ad nauseam the act of voting for who stays or who leaves the island, or house, or business venture, or stage, or weight-loss farm, or jungle, or dance floor, or kitchen. Even voting in the post-katechontic order is nothing more than the act of asserting whom I "like/dislike," for whatever reasons they might be. It is nihilism in its purest form. It is the "Why bother? They're all the same anyway" converted into everyday reality and political farce now referred to as both "entertainment" and "democracy," devoid of any distinction between the two.

In this light the post-katechontic — the global absolutism of capital and therefore of subsumption — signals the historical limit of "a domain of questioning, or of absolutely preliminary research" (Derrida, *Aporias*, 42). It signals the demand for thinking but not necessarily for the definitive acquisition of *knowledge* and *certainty*, since they have been folded into each other. More than ever, surplus value on a global scale and the force of the ontology of the subject that seeks and guarantees its extension reign supreme as both sovereign decontainment and neo-katechontic energy *simultaneously*. Upon the demise of a specific hegemonic apparatus, restraining structure, or, indeed, any regulating idea other than those of unmediated value extraction, accumulation at all cost, and the corporate redistribution of bodies marked by the demands and violence of commodity fetishism, in the post-katechontic turmoil and violence of contemporary capital all claims to hegemony seem to be increasingly indistinguishable from naked domination. As such, contemporary endemic conflict is the means by which, and the limit at which, the duopolistic market-state uncovers itself *as* the movement of global capital itself, to the extent that the shift to the neoliberal state form inaugurated the subsumption of the state to capital, thereby indicating the transfiguration of modern forms of sovereign power into the force of a post-sovereign extension that consumes itself in its perishing and has been doing so since the 1970s. At the level of everyday experience, we have passed from poverty understood in Marxian terms as the nonsatisfaction of material needs to a generalized exposure to an undifferentiated lack/excess devoid of any given sense of collective experience in the order of the symbolic. Herein the worker becomes a self-entrepreneur or a debtor, trapped either way, and without a way out (Alemán, *En la frontera*, 36). We can talk until the cows come home about the internal mechanisms of Marx's understandings of the commodity form and its social relation. We can vie for precision and correctness in our formulations. But that does nothing to assuage the ultimate sterility of such an enterprise to the extent that it merely reconfirms what capital has already extended as the immanence of the everyday.

What can we understand by this? What I am suggesting is that with the post-katechontic advent of contemporary globalization the work of thinking is confronting a predicament in which the metaphors of our inherited modern (bourgeois, and therefore also proletarian) political and cultural forms — subject, history, nation-state, "People," fraternity, equality, liberty, consciousness, etc. — uncover a crisis of limitations and of ongoing ruination.

For this reason, the post-katechontic announces a singular and urgent opportunity for thinking, to the extent that our inherited metaphors regarding the political appear to be increasingly exhausted, though no less vehement in their reactionary resurgences. In this sense, the post-katechontic does not imply that "one leaves the metaphorical element of language behind, but that in a new metaphor the previous metaphor appears as such, is denounced in its origin and in its metaphorical functioning and in its necessity. It appears as such" (Derrida, *Heidegger*, 190). With this in mind, post-katechontic decontainment is the uncovering, and in the uncovering the denaturalization, of the modern metaphorical functioning of the history of Christian metaphysics, its political theology, and its modern Promethean will to power. It is already too late.

Within the ontic order of globalization decontainment names the dilemma that currently lies at the heart of sovereignty's increasing inability to mediate socially, politically, institutionally, or culturally between the history of modern political space, historicity, and the history of Logos (God, the mortal God, the sovereignty of the One, the "People"), that is, between constituted power and its economies of restraint organized within the dimensions of a republican, national, and interstate world system. The simultaneous coming forth, exhaustion, and withdrawal of the modern metaphorical functioning of the history of Christian metaphysics marks at the political level the eclipse of the nation-state's traditional forms of mediation, which is not the same as saying that the state is no more or will disappear.

Decontainment is ascendant post–Cold War and postnational anomie — the globalization of the indistinction between *nomos* and *anomie* — in action. It is the opening for all to see, the evidencing (historically, institutionally, culturally, politically) of the closure of the metaphysics of sovereign power and the painful and confounding glimpse of a hollowing out of Enlightenment understandings of the political, understandings that were already ungrounded, utterly contingent, in the first place. In the grip of this post-sovereign hollowing out and *ungrounding* of the dialectic between anomie and *nomos*, the Left remains enthralled to the myriad subjectivations of the Enlightenment tradition, while the evangelical soldiers of the Right march onward, railing against all evidence of the degrounding itself, striding into battle after battle in order to cast the malaise of *groundlessness* into oblivion with more and more morality, private property, law, bigotry, identity, subjectivity, will to power, Christian value, civilizational superiority, denial (from the Shoah to climate collapse to the COVID-19 pandemic), and, of course, nihilism. Such certainty, however, is only ever catastrophic. The ideological struggle between Left and Right is now staged as a human destinal battle between the will to power of subjectivity versus the will to power of subjectivity (socially conservative moral law, economic austerity, and naked militarized sovereign power as salvation versus social regulation, identitary inclusion to an extent, and naked militarized sovereign power as salvation). On both sides it is a battle to the death for the endurance of the subjectivism of the *I* of the "I endure." But the *perishing* that underlies all duration is manically — and unsuccessfully — concealed.

Conservative politics promises nothing more than a fake epochal destiny enveloped in naked domination and the forging of anomie (no hegemony necessary, just the will to power, such as that of a society armed to the teeth in the name of the constitutional freedoms of the white men of the eighteenth century, while the rights of women, people of color, and non-normative sexualities in the present are ignored or undermined on a systemic scale). So-called progressive politics promises not an epochal destiny but something somewhat better than the conservative alternative, between the humanist chimera of hegemony and the actuality of anomie (no domination necessary, they say, though everyone knows that hegemony is in fact a form of domination, or the will to power with hopefully slightly better intentions). Democracy traverses both options, and you can vote for open domination or for the chimera of a hegemony that no longer exists and that the global economy, the global quest for the extraction of surplus value, cares next to nothing about (think Greece in 2015 or Venezuela in 2019). The only other thing the Left has to offer is the quest for a new master discourse in the name of socialism or Revolution, which up to now at least is also the promise of a new-old deal and the hope for a slightly better master than in the past.[36] At both ends of the political spectrum — a spectrum that is increasingly insignificant — we experience the avid imposition and consumption of the law and the consumerism of the images and rhetoric of the nomic, the thetic, and the conspiratorial. At both sides we now confront a battle between opposing forms of will, which, as will, are not actually in opposition.[37] They are both intended to recuperate a sense, the very sense, of *nomos* itself, thereby proving that what reigns is in fact anomie not as a counterenergy to *nomos* but as that which the post-katechontic never ceases, in performative terms at least, to generate and to strive to close, to silence and to cast into oblivion, or to capitalize.

But the performance has gone awry. National laws no longer contain or regulate the *technology* that drives global financial capital; international laws no longer regulate war; the Catholic narrative of the existence and regulation of universal human rights is increasingly moribund. The growing inability of humanism to mediate its nomic relation to the barbaric, and, as such, its ongoing inability to arbitrate the unleashing of ferociousness as the new norm, indicates the exhaustion of the ability of humanism to conserve, restrain, or guard against genocide, slaughter, expulsion, injustice, racism, ethnic cleansing, or sexual violence. The Left protests, often quite rightly but in the absence of an alternative vision, while reactionary forces advance their claim to the constitution of the destiny of an epoch in the name of God, law, property, and civilization. However, since the forces of reaction fall short of every promise, they merely demonstrate over and over again, and with growing vehemence, that there is no new epoch, no current epoch advancing a new Age, merely the subjectivism of the nomothetic will, which is nothing more than the exacerbation of all the symptoms of the old epoch (modern racism, imperialism, fascism, nationalism, etc.).

The Right promises complete transformation, but it projects the performance of will and force, the benefits of absolute unity behind the sovereign, protection from all "invaders," and a form of jouissance predicated on willful subordination to the master, who is portrayed as the embodiment of the new epoch. For his faithful followers, for example, Donald Trump is the body of the modern katechon who is personally responsible for containing, arresting, and withholding anomie (which now refers to virtually everything except white nationalist and corporate privilege) despite the fact that his thought and speech range between the garbled, the malicious, and the Twitter rabble rouser. Trumpism is a reactionary coagulation ("Fuck your feelings! And history too!" etc.) in the face of the never-ending fluidity of post-sovereign technological and capitalist domination on a planetary scale (coagulation and fluidity, the two aporetic energies that constitute *stasis; the* post-katechontic bellicose energy of the market-state duopoly in action).

For this reason, decontainment names the seismic shift in, and the perishing of, the katechontic function of the nation-state in postneoliberal times. It brings forth the historical ungrounding of all epoch-making will (the exhaustion of the time of empire, emancipatory decolonization, nation building, development, progress, etc.). It registers the virulent reaction against that historical ungrounding of all epoch-making will through the exacerbated katechontic performance of past wills (imperialist, nationalist, nativist, neofascist, racist, heteronormative) extended in the name of renovation, greatness, and the tribal rejection of all forms of difference (of disagreement, any perceived form of queerness, anything labeled "alien," or non-white, etc.). But there is no real political victory to be had in the post-katechontic order because to the extent that katechontic power institutes itself within the dimension and principle of anomie, the latter was always "destined to triumph" (Cacciari, *The Withholding Power,* 51). The Right acts like this is not and never will be the case. But it is increasingly clear that even though its claims to and passion for katechontic order oppose rhetorically the advance of anomie (*"Build That Wall!"*), they do so by becoming an integral part of anomie's history. For this reason, in order to endure, the Right can only drive its force to greater violence via the multiplication of fake battle fronts and crises; it can only engage in the preservation of the energy of chaos as a means of "combating" it while perpetuating it. In this scenario katechontic energy either folds back on itself in the form of turmoil or, when the proverbial river overflows its banks, force is deemed necessary in order to stifle decontainment. Such is the instrumental political imagination underlying the Trumpian fabrication, manipulation, and perpetuation of the Central American migrant/refugee crisis of October/November 2018 onward, the events that unfolded in the wake of George Floyd's murder on May 25, 2020, and the paramilitary occupation of the streets of Portland by federal forces in the run-up to the 2020 presidential elections.

The Left, on the other hand, acts but is not yet able to formulate a thinking beyond indignation, better intentions (the final vestiges of Christian pastoral power), or an attunement to the renunciation of all epoch-making wills. It is as katechontic in nature as the Right. It only knows it does not want to be like the Right, which is no less of a nihilist position in which to find oneself. What is clear, however, is that post-katechontic global turmoil, or decontainment, is the active exhaustion of the history of a certain modern understanding of arché, of principle, rule, representation, and of the social and legal bonds forged between citizens in the formation of the Republic and the modern nation-state. Having said that, it is now *also* the resurgence in their purely nihilistic forms of all things exhausted, as both Right and Left attempt to hang on desperately to principle, rule, and representation in order to conceal the reality and realization of the closure of the metaphysics of the modern state and of the entire Westphalian order that underpinned it for centuries.[38]

All of this brings us to the question of the decision. We are saturated by images and the performance of an order of decisionism on a global scale, in which oligarchs and strongmen do and say whatever they feel like saying and doing, such as eliminating enemies at will or criminalizing absolutely anyone deemed to be "inferior," because they are economically dominant and therefore can. The political struggle of the Right is to uphold the symbolic bond between God and the "mortal God" in such a way as to sustain at all cost an ontic relation to the final Judgment (the transcendental projection of all katechontic power) in the name of a moral *nomos*. The "secular" Left hasn't quite worked out what its relation to the Christian age of Judgment could or should be, or whether it is okay to have the Final Judgment still be the essence and ground of every political decision, because questioning such a thing might imply deconstructing its own relation to Christian and secular Promethean metaphysics (subjectivity, faith, salvation, the Good).[39]

It is obvious that from the perspective of capital alone, the contemporary can be seen as a constant battle for and against decontainment, for limitless accumulation versus the state territorialization of its own reproductive force extended in conjunction with the overcoming of all the "others" — such as *other* modes of production and *other* social identities — that it identifies for subjugation, transformation, or destruction either in its wake or on its most distant horizon. In the era of the bourgeois integral nation-state, the role of sovereign power was to mediate between the forces of territorialization, deterritorialization, and the People via the regulative force of the Law and the fabrication of a hegemonic social apparatus. In Benjaminian terms, modern sovereign power was law-preserving violence. However, it is now clear that the current deterritorializations of capital are initiating multiple forms of breakdown in the very measure and subjection of normlessness, or of anomic exceptionality, in their relation to the nomic world of the law.[40]

In the decontained, post-katechontic world of globalization anomie is no different from, or the constitutive outside of, hegemony or of nomic order and representation. Now it is increasingly indistinguishable from human existence as an extension of war, or as the very force of value extraction on a global scale. Capital frees up military and paramilitary flows and guarantees their extension in the name of a "securitized" peace that is indistinguishable from a generalized state of dynastic, patriarchal warfare. This not only turns the long-standing political ideologies and belief systems of "Left" and "Right," the meaning of the public, labor, the concepts related to notions of war and peace, or the military and the civil on their heads. It renders them in-different — biopolitically equivalent to one another in the face of the absolutism of post-katechontic capital — and scatters them in their indifference across geographical boundaries and individual, public, and institutional domains.

Within this scattering, violence becomes self-serving, undermining sovereign legitimacy yet also installing transparent *illegitimacy* as merely the necessary exercise of power.[41] Within this context it is only ever debatable whether capital actually "needs" the state, or whether the post-sovereign state can ground itself as a restrainer in the face of capital, since the model itself is that of the market as the unstable meeting point for all the fiduciary expectations for its competitor-citizens, but without sustaining meaning (representation) or foresight (knowledge) (Bazzicalupo, "Populismo y liberalismo," 373) beyond the terms of "growth," which apparently is a synonym for everything "Good."

The disciplinary production of modern subjectivity as addressed in much of Michel Foucault's work on the reproduction of specific institutional structures in the eighteenth and nineteenth centuries appears charming in comparison to the contemporary biopolitical domination and immanentization of the body and mind. Within the context of contemporary endemic conflict, or global war, Massimo Cacciari notes that "any nostalgia for the catechontic powers will only appear as will to powerlessness . . . no new empire can fill the void left by their loss of power" (*Europe and Empire*, 155). He is right, but this also explains why in *The Withholding Power* (2018) Cacciari struggles to come to terms with the definitive eclipse of the Promethean age. Cacciari, after all, is a katechontic thinker of the post-katechontic.

In contrast, we could suggest that contemporary thinking must reckon in one way or another with the voiding of epochality itself, in the process recognizing the surrender of all historical figures of the common (republic, empire, multitude, community, state, space, etc.) in the face of a certain end of sovereignty (which, as already noted, is not the same as what Francis Fukuyama proclaimed at the beginning of the 1990s). Cacciari laments that "the idea that such conflict could have an outcome other than that of its own perpetuation is as senseless as the nostalgia for empire. . . . The multitudes are just as far from the angels of the apocalypse as the actual states are from Hobbes's 'mortal god,' and just as far as the great political and economic spaces of today are from the Roman Empire" (*Europe and Empire*, 155).[42] The modern inheritance of the *koinon*, or "gathering," is increasingly moribund, though increasingly essentialized, enforced by the reactionary political forces of the present and desired by the champions of "the commons" as the only political form or common sense available. This accumulative demise, or perishing, of "gathering" emerges hand in hand with the twilight of sovereignty, and from now on it just might become unavoidable as a basic facet of the everyday, despite all claims to, and desires for, the biopolitical or authoritarian conservation and sustained value of specific ways of configuring one form of life over and above others. For this reason, the exhaustion of modern forms of sovereignty must be faced head-on rather than sublimated into a new epoch of sovereignty, for in post-sovereign turmoil it is becoming increasingly unclear what the relation is at all between the common good and the common as a good (Nancy, "War, Right, Sovereignty—*Techne*," 136–37). COVID-19 is the tragic revelation of this problem, for the question of the common good in the United States and beyond is reduced to the libertarian choice between absolute biopolitical mismanagement and the freedom to exercise one's right to infect others and to die free of governmental regulation. In the era of COVID-19, does "the People" wear a mask or not? What is the distance necessary for the common good and for the common as a good? What is the relation between that distance, or proximity, and the individual and societal death drive? This was never a trivial question, but now it is more pressing than ever.

In *The Passage West*, Giacomo Marramao cites Jean Luc Nancy's *The Gravity of Thought* in order to highlight the need to traverse the empty space left by the exhaustion of prior significations such as "community," "the commons," the "city," the "nation," the "fraternal," "equality," etc.: "The West, in its accomplishment, asks us to neither revive its significations nor to resign ourselves to their annulment, but rather to understand that from now on the demand for meaning has to go through the exhaustion of significations" (8).[43] This *going through* is Marramao's *passage*, which a thinker such as Carlo Galli diagnoses but falls short of fully addressing, because he deconstructs the Schmittian legacy only to conclude in favor of a better *nomos*. Marramao's *passage* through the exhaustion of significations evokes Nietzsche's transvaluation of values as a means of opening up our legacies to a thought of *becoming* in which what has remained inaudible can become audible. This thought of becoming—of the passage through our inherited metaphors (of value, morality, virtue, etc.) in the name of *becoming*—Nietzsche refers to this as "nobility," though, it might be said, it still falls short of destroying the work of value itself.

Given all of the above, it is important to note that it remains unsatisfying merely to utilize the term "decontainment" as a synonym for "global war" or for the post-Westphalian condition alone, since utilizing it in that purely sociological form as a mere fact of life, as a banal indicator of "lived globality," does not provide for the grounding of the reasons why the word and the phenomena it indicates are particularly pertinent to our thinking now. In other words, by using the word merely as a sociological indicator of the fact and experience of globalization, something akin to the preconceptual experience of the ungrounding of certain structures and experiences of containment associated with the history and legitimacy of the nation-state — the Westphalian order — it remains unclear what precisely the word, or the possible approach to the multiple truths contained therein, might make possible.

Why suggest an attunement to decontainment now? And, moreover, why think in attunement with the question of decontainment at all, which is equally only indicative of its opposite, *containment*? How, in other words, can one ground the question not only of decontainment but, also, of the perishing, the withdrawal, the demise, the ruin and destruction that the word appears to indicate? In a way, the word must account for something other than the mere indication that before things were contained and now they are not, thereby suggesting, in utmost banality, that somehow things are not the way they used to be, which is, after all, the constitutive ground for the resurgent neofascism of our times.

Where, then, do things stand with (that is, how do things come to appearance in and through) post-sovereign decontainment? With what tools can we demarcate the limit that decontainment imposes on our understanding? Decontainment (which, as already suggested, is merely a less cumbersome way of expressing the indistinct nature of the simultaneously *post-* and *neo-katechontic* energy of contemporary techno-capitalism in its planetary extension) names the coming forth of a previous order of metaphoricity, which, in its coming forth, immediately withdraws from prior forms and understanding. For example, contemporary populism is indeed populist, but it is not the same as it was in the wake of World War II. Similarly, nationalism now is still nationalism, but it is not the same as that of the nineteenth century; war is war but not for the same reasons or with the same forms as before, etc. By this I wish to indicate that between coming forth and withdrawal there is no dialectical relation between the modern katechon (nation, state, subject-citizen, polemos), for example, and the post-katechontic extension of global turmoil and conflict (or *stasis*). What comes forth and immediately withdraws, in its coming forth, is the deepening crisis of the modern metaphysics of the nation-state, which, again, is not to say that there is no longer such a thing as the state or that there will not be one in the future.[44]

Globalization's seismic metamorphosis brings the metaphysics of both the earthly *autorictas* of the mortal God and the traditional Christian imperial restraining katechon to a threshold of post-sovereign ruination that persists. If we understand globalization, then, not as epochal but as an a-epochal re-situating and redesigning of everything related to the word "We," along with all the conceptual and political legacies and forms of social arrangement that have accompanied it throughout modernity, then words such as "nation," "territory," "power," "control," "freedom," "war," "life," etc. no longer mean what they used to and are therefore in need of further evaluation.

The task, though, is no longer to remetaphorize the katechon and therefore metaphysics, but to learn to become attuned to where the perishing of the modern katechon leaves us; to think not counter to the space of permanent crisis without respite or amnesty, but in light of it. The task is not to rile against the shattering of the bond between God and man in the name of law and order. It is to accept the death of God and of the Promethean humanism that has only ever been God's enlightened cultural sojourn on earth. This allows us to understand the closure of metaphysics as the unleashing of limitless turmoil at the level of the signifier and obliges us to take that destructive/creative energy seriously in order to think from within it, as opposed to thinking in denial of it, or in spite of it, in the utopian hope of its pacification or in the neo-fascist turn against it (which is actually its glorification).[45]

Why? As we saw at the end of Shelley's *Prometheus Unbound*, the tyrant of the shadow world Demogorgon converts Prometheus's act of *parrhesia* into the precondition of a future thetic reality and rhetoric of action. As a result, both Prometheus's act and Jupiter's immediate descent into the abyss are subsumed under a thesis addressing the future normative principles of Good versus Evil, in which Demogorgon the orator prepares the path for a future representational order for the freedom, and demagoguery, of the good subject. In this sense Prometheus's individual act becomes a referent for the modern representational order of an entire hegemonic understanding of action and freedom. Thanks to Demogorgon, Prometheus's subjective defiance is recodified into that of a hegemonic fantasm for all, universalized in the name of a normative measure for subjective freedom.[46] However, in the context of contemporary perishing, the conditions of this recodification are increasingly obsolete, and with it the legitimization of hegemony that accompanies it.

For this reason, we should turn our attention in the direction of *posthegemony*. Posthegemony in what follows is not politics per se, and it always involves a double register. On one hand, it is historical. On the other, it involves an a-principial, and therefore infrapolitical, "abdication of political responsibility," in attunement with an "undercommons" that looms "outside every attempt to politicize, every imposition of self-governance, every sovereign decision and its degraded miniature, every emergent state and home sweet home" (Harney and Moten, 2013, 20).[47] This infrapolitical posthegemony exists at a distance from an organizing principle of power, points at all times to the question of the political, and strives to guarantee that thinking not succumb to the instinctive, nostalgic, or anxiety-laden recuperation and reiteration of modernity's regimes of regulatory representation (biopolitics) or mediated subordination (hegemony). Infrapolitical posthegemony raises questions in light of the material conditions of the present but without presuming to know what our own historical time signifies, or whether the contemporary has a single tendential law *other* than that of existential expropriation on a global scale. It accepts that we are immersed in the protracted and brutally violent closure of the era of bourgeois revolution, nation-state formation, and imperial/national capitalist configurations. In this sense, it does not seek to shake off its relation to the question of the contemporary as a relation to the limits of knowledge, that is, to nonknowledge. On the contrary, it strives to assume and traverse that relation in the name of difference.[48]

In the following, our approach to posthegemony from within the elucidation of the limits of hegemony will allow us to move in the direction of the infrapolitical, as a register within thinking that bears witness to a specific necessity within the time of globalization, which I understand as the time of the end of the representation of historical progress and therefore as the time of the post-katechontic disclosure of the socialized closure of the metaphysics of the nation, the subject, and historicism.

## From Hegemony to Posthegemony

Beyond the specifically Greek notion of ruler, chief, or commander sovereign (*hegemon*), the specifically modern concept of hegemony (and therefore of counterhegemony, which occupies exactly the same ontological terrain as its counterweight and forebear) refers to the modern exercise of domination, authority, representation, political inclusion, and social transformation. It refers to the way domination is installed at the social level and reproduces itself as if it were natural. In this sense it is only ever about the sociological metaphors that make lives make sense at the level of the political and the cultural.

The notion of hegemony emerged and developed in accordance with the historical consolidation and extension of the integral nation-state and its territorial logic of power at the end of the nineteenth century. It is not merely a reference to the supreme authority of the sovereign as the "mortal God" but is directly related to the forging of the modern nation-state understood as "the directive force of historical impetus" (Gramsci, *Notebooks*, vol. 2, NB 7, #9, 161). Hegemony and its *ratio*—the ground of its thinking—underpin the bourgeois integral nation-state as the guiding force of the modern history of progress and development. In the age of the bourgeois revolutions, republican hegemony was forged in civil society in such a way that "social power, in the first instance, flows 'up' to the state, where it is institutionalized and then reproduced as state power flowing 'down' to society" (Robinson, *Global Capitalism*, 73). As such, hegemony distributes itself across leadership, domination, and consent and can be deployed as both *a-nomic* and *nomic* in its arrangements. It can be utilized in reference to the transformational content and political autonomy of a certain Jacobin/proletarian spirit, functioning in the name of revolution (anomie), as much as in reference to the ethical content of a fully regulated society via the extension of class domination through the forging of a specific state apparatus (the Law, that is, as political dictatorship).[49] Hegemony refers, in other words, to a particular form of social domination and modern moral economy in which subordinate groups lend their active consent to domination. For this reason, "projects of hegemony involve not merely rule but political and ideological leadership based on a set of class alliances" (216). Therefore, hegemony always raises the question of the underlying conditions of the heterogenesis of the master-slave dialectic extended throughout any given social spacing. It can provide a grammar for the experience of the incommensurability of freedom and equality in their resistance to constituted power, law, and authority, or it can work as a restraining force by systematizing freedom and indetermination in the name of the moral law, the legislation of sovereign will, and representation.

In *The Gramscian Moment: Philosophy, Hegemony, and Marxism*, Peter Thomas takes umbrage with Perry Anderson's reading of Gramsci in his famous *New Left Review* essay from the 1970s, "The Antinomies of Antonio Gramsci." Thomas does this in part by restating (134) Christine Buci-Glucksmann's (*Gramsci and the State*, 47–48) prior observations regarding the fact that the notion of "hegemony" and our understanding of it stem specifically from the Bolshevik tradition. It is on account of this tradition that the origin and development of the term remain indissociable from the experience, history, and conceptual frameworks that fought to establish the transition from one mode of production (capitalism) to another (socialism) in the late nineteenth and early twentieth centuries (Buci-Glucksmann, *Gramsci and the State*, 48).

In the wake of German unification (1871) and the Italian Resorgimento (1815–1870)—in which the Italian bourgeoisie rose steadily to power via a bourgeois "revolution without revolution," that is, without recourse to the French reign of terror—Gramsci turned to Lenin's 1917 formulation of proletarian hegemony as "dual power."[50] Gramsci did this because "dual power" offered a dispositif of class unification in the proletarian separation from and resistance to constituted state power. Early in the *Prison Notebooks* Gramsci addressed the changing form of political class leadership *before* and *after* assuming governmental power. In this formulation, hegemony referred to political leadership predicated on domination over the class enemy *and* simultaneously on a shift to government power once the class enemy was defeated. Hegemony, then, leads and subordinates.[51] Thomas delves further into the Bolshevik derivation and instrumentalization of hegemony, which Lenin generated within the context of a Russian state form that was essentially feudal in nature (218). For Lenin, Gramsci, and consequently Thomas, hegemony provided and extended a grammar of social content to the anomic force of the proletariat.[52] In April 1917 the dual power that proletarian anomie revealed took Lenin completely by surprise. On April 9, 1917, he published a short essay in *Pravda* titled "The Dual Power," which expressed his astonishment at what was happening before his eyes:

> The basic question of every revolution is that of state power. Unless this question is understood, there can be no intelligent participation in the revolution, not to speak of guidance of the revolution. The highly remarkable feature of our revolution is that it has brought about a dual power. This fact must be grasped first and foremost: unless it is understood, we cannot advance. We must know how to supplement and amend old "formulas," for example, those of Bolshevism, for while they have been found to be correct on the whole, their concrete realization has turned out to be different. Nobody previously thought, or could have thought, of a dual power. What is this dual power? Alongside the Provisional Government, the government of the bourgeoisie, another government has arisen, so far weak and incipient, but undoubtedly a government that actually exists and is growing—the Soviets of Workers' and Soldiers' Deputies. What is the class composition of this other government? It consists of the proletariat and the peasants (in soldiers' uniforms). What is the political nature of this government? It is a revolutionary dictatorship, i.e., a power directly based on revolutionary seizure, on the direct initiative of the people from below, and not on a law enacted by a centralized state power. It is an entirely different kind of power from the one that generally exists in the parliamentary bourgeois-democratic republics of the usual type still prevailing in the advanced countries of Europe and America. This circumstance is often overlooked, often not given enough thought, yet it is the crux of the matter. (1–2)

Dual power, which Lenin refers to as a revolutionary dictatorship and which we can consider as a proto-nomic anomie, or counterhegemony, coming into focus within the context of the death throes of the Russian feudal state form, is the socialized yet incalculable and incommensurable *experience of subtraction from sovereign power* and its inherited affiliations. For Lenin, dual power marks the emergence of a previously unforeseeable weak force without a fully assigned position of power or preordained horizon. Nevertheless, one of the sides in the standoff created by dual power provides a specific counterorientation to the state by restraining its ability to reproduce a claim to legitimacy. According to Lenin, this weak force — which is "often overlooked, often not given enough thought" — is in fact "the crux of the matter," for this *gegemoniya* denotes a challenge to the reigning feudalism of the moment. It is a democratic opening of proletarian self-determination and self-mastery capable of bringing the edifice of sovereign feudal authority to its knees, in large part because of its distance from constituted power and from the sovereign calculation of distributions that it imposes across political space. In Lenin's dual power, proletarian hegemony denotes the experience and distribution of freedom and equality beyond the grasp of constituted sovereign calculations, determinations, and measurements. Indeed, it is its incalculability from within the realm of sovereignty — "*Nobody* previously thought, *or could have thought*, of a dual power," as Lenin puts it — that gives the hegemony of dual power its appearance as a democratic, transformational force. Having said that, to the extent that dual power is essentially another name for anomie, or for counterhegemony, it could be said that it still shares the same ontological ground as hegemony because, as "the crux of the matter," dual power should produce, according to Lenin, *the* principle of everything that will carry through into the future.[53]

This sharing of ontological ground is in fact what allows for the postrevolutionary era. Herein proletarian *gegemoniya* shifts from being the embodiment of an anomic dual power — the opening up of a momentary incommensurability via the proletarian subtraction of consent from the authority of feudal sovereign power — to the social coordination of domination through the capture of the legal monopoly of violence embodied in the institutions of the state. As such, the creative spontaneity of dual power comes to be neutralized in the name of sovereign power, and hegemony thereby comes to occupy the place of measurement, calculation, and sovereign representation. It becomes the consequence of a particular form of legislative consciousness, or *nomos*.

In this sense, hegemony represents both the experimentalism of transformational force and its opposite, that is, "the process by means of which social forces are integrated into the political power of an existing state — and as the path along which the subaltern classes must learn to travel in a very different way in order to found their own 'non-state state'" (Thomas, *The Gramscian Moment*, 195).[54] Christine Buci-Glucksmann notes that after October 1917 the meaning of hegemony, as it passed through the Bolshevik revolutionary arc, shifted from the revolutionary content of class-based subtraction to the fortification of specific class relations coalescing within the institutional forms (the law, norms, and ethical content) of the postrevolutionary state. Hegemony was, then, a spacing of political reason that named anomie (the revolutionary experience of self-determination) in order to then pass into *nomos* (the measures of legislative consciousness), resulting in mediated subordination and consent.

Peter Thomas (65) cites Gramsci's discussion of Croce in *Il materialismo storico e la filosofia di Benedetto Croce*, referencing Lenin's contribution to the conceptualization of hegemony: "The greatest modern theoretician of the philosophy of praxis, on the terrain of political struggle and organization and with a political terminology, has reassessed — in opposition to the various 'economistic' tendencies — the front of cultural struggle and constructed the doctrine of hegemony as a complement to the theory of the State-as-force" (qtd. in *Selections*, 56). The history and legacy of Bolshevik hegemony therefore strived to give reason to both the singularity of the event as well as to the history of its gradual subsumption to authority (to the administration of measures, parts, and shares, together with their necessary exclusions or expulsions). Peter Thomas naturalizes this shift at the heart of hegemony as follows: "Dispensing with the pre-Revolutionary opposition of proletarian hegemony and dictatorship, hegemony (over allied subaltern classes) and dictatorship (over the bourgeoisie and aristocracy) were now integrated as complementary moments of the same revolutionary process" (233). As such, they were "sublated" within the representation and reality of the dictatorship of the proletariat converted into state form and "real politics."

In the wake of the Bolshevik experience and of the "passive revolution" of the Italian Resorgimento, the anomic/nomic reason of hegemony determined Gramsci's implementation and development of the term. Buci-Glucksmann has called attention to the ways that this anomic/nomic duality played itself out in Gramsci's *Prison Notebooks*. Central to this process was Gramsci's complementing of Lenin's *gegemoniya* with the formulation of the "hegemonic apparatus," in such a way as to explain the internal processes of the Italian experience and of the bourgeois passive revolution in particular. There is in Gramsci, Buci-Glucksmann observes, a "double process of shift and enrichment from the hegemony of the proletariat to the hegemony of the bourgeoisie, from the constitution of a class to the problematic of the state" (*Gramsci and the State*, 47). This double process of shift and enrichment plays itself out in different ways during the course of the *Notebooks*, in such a way that the concept of hegemony undergoes a transformation in its relation to previous uses: "Up until 1926 hegemony was chiefly used to mean an alternative strategy for the proletariat" (47). As already noted, in *Notebook* 1, for example, the concepts of hegemony and of hegemonic apparatus are not linked directly to the problematic of the bourgeois state but rather to that of dual power and class constitution in a process of revolutionary change. In the later *Notebooks* (7 and 8), however, hegemony gradually extends to cover the structures of the bourgeois state (47). As such, the Leninist derivation in reference to hegemonic anomie shifts as Gramsci begins to explore the "apparatus of hegemony" in reference to the bourgeois mediations of class via the educational apparatus, the cultural apparatus (literature, museums, libraries, etc.), the organization of information, the everyday environment, town planning, and the influence of apparatuses inherited from an earlier mode of production such as the church and its intellectuals (48). Gramsci found that hegemony is not only an explanation of that which is heterogeneous to constituted power — the weak incommensurable experience of Lenin's *gegemoniya* — but that it is a function of the institutional mediations and calculations of state legislative consciousness in which the "hegemonic apparatus" suppresses the experience of *gegemoniya* by translating it into the language and mediations of *nomos*, into the bourgeois forms of the integral nation-state.

Hegemony in this sense inaugurates a sociological reason and politics that both enable and refute the singularity of the event. The incommensurability of revolutionary equality and freedom succumbs to the restraining force and reason of the integral state form while presumably remaining at all times the phantasm that haunts it from within. As a result of this dialectical drama — or this always incomplete and never fully successful demand for the sublation of anomie — the thought of hegemony always upholds a constitutive yet contradictory relation between extension and crisis, in which the latter is inevitably the logical outcome of the former: "Any use of a model of integration also requires a model of disintegration, Gramsci's theoretical and methodological couples being bipolar. No theory of hegemony, in other words, without a theory of the crisis of hegemony (or organic crisis); no analysis of the integration of subaltern classes to a dominant class without a theory of the modes of autonomization and constitution of classes that enable a formerly subaltern class to become hegemonic" (Buci-Glucksmann, *Gramsci and the State*, 58).

The logical consequence of this is that the "more authentically hegemonic a class really is, the more it leaves opposing classes the possibility of organizing and forming themselves into an autonomous political force. . . . The concept of hegemony, therefore, is not exempt from a theoretical ambiguity of its own" (57–58). This latter insight is largely ignored by contemporary neo-Gramscian philologists, in active concealment of the fact that hegemony can be both a principial (Promethean) function that belongs internally to the unfolding of an event and also a turn against itself.

But this is worth dwelling on. The more authentically hegemonic hegemony is, the more open to counterhegemonic theoretical and practical challenges it becomes, since its coercive frameworks become more embedded, sedimented, and naturalized as the common sense of society. As a result, those same coercive frameworks become more open over time to the emergence of "arbitrary" aims, energies, and forms of questioning. Hegemony's success is in fact its Achilles' heel, since freedom within the framework of hegemony can only ever be predicated on the desuturing and denaturalizing of hegemonic subsumption and its institutional apparatuses, with the wager being that the political has to do more than content itself with the translation of anomie into *nomos*, immunizing itself continually against the hegemonic phantasm that it itself has subsumed. Accomplished hegemony is born either from within the potentiality of an event (revolution) or from within the socialization and institutionalization of a bourgeois moral economy ("passive revolution"), but no matter what its origin, it is only ever the force of restraint — or *katechon* — against the appearance of its own phantasm.

Peter Thomas's *The Gramscian Moment* provides us with symptomatic insight into the conceptual and practical limitations of philological fidelity to Gramsci's passage through hegemony. For Thomas, Gramsci's thought "provides us with a way to reconnect to the decisive political experiences of the socialist movement in the twentieth century, as a necessary precondition for exploring the forms of its possible actualization in our own times" (241). It is true that Gramsci allows us to reconnect to the political experiences of the socialist movement in the twentieth century. What is not so clear, however, is in what way this is a necessary precondition for exploring the contours of a renovation, or a possible inception, in thinking now. Presumably in order to do such a thing, one would need to account primarily for the fact that we are no longer living in the 1920s or in the age of the bourgeois revolutions (a detail that contemporary neo-Gramscians generally ignore in the name of fidelity to the Father and his political circumstance). Toward the end of *The Gramscian Moment*, Thomas expresses mild reservations about the notion of *hegemonic apparatus* in its relation to the task for contemporary thinking:

> Today, this notion invites us to reflect upon the institutional dimensions of contemporary philosophical practice and the ways in which, precisely as philosophy *qua* philosophy and even in its radical forms, it is integrated into and overdetermined by the bourgeois integral state,

as a mechanism of conformism and condensation of social relations of organization and comprehension into relations of speculative command. (450)

Contemporary thinking, Thomas suggests, is perhaps overdetermined by its conformism to the ontology of the commodity form and to its modern state form. If we add to Thomas's passing caution the relation between contemporary philosophical practice and the shifts in the international division of labor we now call post-sovereign globalization, then it might be said that just for a minute Thomas points toward the conceptual and political terrain that his own work cannot account for, that is, toward the contemporary global configuration of capital and its historical relation between philosophical conformism and speculative command. In the book's final pages, however, the author steps away from the possibility of thematizing the limitations of hegemony and of hegemony thinking, in such a way as to reinstate origins and thereby remain firmly entrenched within the limiting terra firma of genealogical fidelity to the paterfamilias:

> Just as politics is a necessary moment in the elaboration of a social group's or class's project, if it will not remain confined to a merely corporative existence within the project of another class, so philosophy — or the elaboration of philosophy as a conception of the world, conceived as an ensemble of concepts or social relations of knowledge for grasping and transforming "reality" collectively — also constitutes a ineludible moment in the formation and striving for coherence of a social group. If the subaltern classes do not elaborate their own hegemonic apparatus capable of challenging the relations of force condensed in the established "political society" of the bourgeois integral state, they will remain subaltern to its overdeterminations. (452)

The reasoning here is clear: The Gramscian conception of the bourgeois integral state — that is, the state that came into being as a result of the passive revolution of the Italian Resorgimento in the nineteenth century — is still the state form that reigns over, and through, our understanding of the political. Within the context of this state form, Thomas assures us, if the subaltern classes do not lead and subordinate — that is, reason politically in such a way as to subalternize via the dictatorship of the proletariat and the mediated domination of its hegemonic apparatus — they will remain subaltern. For Thomas, in other words, there is no historical, political, or conceptual distinction to be made between the global configuration of forces in the second decade of the twenty-first century and Antonio Gramsci's evaluation a century before of the historical processes of the nineteenth century and the formation of the integral nation-state in postfeudal Italy. Clearly something here does not add up, since we remain captured in the language, theoretical deployments, and political consciousness of the hegemonic understood as the reasoning that leads to the fabrication of a determinate system of moral life in the passage from feudalism to modernity, with absolutely no recognition of the validity of anything that might refuse to be subjected to the principial function and subsumption that makes that law and its history (Schürmann, *Broken Hegemonies*, 178). By this I mean to indicate that in Thomas's neo-Gramscianism the place of the subaltern and, indeed, of the subject is only ever *under* the historical law of the development of the bourgeois integral nation-state and therefore *under* the law of the ontology of the commodity form itself. The best we can aspire to in this stiflingly normative scenario is the repetition of origins and of previously given patterns and orders of legibility. However, it is hard to see how the repetition of origins can foment a project reimagining a notion of the political, never mind an exodus from the metaphysical subjectivism of the political, predicated on circumnavigating the modern conditions of a political consciousness that was forged in the epoch of the bourgeois integral nation-state. *The Gramscian Moment* places political logic once again on the side of the extension of norms, regulative representation, and the authority of practical rule. Therein reason posits itself once again, and only ever, on the side of the Promethean police order and the integral state, which, as a state form ensuring the participation of the People in the framework of its institutions, has already been superseded by, and will remain superseded in, the post-katechontic order of global capital. Thomas's formulations reproduce, and maintain no critical relation to, the limitations internal to the foundational concepts of political modernity.

In contrast, we might do well to recognize that there is in fact a significant yet passing moment in Gramsci's *Prison Notebooks* that we can opt to take seriously or, if we were to proceed like faithful neo-Gramscians, ignore or merely accept as a sociological necessity. The moment in question comes to light in *Notebook* 4, #38, "Relations between Structure and Superstructures" (*Notebooks*, 2:177–88), in which Gramsci addresses what he refers to as "the crucial problem of historical materialism." This crucial problem refers to the question of how to address the way that methodological criteria acquire their full significance in the analysis of concrete historical case studies such as the French Revolution or the Italian Resorgimento. Gramsci concludes this section by observing that the question of methodology and historical specificity must be "conducted within the ambit of the concept of hegemony" (187).

Herein Gramsci provides us with two figurations of hegemony and, moreover, with two sizeable historical and conceptual limitations. The first conceptualization refers to hegemony as the formation and universalization of a sense of economic, political, intellectual, and moral unity in the relation between one "fundamental social group" and other subordinate groups. Hegemony is, in this sense, the modern social formalization of the One. Gramsci proceeds, however, by signaling, and by skimming over, one absolutely crucial limitation to the concept:

> The state-government is seen as a group's own organism for creating the favorable terrain for the maximum expansion of the group itself. But this development and this expansion are also viewed concretely as universal; that is, they are viewed as being tied to the interests of the subordinate groups, as a development of unstable equilibriums between the interests of fundamental groups and the interests of the subordinate groups in which *the interests of the fundamental group prevail — but only up to a certain point; that is, without going quite as far as corporate economic selfishness.* (180, italics mine)

Corporate economic selfishness is not only antithetical to the inner workings and extension of hegemony; it destroys it. This is the case because, in Aristotelian terms, it extends the victory of the appetites over "reason without appetites" and life governed by the automatism of the drives over reason.[55] The second conceptualization worthy of emphasis reads as follows, as Gramsci returns to that "certain point" at which hegemony ceases to be hegemonic. Now, however, he considers it specifically from the side of the subordinate groups:

> The fact of hegemony presupposes that *the interests and tendencies of those groups over whom hegemony is exercised have been taken into account* and that *a certain equilibrium* is established. It presupposes, in other words, that the hegemonic group should make sacrifices of an economic-corporate kind; these sacrifices, however, cannot touch the essential; since hegemony is political but also and above all economic, it has its material base in the decisive function exercised by the hegemonic group in the decisive core of economic activity. (183, italics mine)

Here the subordinated groups have to feel that their interests are being represented by the state government. For Gramsci, hegemony is the political representation of good intentions toward subordinate groups whose "interests and tendencies," whatever they might be, have to be "taken into account" by the "fundamental social group" — but *not too much and not too little* — while the economic interests of that fundamental group must prevail at all times, but *only up to a certain point.*

Hegemony for Gramsci is a practical economy of tumult held in reserve, a force of legibility and of restraint against the abyss of an irreducible loss of meaning that functions equally on both sides of the equation conjoining the fundamental and subordinate groups. It is the never-ending calculation and balancing act between fully comprehensible and representable means and ends, involving the virtuous politics of restraint and immunization against "corporate economic selfishness" and disequilibrium, which could probably be understood as the potential demise of equivalence, or imminent turmoil. As a result, hegemony is the constant maximization of the active subsumption of the everyday under specific laws of comportment. *Corporate economic selfishness* and, in conceptual terms, generalized unintelligibility, are what lie on the conjectural "other side" of that *certain point* at which the terrain of hegemony — the hegemonic balancing act and enclosure — confronts its limit. Similarly, tumult destroys hegemony.

Ontologically, the "crucial problem of historical materialism" is essentially pastoral, and therefore katechontic, in nature. It is the never-ending determination of the proper steering of all human action and morality toward the political techniques and rationalities of sociopolitical containment. It is the constant determination and instrumentalization of the proper character of modern domination, which is perceived to be better than what Demogorgon referred to in *Prometheus Unbound* as "the appearance of tyranny." By definition, hegemony is the reduction of experience to the domination of instrumental reason. The real — understood as all those aspects of human existence that are not immediately subject to the *ratio* and moral order of hegemony — remains beyond measure, presumably in the realm of the posthegemonic. The real for hegemony would be the threatening realm of the retreat from politics or even the infraexcess of hegemony that cannot be enforced. As such, "the crucial problem of historical materialism" is the tyranny of instrumental reason that is internal to it, the limitations of that domination, and the fact that it is never historically or materially capable of accounting for what remains beyond its constitutive reductionism, beyond the common sense of its modern *ratio*, or beyond the underlying Christianity of its pastoral power reconverted for Gramsci into the possibility of communist productionism and intelligibility. It is for this reason that the historical archive of the subaltern classes "is necessarily fragmented and episodic" and that "every trace of autonomous initiative is therefore of inestimable value" (Gramsci, *Notebooks*, vol. 2, NB 3, #14, 21). The question of legibility raised in the historical archive by subaltern fragments and traces of autonomous initiative points toward the paradigmatic limit that brings hegemony to confront the improper — the unpolitical, "spontaneous," presymbolic, or merely uneducated — realm of posthegemony. For Gramsci, then, the only good subaltern is the one who can be, or already has been, transformed by means of education into "a modern mentality" (vol. 2, NB 3, #48, 49). The subaltern classes should learn to balance spontaneity with conscious leadership in order to become the *constitutive outside* of the modern political *ratio* of hegemony and the forms of unification it demands. Nothing on *the other side of* the constitutive outside — this zone of filial adherence between inside and outside — is worthy of consideration. It signals a mere abdication of political responsibility to be avoided at all cost. For this reason, Gramsci considers that the bourgeoisie is the prime example, worthy of imitation, of a subaltern class that attained its "autonomy" via the formulation and extension of reason (vol. 2, NB 3, #90, 91–92).

But with the advent in the 1970s and 1980s of the neoliberal ethos of unfettered *corporate economic selfishness* unleashed on a global scale — that is, of Deng Xiaoping's adage that "to get rich is glorious" — Gramsci's understanding of hegemony as the proper, ethical steering of human action toward the technicity of sociopolitical containment and its modern forms of representation has crumbled. A line has been crossed definitively. It is already too late for the *modern* understanding of the epoch and *ratio* of revolution in permanence. According to Gramsci's own definition of hegemony, it is clear that for decades now we have been immersed in the realities and conundrums of the *posthegemonic*. But that does not mean that the historical Left has done much to challenge its relation to the administration of regulatory representation and subjectivity in the face of the fully decontained commodity form, of the perishing of the very idea of hegemony, and of the *ratio* that tried so persistently to delimit an ontology of presence and of absolute legibility in the name of freedom, equality, and revolution.

How, then, has the Left addressed the posthegemonic realm that Gramsci could not, or did not want to, name because it exceeded the productionist *ratio* and moral order of communist social uniformity, discipline, consciousness, and legibility? It is well known by now that, in the wake of the exhaustion of the bourgeois revolutionary period, the ongoing crisis of the integral nation-state, and the emergent shift to the neoliberal market-state duopoly, in their 1985 book *Hegemony and Socialist Strategy* Ernesto Laclau and Chantal Mouffe set out to reevaluate and revitalize the notion and place of the concept of hegemony for contemporary political philosophy and practice, observing that what was at issue in the newly emergent neoliberal era was "the very articulation between liberalism and democracy which was performed during the course of the nineteenth century" (171).[56]

Laclau and Mouffe set out the problem of hegemony fully cognizant of the major shifts that had occurred at the heart of the political in the post-1948 (Bretton Woods) period. Who, they ask, is the agent of hegemony? Previously, the answer had been clear: "We have already seen the answer that the Marxism of the Third International gave to this question: from Lenin to Gramsci it maintained that the ultimate core of a hegemonic force consists of a fundamental class" (134). Now, however, they say, the Leninist class determination — the *gegemoniya* of the proletariat — has become so ungrounded that "unfixity has become the condition of every social identity. The fixity of every social identity in the first theorization of hegemony proceeded from the indissoluble link between the hegemonized task and the class that was supposed to be its natural agent. . . . But, insofar as the task has ceased to have any necessary link with a class . . . there are no privileged points for the unleashing of a socialist political practice" (86–87).[57]

The classic discourse of socialism was, observe Laclau and Mouffe, that of "a discourse of the universal, which transformed certain categories into depositories of political and epistemological privileges. . . . It was, finally, a discourse concerning the privileged points from which historical changes were set in motion — the Revolution, the General Strike, or 'evolution' as a unifying category of the cumulative and irreversible character of partial advances" (192). The authors note, however, that the 1980s signal "the displacement of the frontier of the social" (176), insofar as in the neoliberal deterritorialization of capital "a series of subject positions that were accepted as *legitimate differences* in the hegemonic formation corresponding to the Welfare State are expelled from the field of social positivity and construed as negativity — the parasites on social security (Mrs. Thatcher's 'scroungers'), the inefficiency associated with union privileges, and state subsidies, and so on" (176). As a result of the displacement of the frontier of the social inaugurated by the redimensioning of the economic and territorial logic of state power, for Laclau and Mouffe gone are the dictatorship of the proletariat and the exclusivity of social class (since class struggle, they say, no longer determines the political).

Even though for Laclau and Mouffe there is no longer a predetermined subject of hegemony, hegemony itself remains (at least rhetorically) at all times constitutive of political subjectivity. It is in the wake of the proletariat that "the People" and the emergence of a certain relation of indistinction between hegemony and populism come into view as *the* new institution of the social: "Claude Lefort has shown how the 'democratic revolution,' as a new terrain which supposes a profound mutation at the symbolic level, implies a new form of institution of the social. . . . Democracy inaugurates the experience of a society which cannot be apprehended or controlled, in which the people will be proclaimed sovereign, but in which its identity will never be definitively given, but will remain latent'" (186–87).[58] The question for hegemony, in this supposedly new ontological figuration of the political, is the way it addresses its relation to that which cannot be apprehended or controlled, namely, "the People," or democracy, which, in this case, appear to be synonymous.

However, what I am interested in highlighting in this regard is the way that Laclau and Mouffe's theory of hegemony is predicated on a not-so-covert decisionist thrust that, while not being furnished with a specific Schmittian vocabulary of its own, is nevertheless far from being disassociated from the Schmittian, and therefore katechontic, conception of the political.[59] In *The Origins of Totalitarianism*, Hannah Arendt referred to Thomas Hobbes's Commonwealth as "a vacillating structure" that "must always provide itself with new props from outside; otherwise it would collapse overnight into the aimless, senseless chaos of the private interests from which it sprang" (142). Similarly, hegemony theory in Laclau and Mouffe is a Hobbesian katechontic affair concerning the need to guard against chaos, which the authors now refer to as "the implosion of the social and an absence of any common point of reference" (188). As already noted in this Passage, for Schmitt the katechon guarded against the coming of the Anti-Christ and translated the theology of history into the time of empires. For Laclau and Mouffe, hegemony guards against the implosion of the social and translates the crisis of bourgeois capitalism into the time of "the People" (though the relation among leftism, populism, fascism, and, indeed, capital remains unresolved).

It is hardly surprising, then, that Laclau and Mouffe's theory of hegemony should rest on the question of the decision in relation to undecidability, groundlessness, and incommensurability. In their 2001 preface to the second edition of their 1985 book, the authors characterize hegemony as a decisionist ontology designed to carry out expansive work on the terrain of undecidability: "If undecidables permeate the field which had previously been seen as governed by structural determination, one can see hegemony as a theory of the decision taken in an undecidable terrain" (xi). Laclau and Mouffe's insistence on hegemony's ability to decide on what they call "the undecidable" clearly references the essential work of incommensurability that lies at the heart of any notion of freedom or of democratic politics. However, hegemony in Laclau and Mouffe is a politics designed to displace indetermination in favor of intelligibility, measurelessness in favor of calculability, ambiguity in favor of certainty, undecidability in favor of the decision. In this work *against* the existence and force of incommensurability, it is the category of "equiva-lence" that mediates between and alleviates the potentially negative effects of dissymmetry and difference that might lead to undecidability.[60]

What is the logic of the articulating decision in its relation to an antag-onistic terrain? The answer to this question is strikingly simple: The politi-cal thrust of hegemony is to decide on externality in order to guarantee the reduction and closure of the social field to a certain form of intelligibility articulated across a radically open social sphere. The work of hegemony is to open up to externality, but to open up in order to close down undecidables via the decision, which is, precisely, the dilemma confronted in Gramsci's political ontology. When the authors describe hegemony as a theory of articu-lation, what they mean is that it is a theory of political decisionism in a space no longer anchored — in a relation of fixity — to the social pact enforced by the sovereign will of Hobbes's Leviathan or by its katechontic surrogate: the bourgeois integral state.

Hegemony for Laclau and Mouffe is "a space in which bursts forth a whole conception of the social based upon an intelligibility which reduces its dis-tinct moments to the interiority of a closed paradigm" (93). What does hege-mony "burst forth" against and strive to reduce and close? Again, the answer is clear: "It is because there are no more assured foundations arising out of a transcendent order, because there is no longer a center which binds together power, law, and knowledge that it becomes necessary to unify certain political spaces through hegemonic articulations" (187). Hegemony is a surrogate force working in the wake of the integral sovereign state in order to bind together subjectivity and experience as an assured foundation for the political, across a social terrain in which transcendent sovereignty has been supplemented by societal unfixity (or by an emergent biocapitalist power on a global scale). Hegemony, then, is grounded in an act of openness to the constitutive outside but simultaneously in an act of closure and constraint, for openness or lack of unity — lack of all reference to unity in the wake of the end of the era of bour-geois revolution — is, they say, as dangerous as the restoration of authoritarian unity (or closure). Hegemony, then, constructs a bridge between eschatology and political thought in the wake of the integral nation-state:

> If there is no doubt that one of the dangers which threatens democracy is the totalitarian attempt to pass beyond the constitutive character of antagonism and deny plurality in order to restore unity, there is also a symmetrically opposite danger of a lack of all reference to this unity. For, even though impossible, this remains a horizon which, given the absence of articulation between social relations, is necessary in order

to prevent an implosion of the social and an absence of any common point of reference. (188)

Hegemony is the exercise of an unceasing *proto-nomic* decisionism, a never-ending and, as they say, impossible nomic judgment on a world that remains heterogeneous to hegemonic reason. As in the case of Gramsci, the sole function of reason for Laclau and Mouffe is to constantly measure, calculate, and decide upon the incommensurable relation between what constitutes too much unity (authoritarianism) and what constitutes too little unity, which they refer to as "a lack of all reference to this unity." When, one might ask, is too much unity too much? When is too little unity too little? To decide on this is "impossible," they say, but we must do so anyway, because if we do not, hegemony will cease to exist and we will succumb to the chaos and lawlessness of social implosion or to an infraexcess of the political. For Laclau and Mouffe politics is, as it was for Hobbes, Gramsci, and Schmitt, the right to decide.

Thus, in the wake of the bourgeois integral state, in Laclau and Mouffe, as in Lenin and Gramsci before them (though with a different vocabulary), hegemony is a katechontic decisionism designed "to prevent an implosion of the social and an absence of any common point of reference." For whom? Since class is no longer the privileged point of articulation, we would have to say that it is for the hegemonizers and their constitutive outsides, since hegemony in the era of "the People" works katechontically for both Left and Right.

In this sense, the fear of social implosion is the law that determines the infrastructure of the *undecidables* that render all decisions, *as* decisions, conceivable (Levinson, *Market and Thought*, 155). The constant danger for hegemony, of course, is that its essential antagonism lies in that which remains external to its own reason and intelligibility (world, real, subalternity, suffering, the presymbolic, etc.). Openness to the constitutive outside (anomie) and its subsequent domestication (*nomos*) is the theory's essential proposition, and therein also lies the theory's essential Hegelianism. As such, the relation to openness, while necessary to guarantee closure, is fraught with problems: "The first problem concerns . . . the external moment which hegemony, like any articulatory relation, supposes" (138). The problem appears to be a question of measurement: How anomic can anomie actually be? This depends upon the level of *recognition* there is in the relation between inside and outside. In Laclau and Mouffe's formulations, hegemony can be a friend to its real or potential enemy — that is, to its constitutive externality — only as long as that externality recognizes the legitimacy of the opposition: "A hegemonic formation embraces what opposes it, insofar as the opposing force accepts the system of basic articulations of that formation as something it negates" (139).

In this formulation hegemony can be a friend to its negation (other, anomie, or enemy) only when the latter recognizes and accepts that the former has the ability, right, or power to decide on the terms of their oppositional relation. But in order for that to happen the latter has to accept the validity of the former's symbolization of them as a potential negation, or enemy. If they do not, they are, in Hegel's terms, mere rabble.[61]

Hegemony's constitutive outside is its anomic negation (its necessary enemy), a negation that remains at all times internal to (and therefore a friend of) hegemony's self-unfolding and extension. Hegemony in this sense is constitutive of a certain conception of the political in which there can be absolutely no event or disjunction, for an event occurs only at a distance from the symmetrical reasoning of the friend-enemy relation, at a distance, that is, from knowledge, reason, calculation, and truth (Derrida, *The Politics of Friendship*, 30). Hegemony in relation to this constitutive (and therefore internal) externality is already, and only ever, a turn and a return to the self-constitution of hegemonic reason, of the reduction of the world to the sovereign One, whereupon the enemy is assigned a single place as a constitutive relation to the friend (hegemony). The constitutive outside is only ever constitutive of *nomos*, or is destined to be politically inexistent. Reason in this logic is always already immunized against any possible *alter*—against anything other than the law of hegemony, any originary heterogeneity, or the unconditionality of the nonfriend (222)—for difference here is only ever a function and extension of the selfsame, and the friend and enemy share fraternally in the self-legitimating acknowledgment of their hegemonic negation and positive captivity.

Anything outside of this fraternity—anything truly *alter*, truly *queer*, or infrapolitical—is just not of the order of the political and is not addressed by Laclau and Mouffe. Hegemony, then, is a question of pacifying and administering the negation of externality from within, in order for chaos—the implosion of the social, or the void—to not ensue. Indeed, this leads to the following question: From where are the terms of the oppositional relation to externality defined? The answer is by now predictable: "The *place of the negation* is defined by the internal parameters of the formation itself" (139). In other words, the constitutive outside that accepts and acknowledges the validity of the hegemonic articulation has no language other than that of the hegemonic formation, and there is no *alter* available at all, because by definition such a thing does not respect the normal conditions of hegemony's articulation with the outside. The oppositional negation of hegemony—hegemony's necessarily external yet constitutive hostility—is in fact the closest, most familiar, and most intimate friend and brother.

Laclau and Mouffe state the following: "The theoretical determination of the conditions of extinction of the hegemonic form of politics, also explains the reasons for the constant expansion of this form in modern times" (139). As such, they indicate that the hegemonic articulation is a struggle against the death of the interiority of a closed paradigm (*nomos*) that is nevertheless open to its constitutive outside (anomie) (143–44). Hegemony in Laclau and Mouffe strives to territorialize — to give representation to and to contain — a will based on dedifferentiation or subsumption, as a means of *overseeing* a fundamental bond between the social field and the reason of subjective command.

As in Lenin and Gramsci, hegemony theory in Laclau and Mouffe is a reductive schema of self-familiarity; it is the extension of a phallogocentric sameness designed to exorcize from the social field all thought and practice grounded in *alterity*. Hegemony is the existential negation of the *alter*; the potentially infinite remove, which is the real enemy.[62] There is no room here for the impersonal nonfriend that underlies all democratic thought and practice, for this anonymous figure indicates the potential implosion of the social — post-katechontic lawlessness — that hegemony works to restrain and contain. Laclau and Mouffe's theory of hegemony is a reason grounded in the absolutely necessary closure of anxiety, unleashed against *alterity* in an attempt to suppress all that is heterogeneous to the reductive reasoning of the hegemony-externality, *nomos*-anomie relation that remains internal to the hegemonic articulation. It is, as in the Schmittian apparatus, a conceptual framework designed katechontically to restrain and contain categorical and practical uncertainty, incalculability, and incommensurability, and it is extended in the name of subjective sovereign decisionism now inflected toward what the authors call "a radical democratic politics." But as Laura Bazzicalupo puts it: "In Laclau's schema something does not add up" ("Populismo y liberalismo," 368).[63]

Similarly, the question for us is how to consider the material conditions of globalization at a distance from, rather than in the shadow of, the forms of containment imposed by the inherited metaphoricity of the Paulist katechon and of the neoimperial eschatology — the Christian metaphysics — that accompanies it. How, in other words, can one do the following:

> Imagine a political act whose primary determination is to move beyond phillocentrism, beyond community, beyond translation, and not against an enemy but toward the non-militant region from which all militancy and every partisan modality emerges? Not toward neutrality or pacifism, but against all enemy partisanship, which is also the impossible preventive partisanship of the friend, or of he who feigns to be so (for there are no friends). (Moreiras, *Línea de sombra*, 84)

Many on both Left and Right will respond that politics is only ever the work of representation and containment and therefore that such a question is invalid because it is nihilistic or impossible to implement as either policy or real political legislation, curtailing affective investments in specific nomenclatures such as parliamentary democracy, communism, humanism, populism, or militancy. One could only respond that such a formulation is only ever preparatory of a form of thinking and acting that offers an alternative ground from that of the Christian onto-theological quest for political and subjective restraint and containment.

The modern geometries of containment such as the nation-state, "the People," or "the Party" no longer do the work they did even a few years ago, and the nomenclatures themselves appear increasingly to be the melancholic symptoms of a dominant Right and of a postimperialist Left more interested in rescuing the validity of prior forms than in examining the material conditions of the current posthegemonic conjuncture. The easy path is to err on the side of fidelity to the reterritorialization of modern legislative (that is, hegemonic or militant) consciousness as the only progressive horizon available to us in deterritorializing times. Perhaps ironically, this is also the position of the Vatican, but without the political militancy.

While hegemony and the militant subject emerged and developed in response to the historical extension of the integral nation-state and its territorial logic of power in the years following the Paris Commune, globalization has developed out of the definitive overextension and hollowing out of the bond between the territorialization of power, the history of that power's legislative consciousness (including the phallogocentric history of the modern subject), and modernity's relations of property legislated on the terrain of interstate modalities of war. The need to delay the end of the time of Euro-Atlantic empire — and therefore to restrain the history of its ultimate demise — has conditioned the desire for a strong decisionist concept of the political, which is what we see more or less camouflaged in Laclau and Mouffe's theory of hegemony, in the model of a virtuous subjective fidelity advanced by the communist hypothesis, and also at the heart of Trumpism's founding commandment ("Make America Great Again!").

We are still thinking and acting within an ontological tradition that is increasingly obsolete, or reactive. This raises the validity of the following question, the consequences of which have been largely ignored: "Is it possible to salvage some kind of anti-systemic productivity in our transitional times for a mode of knowledge that would seem to depend almost entirely on epistemological models bequeathed by modernity at the very moment in which modernity becomes a thing of the past?" (Moreiras, *The Exhaustion of Dif-*

*ference*, 76). In an era in which capital has no exteriority and no alternative (I know, alternatives are all around us in their minuscule and myriad forms, and yet . . .), is there a viable way to think something other than the technical reproduction of the given, when the given is the destructuration and post-sovereign decontainment of modern conceptions of political space without inaugurating any true difference in the present?

It is now clear that neoliberalism has ushered in the closure of the national bourgeois era, that is, it has brought about the exhaustion of the imperial interstate system in its specifically territorialized capitalist forms. Jelica Sumic defines the ensuing globalization of capital as *the ongoing dismantling of the preexisting system* of bourgeois territorialization and therefore as the ongoing dismantling of the existence of emancipatory politics as the Promethean detotalization of totalization. She thereby raises the question of the relation between modern emancipatory politics — populism, for example — and the increasing obsolescence of national political space and of the nation-state as the symbolic Other of "the People":

> If the subversion of the master's closure is not sufficient to account
> for an emancipatory politics more attuned to the deadlocks of global-
> ized capitalism, that is because the latter is articulated to the non-
> existence of the Other, and has as its structural principle a "general-
> ized metonymization" that from the outset excludes the possibility of
> closure capable of rendering any given situation "legible." Our point
> is that the possibility of an emancipatory politics changes fundamen-
> tally when the master's discourse yields to "generalized metonymi-
> zation." Or to be more precise, the total hegemony of a discourse
> that is structurally metonymic, the capitalist discourse, has decisive
> consequences for the transformative power of politics, ultimately, for
> its capacity to change the transcendental regime of the present world.
> What characterizes the globalized capitalist discourse is precisely that
> there is nothing left that serves as a barrier. . . . In the current space of
> discursivity, the notion of place itself is strangely out of place. What
> is more, with the category of place thus rendered inoperative, it is
> one of the key categories of emancipatory politics, the notion of lack,
> necessary to the subject for it to sustain itself in the symbolic Other,
> that becomes obsolete. . . . In the absence of the master signifier
> which would render a given situation "readable," the subject remains
> a prisoner not of the Other that exists, but of the inexistent Other, or
> of the inexistence of the Other. ("Politics in the Era of the Inexistent
> Other," 9–10)[64]

If populism is the division of the field of the political into the subjectification of a *We* and therefore, via its logical extension, also into the subjectification of a specific *They* (the anti-*People*)—both of which position the subject
as the effect of the signifier that expresses itself via the language of, and in
relation to, the Other—we would do well to recognize that it is increasingly
unclear in globalization how to identify *concretely* who the *anti-People* are,
where they are, and what they are doing, since the conditions of exploitation
are always already both *offshore*—at the other end of the world—and also
at the very core of individual and collective desire and identification. In the
epoch of conspiracy theories run amok, the *They* springs up anytime for apparently any reason, and, as its logical extension, so does the *We* against whoever
it might feel is conspiring against them. The *They* becomes absolutely anyone
who does not fit into the specific abstractions and values of any one tribal
group: *We*. Hence the upsurge in populism in recent years is the direct result
of the real and apparent *decomposition of the Other* as a fully identifiable *They*.
Perhaps it is for this reason that contemporary populism is the extreme exacerbation of an unconditional subjectivity, and subjectivism, that has always
presented itself at the modern heart of the political.

If populism is the metaphysical actualization of representation in action,
then we can see that it is the coming into being of a *We* that over a period of
time comes to understand itself as the object of its own consciousness. In this
sense it is the actualization of the subject-object relation itself and, as such,
the container of *techne* at the level of the political (understanding *techne*, as
Martin Heidegger puts it, as the societal extension of the affirmation "*I represent something*"). This has always been the case. But in light of the shifting
terrains of globalization, in which the *I represent something* is increasingly
meaningless in its nomadism and deterritorialization and increasingly virulent
in its demand for gathering, perhaps we can now indicate that contemporary
populism is the emergence of a drive for the political that is determined fully
by *the ongoing crisis of the preexisting spatial system* rather than by the epoch
of the spatialization of the integral bourgeois nation-state. Populism is now the
expression of the crisis of the populist and governmental forms that guaranteed a transition from archaic kinship forms to modern notions of citizenship
and social inclusion. With the ongoing dissolution of the bourgeois imperial
order and the collapse of national capitals sutured to the discourses of economic development and underdevelopment, of dependency, of centers and
peripheries, and therefore of insides and outsides, the populism that used to
appear as the performance of the territorialized sovereign legitimacy of "the
People," as an internal political subjectivation, now appears as the affirmation of a desire for something—sometimes for absolutely anything—other

than that of full exposure to the vagaries of, and total subsumption to, global capital.[65]

In Gramsci's interpretation, there is a "certain point" at which the practice and field of hegemony — its restraining force — kicks the bucket. This certain point is the real as the infraexcess of the instrumental reason of the political. This infrahegemonic excess is the historical raison d'être of *posthegemony*, which, as already suggested, is the thematization of the limits of hegemony and of hegemony thinking via the extension of an intellectual *infidelity* to the conceptual confinements and calculations of the integral interstate *nomos*, to its dialectical faith in the consolidation of the hegemonic apparatus, and to the regulatory (biopolitical) representation of the place of the subject. Reiner Schürmann has defined in the following terms the task of a thought that does not surrender itself immediately to the determinate conditions of hegemonic fraternization: "The history of hegemony belongs to the history of norms, it names the authoritative representation that serves to constitute the phenomenality of phenomena and thereby to legitimize all theoretical and practical rule. But there is always a fantasm that cannot be exhausted in regulatory representations" (*Broken Hegemonies*, 6). What remains unaccounted for, and what the tradition has concealed, is the question of what regulatory representation cannot capture or domesticate. Biopolitics, together with all the impolitical philosophies that ultimately affirm it as a form of transformative thinking, remains subject to the history of norms extended throughout the trajectory of the era of bourgeois revolution and the integral nation-state.[66]

In contrast, infrapolitical posthegemony exists and is deployed in the wake of the apotheosis and closure of the era of bourgeois revolution and the integral nation-state, as a thinking attuned to an existential analytic that cannot be exhausted in the history of our modern regulatory (biopolitical) representations. The conceptual and practical weight we assign to the *closure of metaphysics* — or not, as the case may be — is absolutely central to this discussion. With the death of God (Nietzsche) and the destruction of the metaphysical–onto-theological ground for thought (Heidegger), we confront the closure of metaphysics hand in hand with the advent of absolute technological enframing (*techne*) on a planetary scale (which is not to say that Nietzsche and Heidegger are complicit with that advent). In *Broken Hegemonies* Reiner Schürmann offers the fundamental diagnosis that in the current epoch, which he reads as *the closure of epochality itself*, we are witnessing the gradual and unforgiving breakdown of any *arche* previously capable of mobilizing thought and action. In this sense, the time of the closure of metaphysics is *an-archic* (in which case, neoliberalism is merely a symptom of, and the attempt to further conceal, a far deeper conceptual-existential conundrum). The closure of metaphysics does not indicate a transition to other forms, for here there is no Hegelian *Aufhebung* available (unless the sovereign decisionism of so-called real politics intervenes to oversimplify matters for us, which, of course, it strives to do on a daily basis but fails).

Within this overall context of decontained turmoil, the *infrapolitical*— the ontological difference or distance from the political that always flows beneath the political (Moreiras, "Infrapolítica y política de la infrapolítica," 56)— remains inextricably linked at all times to posthegemony and is essential to any possible formulation of a democratic thought and practice at this time. Jorge Álvarez Yágüez ("Crisis epocal") posits that what is at stake is a thinking that is *other* than that of the inheritance of the *koinon*— which is the originary principle or foundation (*arche*) that guarantees the possibility of a relation to the One (to the Aristotelian *pros hen*), thereby determining our understanding of the common, the public, the res publica, *nomos*, the commonwealth, the people, biopolitics, and the modern structure of sovereignty. What we understand to be the common is, in all its historical variants, the fully determined, principial relation to the One. Obviously, the emergence of the nation-state as the principal foundation of the post-1648 Westphalian world order and the ascension of individual consciousness as the *arche* of the bourgeois Enlightenment subject in post-Renaissance philosophy and politics are refortifications of an originary concept— the One, the Subject, consciousness, etc.— that has been waning and reinstating itself forcefully, reactively, for centuries. Such refortifications and iterations have been fundamental for the historic territorialization of capital and the modern nation-state. Communitarianism, the commons, neocommunism, and decolonial thought are all theories of a will to power grounded not in the closure of metaphysics but in the decisionist/ subjectivist *closure of the closure of metaphysics* extended in the name of the domination of the ontology of the subject experienced as freedom.

Infrapolitical posthegemony, on the other hand, bears witness to the fact that these positions are the embodiment of the nihilism that already possesses us (*techne*, the will to power, or the calculations of the relation between means and ends). For this reason, infrapolitical posthegemony merely strives to advance a thought that remains at a distance from the nihilist legacies of subjectivist decisionism that we have inherited from modernity and its Latin-Romanic, humanist antecedents. To reduce our nihilist subjectivist legacies to rubble, to a point of suspension or inoperativity, is to think and write in preparation for a clearing, a renovation and potential turn in our thinking that might be capable of clearing away the subordination of freedom to the ontology of subjectivity and to the modern history of its katechontic and biopolitical deployments.

## Why Bother with the Infrapolitical?

The infrapolitical register in thinking derives from the realization that a turn away from the political calculations of neoliberal and postneoliberal globalization, in which the "postneoliberal" refers to the effects of neoliberalism applied and now experienced as both post-sovereign state form and unbounded planetary and human value extraction in extremis, is incumbent upon us. Such a turn strives to approach the task of thinking from within the inhabitual, which begins with the dismantling of the primacy of the political over existence, which can only be offered via the reassessment of the thinking and experience of *existence* as being-toward-death.

We can now say that the infrapolitical is the thinking that flickers on the tremorous limit at which the end of the representation of historical progress is finally realized and the metaphysical indulgences of previous vital political and ideological illusions (such as the bourgeois foundations of fraternity, equality, and liberty) flounder and run aground, rising up, nevertheless, in increasingly vitriolic forms as subjectivist reactionary demands for definitive (nationalist, populist, or identitarian) decisions, resolutions, or truths regarding the twilight of the modern.

To reiterate, attunement to a specifically infrapolitical register in thinking gives no credence to the overcoming of political disenchantment in the name of fidelity to the unifying inheritance of "the commons" or of a "communist hypothesis," since the infrapolitical comes to the fore in the realization (which cannot be merely confused with eschatology) that "nothing remains any longer in which the hitherto accustomed world of humankind could be salvaged; nothing of what has gone before offers itself as something that could still be erected as a goal for the accustomed self-securing of human beings" (Heidegger, *The History of Beyng*, 154). The infrapolitical sits on the side of conceptual reassessment, of backtracking, rather than on the side of commandment and prophecy. It is this differential gesture and perception that orients it toward a possible inception in thinking.

In Marxian terms, while the Westphalian interstate system that reigned until 1971 came to be an imperial-national order capable of fomenting but also of mediating and restraining competitive relations between the relative values (GDPs) of national bourgeoisies — in other words, while political and economic modernity was anchored for centuries in the calculable and therefore representable (or at least agreed-upon) value of gold (and then in arbitrarily fixed exchange rates still held to the value of gold after the 1944 Bretton Woods conference) — our current demetalized, "dollarized," and fully unrestrained quest for surplus value on a planetary scale has unleashed the violent demise of an economic and political architectonic grounded in geographical and economic commensurability, thereby producing an ever-changing and deterritorializing shift in, and never-ending conflict between, different manifestations and perceptions of the very idea of value (relative and therefore absolute).

Contemporary global capital is predicated on the anchorless, deterritorializing, increasingly rapid circulation of and competition between relative values and on the opening up of ever-new fault lines and border zones for the further extraction of value. These postnational frontiers inaugurate the dismantling of traditional legislative mediations and legal structures (the modern state form, for example) to such an extent that the *anomie* that has always been internal to *nomos* becomes, in its post–Cold War ascendance, the active and ongoing *perishing* of the modern state's ability to mediate between *logos*, constituted power, political space, and modern forms of institutional restraint.

Globalization is the setting in motion of the demise of the modern mediations of relative value. It is their displacement into a monstrous quest, beyond all certainties regarding the value of value itself, for the absolutization of surplus value. Furthermore, it is capital's gigantic quest for the ultimate spoils of self-destruction that allows us to glimpse the unrestrained world of an absolutely decontained civil war (of *stasis* fully unleashed on a planetary scale), which is nothing more than the ongoing perishing, the very form of ending, of modern political space itself *without* an alternative sovereign order or topographical arrangement in sight and, hence, with no enduring location from which to anchor negation, transgression, or transcendence.

It is clear by now that the contemporary indistinction between war and peace on a global scale marks the active and ongoing destruction of Kant's attempted yet impossible approximation to perpetual peace and to the interstate order of restraint.[67] As Heidegger (*The History of Beyng*, 154) put it, "What is as yet ungraspable, and yet imposing itself and intruding everywhere in the realm of the uncomprehended, is the disappearance of the distinction between war and peace." It is as a result of the active disappearance of this distinction between war and peace — a disappearance that inaugurates the invalidation of the regulative idea of reason itself and, as such, of the very presence of reason — that the infrapolitical comes once again into sight with no founding principle or specific methodology to orient or determine it.

Having said that, what is suggested by the suffix *infra-* (rather than by, say, the *sur-* of surrealism or the *meta-* of metaphysics) is the necessity of an engagement with the horizon and materiality of ruination, perishing, finitude, and death. It does not operate solely in the name of an "actuality" of politics. While coextensive with the political, it strives to destroy the ontological presuppositions of the political. For this reason, the infrapolitical register's primary differential gesture toward thinking is located in its attunement to the existential, rather than just to the moralizing political indignations of both Right and Left, which highlight the distinct forces of humanist subjectivism.

On a purely sociological level one can look toward symptoms such as the ongoing political and social debacles experienced under the auspices of the COVID-19 pandemic, Brexit, Catalonian secessionism, Hong Kong, Chile, or Ukrainian, Brazilian, Bolivian, and Venezuelan "democracy," to name just a few, or the vociferous yet somnambulistic claims to a collective recollection of a time prior to the current catastrophe via the "Make America Great Again!" brand. But one can also consider the myriad forms of right-wing movements that range from the "cultural" defense of the welfare state by wholesome Scandinavians embracing the historical values of the extreme Right or the flagrantly racist and misogynist neofascist Right (Vox) in Spain gaining fifty-two parliamentary seats in the name of the defense of "our Western culture" to the blatant anti-immigrant racism and defense of the land against all non-white "invaders" voiced in *Build That Wall!*" One can also ponder, of course, the globalization of financial austerity and the collectivization of public and private debt that accompanies it, or the resurgence of right-wing governments in Latin America after over a decade of attempted progressive reform connected directly to soaring global commodity prices. We can look in the direction of unfettered resource extraction, mass global migration, climate change, terrorism, cryptocurrencies (the votaries of which broadcast nothing less than the algorithmic "decolonization" of currency itself in the name of planetary deliverance!), artificial intelligence, split-second financialization and high-speed trading, the passing of the utopian horizons not only of worker emancipation but of the former global "periphery" in its entirety, the increasingly extensive resistances of injured microidentities, narco-accumulation, "global war" . . . the list is endless.

The question "What is the world coming to?" is now the most banal expression of perplexity regarding the nature and character of our times and simultaneously the most conceptually impenetrable of all possible questions. It is certainly more bewildering now than it was just a few decades ago, when President George H. W. Bush prophesized that the collapse of the Soviet Union would mark the beginning of a New World Order. In the wake of the Cold War the idea of a specific post–Cold War order, of a historical direction anchoring individual and collective destinies and endeavors, or the very idea of a specific *nomos* of representation and of representability, is no longer available.

It is no longer even clear whether the term *interregnum*, which remains implicit in the previously enumerated symptoms, is sufficient to lend consistency to our understanding of the current predicament. Despite Antonio Gramsci's well-known appropriation of the term in reference to the spiritual and moral crisis of European capitalism in the 1920s—"The crisis consists precisely in the fact that the old is dying and the new cannot be born; in this interregnum a great variety of morbid symptoms appear" (*Notebooks*, vol. 2, NB 3, #34, 32–33)—the word *interregnum* is in juridical terms still the secret placeholder of a claim to the rehabilitated destiny of a specific notion of epochality and its particular form of sovereign rule. It denotes both a time of sovereign suspension *and* the containment within itself of the unsuspending of suspension. *Interregnum* remains at all times *"future-oriented"* (Schürmann, *Broken Hegemonies*, 152), silently containing the promise of an epoch-opening uniqueness or of a historical negation of sorts. Now, however, it is beginning to appear that the promise of the latter—of the contained and implicit rehabilitation of the linear time of progress from within the *interregnum*—remains definitively beyond our grasp. The perishing of that time is extending its force everywhere in the form of generalized turmoil and perplexity while also inaugurating the demand for a different nomenclature indicating something so post-epochal and so post-sovereign in nature that it would have no political or philosophical name other than that of infinite *ruination*. In the 1920s Gramsci lamented Europe's inability to constitute a renewed (communist) epoch. In the 2020s the lament itself is beyond repair.

The figure of the "mortal God" and its regime of representation are falling apart at the seams, but they are doing so without embracing the roots of a new Age. Nothing here can be resolved, for "with the emergence of a new regime of mastery that knows no limit, no outside, negation no longer constitutes a true principle of creation. . . . Negation, instead of constituting a *condition sine qua non* for the emergence of some epoch-breaking novelty, remains capable of doing away with the old yet proves to be powerless in giving rise to a new creation" (Sumic, "Is There a Politics in Psychoanalysis?," 3). We can merely glimpse that while in former times "force [was] the midwife of every old society pregnant with a new one. It is itself an economic power" (Marx, *Capital*, vol. 1, 916), in the contemporary order of planetary value extraction and of the ongoing closure of historical progress we have plenty of economic power and force but are left devoid of the transitional linear time required of a new birth, commencement, or avant-garde of any kind. We are well on the way to losing the epochal promise of representation arrested and contained silently in the *inter-* of the *interregnum*. Echoing Reiner Schürmann, our epoch is simply the *terminus* of epochality.

The term *impasse*—which is always open to resolution via a sovereign or subjectivist decision—is no less problematic than *interregnum*. Having said that, it is what precisely underlies and haunts the decisionist terrain of both

the populisms and the sovereign authoritarianisms of contemporary globalization. The absolutization of the impasse is what is concealed beneath the
demand for meaning at all cost ("Make things make sense again!"), as if the
true meaning of the Age could be revealed as a result of the will to break with
the experience of a political dead end that is nevertheless constitutive of the
never-ending circulation of the market-state duopoly.

It is as a result of all the above that in the passage from the katechon to the
post-katechontic and from hegemony to posthegemony I have proposed the
term "post-sovereign *decontainment*" in order to indicate that it is no longer a
question of an old epoch that is coextensive with a linear temporal transition
toward the contours and possibility of a new destiny, of a new epoch of representation. It is simply globalization (which by now cannot even be understood
in the same terms as "late modernity" was just thirty years ago) as a perpetual
form of hollowing out and ending. It is no longer a question of Prometheus
bound or unbound. Promethean thinking is moribund, overcome by a historical and conceptual perishing that is incapable of positing anything new in its
place. This *an-epochality*—the boundless disaster of epochality itself—raises
a number of questions, one of which is that of the tendential patterns, if any,
which endure in the persistent, limitless turmoil that is the late neoliberal,
global order.

As already said, progress and development are on the wane, certainly, and
how could they not be? We are living in a state of rapid retreat from the
founding metaphors of the entire Enlightenment tradition, including those
of the liberal subject, democracy, the human, the Nation, the Republic, and
the interstate order of warfare between sovereigns. As a result, our modern
organizing principles—other than those of limitless economic "accumulation by dispossession" (Harvey)—are withering away in the face of planetary
resource extraction and different forms of proxy war waged as a means for gaining access to surplus value at all cost, while the modern (Kantian) ideal of establishing a connection between thinking and acting—the relation between
securing a rational foundation for the knowable and then conforming society's
daily actions to that foundation—has definitively run its course (Schürmann).

Beyond technology, individual self-interest, and the relentlessly unforgiving topographies of Thomas Hobbes's *war of all against all* there is nothing
to replace the *nomos* of the Cold War, which is probably why the question of
*ethics* has become so commonplace in its well-intentioned regurgitation of
liberalism. In globalization the world is coming to nothing, or, there is nothing for the world to come to other than surplus value and destruction, since
globalization itself conceals the coming to presence of *world* (Nancy, *The
Creation of the World or Globalization*). For this reason, the relation between

thinking and acting is dominated increasingly by the instrumentalization of *techne* alone, and capital is increasingly extractive in nature. Meanwhile, the subjective will to power, or nihilism, which manifests itself not only in the political staging of the oligarchs and their acolytes but in increasingly belligerent exhibitions of populist and institutional racism and gender violence, is the one thing that reigns unchallenged, confronted for the most part only with better-intentioned contrary wills but not necessarily with anything *other than* the will to power.

No doubt it will be proclaimed by many academic devotees of the resurrection of modern revolution and universal emancipation—by the museum curators of the dialectical path to absolute spirit, the academic philological bourgeoisie in search of a loving master and world picture still anchored in the Enlightenment doctrines of the subject ("Behold! Our Truth!")—that such a diagnosis suffers from all the decadent, pessimist symptoms of a leftist melancholy that, tainted ironically by Hegel's "beautiful soul" (the self-cloistered cult of the beauty of holiness), is more attuned to a state of self-hypnotized inactivity (pessimism, nihilism, or merely "deconstruction," which is used increasingly as if it were an affront in itself) than it is to concrete moral action (militancy, "real politics," or "historical materialism"). But in the infrapolitical register there is no longer any optimism to be placed in either salvation from barbarism or in a *beyond* to disenchantment, which is the underlying desire for a good part of the Left's boundless fidelity to the subjectivization of the subject, as if more of the same could provide a definitive resolution.

As already noted, the point of departure for the infrapolitical register is conceptual attunement to the full exhaustion of all historical representations of progress, which, of course, is very different from suggesting that Marx, for example, was wrong or that the infrapolitical is antithetical to the act. What the infrapolitical register in thinking proposes to circumvent are the facile theologisms of the will to power, its metaphysical attachments to historicism, hegemony, and the vacuous promises of a *beyond* to disillusionment grounded in the political will of the militant subject. For this reason, the infrapolitical register in thinking remains attuned to the *posthegemonic* shadows that persist outside the calculations of the political.

Infrapolitical posthegemony never takes center stage but plays and toils in the shadows of every political staging. It is always coextensive to politics but without ever being political per se, for, as already said, it is its distance from the political—its safeguarding of a place undetermined by the everyday calculations of means and ends—that preconditions its inventive nonconformity to the political itself. For this reason, it is only ever a democratizing critique of democracy. What is at stake for the infrapolitical register and for the unfamiliar dimension of the possible that it seeks to move toward is the dignity of the human in the age of decontainment, and this in the full realization that humanism "does not set the *humanitas* of the human being high enough" (Heidegger, "Letter on Humanism," 251). There can be no doubt that the humanism we have inherited from modernity has made a fundamental "contribution to the history of the armament of subjectivity" (Sloterdijk, *Not Saved*, 204).[68] In this sense it is nothing more than anthropocentric violence in conceptual and cultural form, since it conceals the *humanitas* of the human while ceaselessly claiming to define and ameliorate it, as it moves along the dialectical path toward the truth of absolute spirit (and all of this in the name of progress, the subject, culture, identity, the Nation, representation, gathering, location, home, the familiarization and domestication of the relation between human and world, etc.). For the infrapolitical register, however,

> thinking does not overcome metaphysics by climbing still higher, surmounting it, transcending it somehow or other; thinking overcomes metaphysics by climbing back down into the nearness of the nearest. The descent, particularly where human beings have strayed into subjectivity, is more arduous and more dangerous than the ascent. The descent leads to the poverty of the ek-sistence of *homo humanus*. In ek-sistence the region of *homo animalis*, of metaphysics, is abandoned. . . . What counts is *humanitas* in the service of the truth of being, but without humanism in the metaphysical sense. (Heidegger, "Letter on Humanism," 268)

What does this indicate? It does not signal that infrapolitics is predicated on finally uncovering the essence of being (the beingness of Being). It indicates thinking in the *arduous service of ek-sistence* (of fundamental ontology), understood as *being-toward-death* as the abyssal path away from the inauthenticity of the modern ontology of the subject, which is also the ontology of the commodity form. For this reason, in the infrapolitical register the *decision of existence* (Nancy) implies exposure to a register of thinking that remains beyond the biopolitical administration of life and the subjectivity that underpins it. It most certainly lies beyond, yet remains concealed by, the primacy of politics or the centrality of subjectivity and the preconceived notions of militant praxis that accompany it.

For the infrapolitical register, the decision is the own-making event of the uncovering of existence as fundamental ownlessness (Nancy, "The Decision of Existence," 102–4). This infrapolitical register is a *quest for an opening* to the thinking of the singular — to *Being as ownlessness* — and, as such, to the thinking of a fundamental modification in our understanding of the act and of our place in the world. This understanding would never cease to uncover the question of the relation between justice and the community of beings, certainly, but would do so in light of Being rather than in light of the biopolitical administration of life and its assignation of social roles, for the latter are only ever indicators of the history of a subjectivist nihilism that underlies the political coercions of hegemony and counterhegemony. The infrapolitical thinks in relation to the comportment of the an-*arche* that extends a relation of nonconformity to the "metaphysical and technocratic reflexes of humanolotry" (Sloterdijk, *Not Saved*, 142).

At the conclusion of a recent book detailing the causes, extension, and deleterious effects of technologically dominated financialization and debt in Brazil and Mexico from the 1970s to the present, Brian Whitener speculates on the possible remaining paths and future determinations for thinking and acting in the wake of neoliberal forms of accumulation by dispossession. The conclusion of this enlightening work reads as follows:

> In the coming years, there will be some who, despite the failure of the neostructuralist policies of the [Latin American] *marea rosada*, will argue, perhaps out of conviction, perhaps out of pragmatism, that we cannot give up on the state as a redistributive apparatus. There will be others who, perhaps taking seriously the above analysis, will link it with literatures on new developmentalism and argue for a return to manufacturing, class alliances, and the like; while others will continue with claims that there is no alternative to capitalism and will shrug their shoulders at the idea of anything other than reform. For those who find those options unappealing, the question will be how to construct — as a storm of the far right builds across the globe — a different political option, one not guided by the hope that the state and capital might solve these paradoxes for us but rather one that builds on and extends the long-standing experiments with autonomy seen in many parts of the world. . . . To pry open an exit from this labyrinth built out of the twin dynamics of surplus capital and population before a hard right turn can only be a difficult project, but it is one which calls us to participate in it, if only because there finally appear to be few other alternatives. (*Crisis Cultures*, 151)

The three hypotheses proposed in this formulation — the revisiting of the state as a redistributive apparatus, the extension of class alliances (which is essentially the revisiting of hegemony), and reform — are common-sense sociological responses to the genuine and ongoing technological disintegration of modern political space and political modernity itself. But rather than three distinct or alternative pathways for the determination of thinking and acting, they offer only equivalence to the extent that they are all conceptually and politically coextensive to the political theology of the modern katechon and to the particular ontological ground of the commodity form (*techne*). They offer a reengagement with an already exhausted form of modern containment, namely, the neo-Keynesian planetary *nomos*.

However, Whitener also proposes a fourth hypothesis for "those who find those options unappealing": "A different political option," he writes, "one not guided by the hope that the state and capital might solve these paradoxes for us but rather one that builds on and extends the long-standing experiments with autonomy" (151). But to the extent that history teaches us that the nation-state system has been captured by the total subsumption of life itself to capital on a global scale, then by definition the ontological ground of the technological abstraction of contemporary finance and manufacturing capital remains intact in the reveries of autonomy. Given the intricacies of Whitener's own analysis of financialization since the 1970s, this fourth option remains unconvincing as a way of prying open "an exit from this labyrinth built out of the twin dynamics of surplus capital and population."

As already observed in this passage through decontainment and posthegemony, there is no autonomous "outside." The true subject of *Capital*, says Martínez Marzoa (*La filosofía de El Capital*, 132), is Western *techne*, with the fetishism of the commodity as a modern form of metaphysics that obscures the fact that it can only be a certain relation to theory — rather than to the fields of political economy, political science, sociology, or, in fact, philosophy — that can grapple with the question of how "to pry open an exit from this labyrinth" (Whitener, *Crisis Cultures*, 151). Indeed, it is precisely within this context that Kostas Axelos's questions become fundamental in their censure of what we might today refer to as the common-sense principles of historicism, sociology, political science, and cultural studies:

> How aproblematical the real remains for Marx! It is a real that he does not demonstrate but that he begins from and then ends up reaching. For him, what is real, true, active, and actual is what is real, true, active, and actual in the eyes of common sense, which is what it actually becomes for everyone after Marx. . . . Does he thus fall short of the movement of philosophy's thought, or does he transcend it in another direction? . . . Posing this question becomes all the more difficult because Marx nonetheless spoke of something "beyond the sphere of actual material production," in which, however, philosophy *ought* to be realized in being abolished. The reign of technique follows upon the

realm of ideas. Technique itself is the secret of material production, the motor force of real becoming. It must first realize itself, in depth and in extent. Will it in turn be transcended? Will there be something beyond technique, beyond, to be sure, global, universal technique? . . . Marx has begun thoughtful reflection on technique. It lies upon us now to think about and to experience technique as a planetary conquering force. (*Alienation, Praxis, and Techne*, 324–32)

It is precisely as a result of the limitations and concealments imposed by sociological common sense that *fundamental ontology*—the question of a turn in thinking and acting toward the ontological difference between beings and Being as that which remains to be deciphered (a turn *Capital* points toward via the constitutive concepts of commodity and value but then camouflages in the very same gesture)—lies at the heart of the wager for the promise of moving in a direction other than that of the ongoing disintegration and perishing—via the turmoil circulated planetarily by the post-sovereign market-state duopoly—of world itself.[69]

With no interregnum or redemptive form in sight, this is not about the life and political form of a new Promethean politics or of a new ontological ground for subjects (or for "the subject" in general) but about tracing the finitude of the political in its distance from existence (*ek-sistence*), as that which always returns as ontologically prior but barred, or foreclosed, in the order of *techne*. Rather than a solution or a flag, it is nothing more than a timorous step toward the possibility of questioning in such a way as to clear away inherited limitations in the realm of thinking and acting. The infrapolitical register is the never-ending rekindling of the shadow of that which is withdrawn from representation, not in order to remetaphorize it but in order to signal the possibility of an existence that remains uncaptured by the *subjectum*, its representations, its hegemonic forms, and the ensuing struggles for recognition to which it inevitably gives itself in the name of politics, power, and, therefore, domination (hegemonic or not).

In the Passage that follows we continue to move in and across the context of a world of ceaseless war and turmoil, or post-sovereign decontainment, in the direction of the ontological difference and in the name of a-principial facticity and freedom from the confines of regulatory representation, or biopolitics.

# Passage II: Narco-Accumulation
## Of Contemporary Force and Facticity

Force, in the hands of another, exercises over the soul the same tyranny that extreme hunger does; for it possesses, and *in perpetuo*, the power of life and death. Its rule, moreover, is as cold and hard as the rule of inert matter.

> —SIMONE WEIL, *"The Iliad*, OR THE POEM OF FORCE"

If there is still war, and for a long time yet, or in any case war's cruelty, warlike, torturing, massively or subtlety cruel aggression, it is no longer certain that the figure of war, and especially the difference between individual wars, civil wars, and national wars, still corresponds to concepts whose rigor is assured.

> —JACQUES DERRIDA, *Without Alibi*

There is nothing on the horizon except for an unheard-of, inconceivable task — or war.

> —JEAN-LUC NANCY, *Being Singular Plural*

Bones here aren't a metaphor for what's past, but for what's coming.

> —OSCAR MARTÍNEZ, *The Beast: Riding the Rails and Dodging Narcos on the Migrant Trail*

## Toward Narco-Accumulation

In *Capital* Marx teaches us that accumulation — "the conquest of the world of social wealth" (739) — is generated in a system of production via the exploitation of labor and the creation of value. However, in the financialized era of debt and deprivation-driven globalization "there is no significant production of new surplus value" (Whitener, *Crisis Cultures,* 201). It is for this reason that "there can only be profit-taking and thus no actual 'accumulation,' in the technical sense, can occur" (201). In the post-katechontic order of technologically driven value extraction, what remains untouched is the ontological ground of the commodity form. Not only does it remain untouched as the specific mode of *being* of the modern and contemporary structure of society, but its decontained planetary extension also saturates species-life with its ever-shifting patterns of biopolitical subsumption and destruction, with the constant reinvention of spatial inequalities and forms of violence, and with juridical and anomic procedures of exclusion/inclusion. What shifts incessantly is the ground — the mode of being of beings captured in a socioeconomic world of "precarity" — determined by and standing in reserve for the needs of technological domination and value extraction. The ontology of technology closes off the fundamental question for the *beingness of being*, or for the intelligibility of a possible meaningfulness, which would be the only horizon of questioning that could now not just shake but potentially destroy the particular ontology of the commodity form, or the ontic mode of being of what is at hand.

From the advent of the Industrial Revolution through to some point in the early 1970s — a "certain point" at which, as seen in the previous Passage, global corporate interest definitively voided the politics of hegemony — the mode of being of the commodity form (no matter how uneven or "combined") had always been sutured to the teleological path of the progress and development of nations and their populations, to the promise, that is, of a future "conquest of the world of social wealth" on a scale never before witnessed in human history. This was the case even in the wake of Auschwitz and Hiroshima, when the 1948 Declaration of the Rights of Man had attempted to resuture the notion of the human to something other than the barbarity of technological genocide. Now, however, the ever-shifting ontological terrain of the commodity form is no longer defined by the ideology of progress but by that of a morass of debt referred to as "growth" and understood as "the relentless process of more and more, of bigger and bigger" (Arendt, *Crises of the Republic*, 179).

Ultimately, what we have been experiencing in the last half-century is a planetary shift, wreaked by the ontology and violence of the commodity form, in the mode of being of beings. The intelligibility of this shift is one of the lingering questions presented to us by the post-katechontic immanence of global techno-capital, or post-sovereign decontainment. Another by no means disconnected question is that of how to determine a path for thinking that does something *other than* reproduce the mode of being, or the particular ontological ground, of the given. How to think, in other words, on the basis of the finitude of the particular ontology of the given?

Following on from the route to posthegemony and infrapolitics traced in the previous Passage, in the pages that follow we will traverse the phenomenon of narco-accumulation — that is, the intertwined and illicit cross-border transit of drugs, arms, and human beings — in such a way as to highlight, via the intimacy of its relation to the extension of violence and to the question of historicity, the mode of being of beings in the post-katechontic order of decontainment (the ontic world of beings in globalization). The purpose in this Passage is to try to determine a path toward the indication of an area of experience *other than* that which is bequeathed to us in the form of the commodity form and the violence that anchors it to specific modes of life. What is at stake in the following, in other words, is the infrapolitical passage toward the question of intelligibility, existence, and freedom, while taking into consideration the complexities of an attunement to the call of fundamental ontology, or *Being* itself.

But first, what can be understood by *narco-accumulation*? Like all accumulation in the era of globalization, narco-accumulation is the pursuit of value extraction in a world conquered by the absolute despotism of a social wealth that is fully coextensive with the outright pauperization of the burgeoning numbers of the postindustrial reserve army. On one level, narco-accumulation is just one more name for the contemporary will to power of capitalism, in which capital projects itself, as always, in two directions simultaneously: (1) toward the absolutization of commodity and surplus value and (2) toward the minimization, within the passage toward value, of the value of labor. In narco-accumulation the body of the migrant worker, for example, enters the domain of value, which is only ever oriented toward subsistence at the best of times, through transterritorial movement, thereby indicating definitively that there is nothing at all *intrinsically* valuable in the body of the migrant/future potential worker.[1] The distinction between entering the service of labor and being discarded entirely along the lines of *bare life* (Agamben, *Homo Sacer*) is as minimal now as it was at the outset of the Industrial Revolution. The only difference is that labor no longer occupies the realm of development, now existing, in contrast, in the wake of progress and of the international struggle for emancipation rather than anterior to it.

But, more importantly for our understanding of this particular post-katechontic phenomenon, narco-accumulation is a name for the movement of the commodity form — drugs, guns, bodies — unconfined by the legal restrictions of the modern state form. It is the active post-sovereign decontainment of the constitutional form. This is the case in large part because it is the market-state duopoly itself that *depolices* its own legal restrictions on unlawful economic activity, while simultaneously performing the *militarization* of the *depolicing* in order to maintain the enactment of a law and order that is not only extremely profitable but, indeed, politically and socially necessary for value extraction because without it the entire national and global economy would collapse.[2] In conjunction with this militarized *depolicing* of the illicit economy, and with its reconversion into the rhetoric of "war," the neoliberal demise of modern political forms spectralizes the representation and authority of prior moments in the history of capital in such a way that "labor power" is reconverted increasingly back into premodern forms of subordination to the order of *caciquismo* such as worker peonage to the overlord, the payment of feudal dues, tithes of passage, indentured servitude, and slavery. In the process, both war and peace move together beyond the treaties and mediations of modern interstate sovereignty and pass over increasingly into everyday premodern forms of organized property theft, maritime and nonmaritime forms of piracy, kidnapping and ransom, and resource value extraction.

In narco-accumulation, the duration of work is no longer the expression of the magnitude of the value of the products it generates and circulates. Rather, narco-accumulation is the world no longer subject to the rational measurability of social wealth, since in the illicit movement of product from place of origin to final point of consumption there is no proportionality between the generation of commodity value and the social form for the realization of human labor. The astronomical wealth it generates is estranged entirely from labor value and is then either hoarded offshore or reinvested — laundered across the entire "legitimate" global banking economy — into the spawning of more surplus value across and beyond national boundaries. Rather than labor power it is *transit* in general, and in particular the existence of the increasingly militarized US-Mexico border complex, which provides the basis for the hemispheric commodity value of the products and raw materials that are always in movement toward the moment of consumption at the final destination.[3]

Marx (*Capital*, vol. 1, 225) tells us that for centuries the value of money, and therefore of value itself, was tied symbolically to the price of gold on the world market. As a result, paper money was an imaginary expression tied to the representation of gold as a specific quantity and value for economic measurement itself. Upon the demise of the gold standard in 1971, however, value began to shed its regulating chains. As a result, with the algorithm-inspired advent over the course of the last three decades of split-second global finance, now the imaginary value of paper money in one economic spatial configuration can cripple the imaginary value of the paper money of another economic configuration within a week or two, and millions of livelihoods can be brought to the brink of collapse within hours. Indeed, paper money as the quantifiable yet imaginary form of expression of value can be either supplemented or displaced entirely. Cocaine can become not just a commodity for sale on the market but the money form itself, a replacement for the paper money that in turn stood in for and replaced the value of gold. More recently, and as already referenced in a note in the previous Passage, possession and use of blockchain technology (the basis for the algorithm of any cryptocurrency) emerged as the source of a metamoney that is now even more groundless than its paper form, as a technologically driven abstraction (bitcoin) of the social abstraction (paper money) of a historical imperial abstraction (gold), which was based previously in imaginary form on the existence of a certifiable amount of a metal extracted and stockpiled above ground in castles, churches, forts, and palaces or in impregnable subterranean bank vaults.

Since the demise of the gold standard, the circulation and exchange of value in the post-katechontic order is now deprived of representational sense, which probably explains why the cultural representations of the industries of narco-accumulation crystallize the entire global movement of illicit drugs, arms, and people via the individualistic melodramas of, for example, one DEA officer doing battle with small bands of Colombian and/or Mexican traffickers. This is a reductive geopolitical, moral, and geoeconomic formalization that captures the phenomenon of narco-accumulation as the ongoing anthropo-logical battle between the goodness of the nomothetic will of the North versus the evils of all equally subjectivist challenges to that will from the other side of the border. In reality, however, narco-accumulation is more than merely a classic moral tale of the battle between good gringos and bad everyone else. It is the very existence and immanence of "world money," that is, of the "abso-lute social materialization of wealth as such (universal wealth)" (Marx, *Capi-tal*, vol. 1, 242). But because it is illicit, it is an absolute social materialization that hides within the sheer measurelessness of a value that dominates our bodies and lives on a daily basis and on a global scale.

While it is true that the term "narco" was created by the state (in the same way the words "criminal" and "bandit" were implanted at times when the "en-emy" could be designated territorially and announced with a degree of clarity in relation to specific individuals or subgroups existing within a specifically defined sovereign territory), now the term "narco" no longer conforms to that individual or group of individuals who are outside the law within a given re-gional or national political space. It applies to the internal daily interactions of all levels of economic, political, police, and military authority, from the local and regional to the national and transnational. It is now indistinguishable from the technical, self-globalizing, sense-making expediency of accumula-tion itself. For example, in socioeconomic and anthropological terms narco-accumulation determines not only the lives of those who participate directly or indirectly in the cultivation, transportation, delivery, and consumption of the enterprise's specific products. It is woven into and throughout the very fab-ric of global capital. In the state of Michoacán, for example, drug cultivation, manufacturing, and trafficking exist hand in hand with the agroindustrial pro-duction and transportation of avocadoes, strawberries, raspberries, and cran-berries, an industry supported directly by transnational capital and its legal markets. It is for this reason that "in the case of the avocado entrepreneurs from the Uruapan-Peribán-Tancítaro region, the presence of organized crime is part of the landscape itself" (Maldonado Aranda, "'You Don't See Any Vio-lence,'" 158). Narco-accumulation determines the working conditions of the underpaid fruit pickers of Michoacán as much as it orients the consumer choices made by the wealthy US suburbanites and hipsters who purchase their imported *narco-fruta* at the neighborhood Whole Foods or downtown food co-op. It is not only that it is part of the landscape. It *is* the landscape.

Narco-accumulation is one of the primary frames for specific insight into the contemporary twilight of the order of sovereignty and of the post-sovereign disturbances it leaves in its wake. By this I mean to suggest that the extension and intensification of the paramilitary force that accompanies and upholds narco-accumulation in its myriad forms, as an overall and increasingly visible "warlike pose or postulation" (Nancy, "War, Right, Sovereignty — *Techne*," 111), is a fundamental yet conceptually fragile dispositif for addressing the question of the limits of the political and, perhaps more importantly, for reckoning with and challenging the current limitations in our understanding of what Giacomo Marramao has called the era of the "twilight of sovereignty" and that we refer to as the tumultuous age of the post-sovereign state. As previously outlined, this is the late-neoliberal era of a fundamental shift in world orderability that stems from the fact and realization that the sun is setting rapidly, though by no means evenly or serenely, on the modern age and, in particular, on the modern age understood in political-theological, territorial, and temporal terms.

Nothing new or different, however, is emergent in the wake of this crepuscule, thereby casting doubt on the very notion of *interregnum*. The contemporary dwells increasingly within the coming forth not of conceptual clarity and certainty — of a certain understanding of a visual economy of truth — but within the yielding of all thinking and practice toward the categorial shadows of a "diffuse glare occurring before dawn and after sunset" (Marramao, *The Passage West*, 85). This diffuse glare, this succumbing, or *perishing*, of all conceptual legacies and inherited certainties is an increasingly generalized condition that radiates sovereign and non-sovereign forms of violence across spaces in which the state no longer holds a monopoly on politics (Galli, *Janus's Gaze*, 121) and in which different forms of non-state force extend unevenly and increasingly across the geographies of the local, regional, national, and global.

There can be little doubt that the twilight of sovereignty that we also refer to as "globalization" is the effect and symptom not only of a fundamental shift in the socioeconomic and political function of "neoliberalism," which David Harvey has referred to as a new era of "accumulation by dispossession" (*A Brief History of Neoliberalism*), but of seismic shifts in the very coordination of the teleological and the eschatological. Globalization — the post-katechontic "twilight of sovereignty," the perishing or withering away of the modern, and the absolutization of the ontology of the commodity form — exceeds the notion and experience of *crisis* (the idea of a mere imbalance or distortion internal to the regulative mechanisms of modern sovereign power) and begins to demand other names and other ways of thinking the relation between war, sovereignty, technology, and the limits of the political. But it demands ways of thinking that no longer point exclusively in the direction of modern sovereign force and the subjectivist will to power that reigns supreme through it and as a result of it.

In other words, from within the twilight of sovereignty we are confronting: (1) the question of the long-standing and ongoing collapse of the modern legacies of the political; (2) the question of how to think at a distance from, and in a relation of difference to, the political in an epoch in which its inherited categories are increasingly inadequate; and (3) the question of a possible turn from inherited patterns of subjectivist force that have been, and remain, internal to the shift from neoliberalism to a fully fledged duopolistic state form in which the difference between market and state, and between war and peace, is increasingly indiscernible and in which force is no longer contained in the modern relation between the nation-state, citizenship, their constitutive exclusions, and the interstate system that regulated them internationally.

Thinking in the wake of the violent shift to the market-state duopoly that we have been experiencing over the course of the last four decades — a post-sovereign duopoly that, as a result of the absolutely fetishized domination of *techne*, only ever globalizes, distributes, moves, or transits the lived force that it itself globalizes — the only thing we can affirm with any degree of clarity is that elucidating the conceptual and structural conditions of the connection between late neoliberalism and the paramilitarization of violence is extremely complex.[4] It might even be impossible to achieve with any degree of thoroughness given the forms of intracapitalist violence that remain untouched by the array of juridical conventions regarding the means of war, or the difference between war and peace, that exist and remain "on the books" as such but do so without meaningful application at the international, national, and regional levels.

To a large extent, it is the systemic ineffectiveness of regulatory mechanisms (for example, the increasing ineffectiveness in the distinction between constitutional law and political legitimacy in their relation to the limit between war and peace) that obliges that thinking move beyond the internal intricacies of *crisis* — beyond the potential tweaking of a faltering interstate *nomos* — in order to contemplate the irreducibility of a conceptual quagmire that for decades has been our common lot, and increasingly so.[5] Within this context words such as *our* and *common lot* become increasingly problematic, increasingly exposed to absolute atomization, disintegration, supernumerary overextension, and reactionary forms of populism, nationalism, and militancy.

As already indicated in the previous Passage, by now it is well known that neoliberalism emerged internationally in the 1970s and 1980s as the ideological and economic justification for the violent dismantling of a modern state form that, in its passage from the nineteenth century, had been predicated on a managed economy and the fabrication of "the People" as a territorially bound fictitious universality, or *fictive ethnicity* (Balibar, *Race, Nation, Class*). As a result of neoliberal dismantling, globalization can be understood now as the uneven passage *away from* logics of power that were built, in both "core" and many economically dependent or "peripheral" nations, on territorialized production coordinated via administrative jurisdiction, capital regulation, and the forging of social pacts between states, elites, and subordinate classes on both the national and international levels. The post-Enlightenment bourgeois order of the integral nation-state, the Fordist integration of production and the organization of mass consumption, and the extension of Keynesian economics and social welfare built on the ideal of a functional compromise between capital and labor in the wake of the "Great Depression" (or on the populist articulation of a progressive, modernizing bourgeoisie mobilizing its alliances against the interests of the traditional conservative oligarchy) — and with all of the above passing over into the post–World War II context of Cold War geopolitics, in which different forms of war and social conflict were relegated largely to the territories of the so-called Third World — have succumbed in recent decades to the increasingly post-territorial transfiguration of all forms of human life into a technologically driven standing reserve for the penetrative force and extension of unfettered capital and value extraction.

As already suggested, almost three decades after the collapse in the early 1990s of the structural spatial restraint provided by the Cold War — in which the planet was divided but also balanced among rival national units existing under a bipolar order of economic, military, and ideological enmity and nuclear deterrence dominated by the United States and the Soviet Union — the external application of neoliberal economic policies to the politics of the modern Keynesian state form has morphed into a fully deregulated and despatialized market-state duopoly, or post-sovereignty. With this shift from external critique and dismantling force to a state-geoeconomic form predicated on socialized militarism, unfettered economic privatization, legal and illegal corporatization (narco- and other forms of illicit trafficking and accumulation), austerity, deregulation, ongoing land expropriation, split-second algorithmic financialization, cyber kill chains, online "advanced persistent threat," organized state cybercrime, and resource value extraction on a global scale, it is only now becoming clear that the distinction between sovereign stability and instability, or between war and peace, has been on the wane, yielding to the shadows of our technologically determined twilight, for decades. As already mentioned in our initial Passage through decontainment and toward the infrapolitical as a necessity, all of the above opens us up to the question of intelligibility and ultimately to the question of "What is the world coming to?"

## Toward Facticity

Almost two decades ago, Alberto Moreiras (*The Exhaustion of Difference*, 90–91) addressed the shift in political form from that of the modern state to the post–Cold War era by signaling the emergence of a shift of historicity that seemed to coincide with the transition from the capitalism of modern discipline to that of postmodern control and finance. Moreiras signals the shift in the following terms: "[Gilles] Deleuze's announcement that the world is on the verge of going from a regime of rule characterized by discipline to a regime of rule characterized by control can perhaps now be supplemented with the notion that the transitional space marked by 'on the verge of' coincides with the time of gradual suffusion of the social by finance capital, in Jameson's terms" (90). Moreiras wonders at what point a line was crossed, thereby highlighting the problem of the temporal horizon — of the very moment — at which a certain shift and form of historicity rises to the surface of understanding. It is here that the question of war and perception come into play: "When exactly," asks Moreiras, "does one society stop being ruled by discipline or by monopoly capital and start being ruled by control or by finance capital?":

> This is like the Aristotelian question about the withdrawing army: suddenly one soldier turns around and flees the scene of battle, then two, then three, then a dozen. At what point can it be said that the army is withdrawing and the battle has been lost? But the question, which is an important one, hides a supplement. It is only at the time of battle that the question can be asked. Only that particular time of confrontation allows for a question about confrontation itself. We live in one such time. (90)

How, in other words, to give language to a moment of perhaps imperceptible transitional conflict between distinct political forms and shifting modalities of war, and how to address the question of historicity that underlies their relation? How can the contemporaneity of the contemporary be determined for thinking and therefore for effective living and acting?[6] At this point in his argument, Moreiras endorses Paul Bové's Gramscian formulation of the post–Cold War period as a time of *interregnum*: "Bové's interregnum refers to 'that place and time when there is as yet no rule, when there are ordering forces but they have not yet summoned their institutional rule into full view'" (90). But this is where the overall sense of intellectual and conceptual *perishing* expressed by Bové and Moreiras begins to move beyond the determinations of the Gramscian echo, beyond the containment of the *interregnum*, in such a way as to open up to the question of *facticity*.[7]

The imprecision of the "when, exactly," Moreiras says, citing Bové, generates "'a particular form of in-betweenness with important implications,'" since
it brings to light "'as yet unfulfilled demands for thinking, a process that can
only be satisfied in a movement that does not work within the tread-marks
of previous intellectual systems themselves principally attendant upon either
modern state formations (and their epiphenomena) or romantic embrasures
of local "struggles" against "global" forces'" (90–91). In this formulation, it
appears that we are on the verge of an absolutely necessary and yet still unfulfilled determination for thinking in relation to what *being* (or *being-there*)
*for a while at a particular time* means. Given our overall warlike posture,
such a form of thinking could no longer proceed exclusively from within the
inherited certainties of *logos* but only at a distance from such an inheritance.
It would inhabit the demands of an oscillating form of reasoning (if such a
thing can be delineated) that is not just somewhere between the modern and
postmodern — between two moments or styles — but, more importantly (and
this via a Janus-like thinking), a thinking within oscillation between *beings*
and the *being* of beings. What we see in Moreiras's approach to Bové is the
suggestion that we confront the question of the times, of our times, in relation
to understanding and making sense, and therefore to mortality, and therefore
to existence.

Almost two decades later we can say with a slightly greater degree of
certainty that that place and time when there were ordering forces but still
no clear institutional rule in full view has devolved into the tumultuous
(para)military domination of the market-state duopoly in full force. To the extent that now the calculation and instrumentalization of the relation between
means and ends is even more forceful than it was two decades ago, to the
extent that "there can only be profit-taking and thus no actual 'accumulation,'
in the technical sense, can occur" (Whitener, *Crisis Cultures*, 201), and to
the extent that the ordering forces are increasingly violent and increasingly
illegitimate in their pursuit of resources, economic advantage, and human
commodification; indeed, to the extent that the ideology of progress that underlies the modern structure of the interregnum is fading into a distant past;
and, finally, to the extent that the thinking advocated by Bové and Moreiras
still remains and might always remain pending, it is safe to say that we remain
ensnared within the question of, and in a fundamental quest for, sense, intelligibility, and meaningfulness that came to light in the post–Cold War period
and that is now assuming increasingly sinister proportions as the weight of
planetary force and extinction becomes more and more palpable. In other
words, the question of the interregnum gives way before the burden of the
factical thrown-ness of meaningfulness itself, beyond the commodity form.

This opens up the question of the relation delineated in the modern tradition between power, violence, force, historicity, and sociopolitical renovation. It also raises the question of the ways in which that relation has shifted, or has been fully consumed, in recent times.

In Hannah Arendt's well-known formulation ("Power and violence are opposites; where the one rules absolutely, the other is absent. Violence appears where power is in jeopardy, but left to its own course it ends in power's disappearance" [*Crises of the Republic*, 154]), power is predicated on the recognition of authority and on the legitimacy of its representations.[8] If this is the case, then Michel Foucault's biopolitics is the rationalized and fully naturalized management and reproduction of power as everyday social and mental life, while the absence of legitimacy, authority, and recognition transforms power into the instrumentalized energy of physical force alone. The latter, for this reason, is both the death of biopolitics and of Arendt's definition of power.

However, the question of temporality — or of *being-there for a while at a particular time* — complicates things considerably. It was on the basis of force that Hegel's speculative dialectic reconfigured the Hobbesian Commonwealth, which was understood as the banishment of the State of Nature, or the force of the war of all against all. The Hobbesian Commonwealth came to be predicated in Hegel on the state's dialectical neutralization of violence in the name of reason and Absolute Spirit, which then came in its Marxist transfiguration to signal the utopic path toward human emancipation in the form of labor and the consciousness of the dictatorship of the proletariat and its determined negation of the bourgeoisie. As highlighted at the beginning of the previous Passage, by understanding force as the midwife of every new society Marxian historicity came to be predicated on the development of a dialectical consciousness grounded in antagonism that was supposedly capable of neutralizing violence and of reconverting it into a society-state designed to guarantee the dictatorship of the proletariat. "Communism" was the ultimate horizon for social reconciliation via the synthesis between proletariat and social power, which, it was thought, would lead to the withering away of the state and, presumably, to the negation of the dialectical politics of recognition between master and slave.[9]

However, what we see in contemporary patterns of force — that is, of planetary post-sovereign decontainment — is the active perishing of the terrain of dialectical consciousness, of the hegemonic apparatus, and of a teleology of progress capable of neutralizing violence and of converting it into a social reason, or power, other than that of the nihilist immanence and forceful extension of global techno-capital. In the twilight of legitimacy, representation, and recognition we are left suspended in the absence of a specifically Hegelian historical consciousness, of a sociopolitical innovation of any kind, and therefore of a functional *interregnum*, for the threshold between Hobbes's commonwealth, the metaphor of the state of nature understood as the constitutive outside that sustains it, and the Hegelian dialectical absorption of violence have withered away into the planetary extension of the post-sovereign market-state duopoly, or nihilism. All of which indicates that Moreiras's concerns regarding facticity and epochality are still germane today, to the extent that they invite us to reflect in a register *other than* that of the modernist faith in the revamping of both biopolitics and the Hegelian dialectic in the name of salvation.

The question, however, is how to move in that direction or, rather, how to backtrack from that faith and its constitutive subjectivism. Certainly, globalization's weakening of clear legal and territorial demarcations is the underlying basis for Carlo Galli's reading of contemporary global capital as endemic and endless *global war*, which he defined in the wake of 9/11 as a "war without spatiality in the modern sense of the term" (*Political Spaces and Global War*, 182), "without frontiers, without advances or retreats," as just "acts that concentrate . . . the logics of war, economics and technology" (162), and that therefore "cannot be seen on a map" (166). However, Galli was not the first in his diagnosis of the relation between the decontainment of modern nomic force, the collapse of the modern state form, and the paramilitarization of violence. A decade before the terrorist attacks on New York and Washington, DC, in 2001, Jean-Luc Nancy had already identified some of the fundamental questions pertaining to the emergence of global war in reference to the first "Gulf War" against the regime of Saddam Hussein, which was waged from August 1990 to February 1991 (that is, between the fall of the Berlin Wall in November 1989, the United States' flagrant violation of international law and national sovereignty in the "Operation Just Cause" invasion of Panama from December 1989 to January 1990, and the definitive demise of the Soviet Union at the end of 1991).[10] Similarly, in *Specters of Marx* Jacques Derrida referred to the end of the Cold War as the inauguration of a novel form of war (62), which he characterized as the definitive demise of an "outdated opposition between civil war and international war" (98). Similarly, in *The Gift of Death* Derrida would speculate in the manner of Carl Schmitt regarding the longue durée of the modern crisis of sovereignty, indicating that the novel form of war emergent in the 1990s had in fact been a long time in the making: "After the Second World War . . . one loses the image or face of the enemy, one loses the war and perhaps, from then on, the very possibility of the political" (19).

This loss is the ongoing post-katechontic *perishing* that is post-sovereign decontainment, which uncovers a secret correspondence with the closure of metaphysics and with the fact that the closure of metaphysics can no longer be contained, set aside, or definitively cast into oblivion by the dialectical, and therefore metaphysical, fables of subjectivity, nationhood, or political hegemony. This loss is the definitive consummation of onto-theology that haunts and traverses everything in the epoch of the end of epochality.

It should be clear at all times, however, that violence in its contemporary military and paramilitary forms is not the sole purview of the post–Cold War neoliberal world and the emergent market-state duopoly, for, to an extent, there is nothing new here. Paramilitary or extralegal force is, and has only ever been, the social manifestation of a structural heterogenesis in the modern sovereign relation between *nomos* and anomie, which underlies and conditions all relations between means, ends, and the conditions of the political. Therein lies a fundamental gray zone in the relation between *nomos* and anomie, which uncovers the thorny and unresolvable relation between power, violence, and force.

While *nomos* is designed to orient force toward the exercise of power — that is, toward the daily operations of a fully harnessed and economized violence, specific political reason, or biopolitics (even when nomic power can also indulge in utter annihilation as a means unto itself) — anomie is the domain of a power that is more likely to be oriented toward, or entirely overrun by, acts of extralegal brutality as a means unto themselves. As such, this is a power that, in its very exercise, uses itself up in terms of its political legitimacy and is transformed into the excess of a force without reserve, even though anomie is also central to the instantiation of every *nomos*. Power and violence, as two distinct yet intimately related manifestations of force, crisscross the relation between *nomos* and anomie in an incommensurable crossing between the telluric (the lowest of the low) and the quasi-transcendental (the mortal God) that structures the relation between irregular and regular military force as well as between sovereign means and ends. It is for this reason that in the relation between power and force, sovereignty is both the highest value and an active drain on the sovereign itself: There is no sovereignty without this outflow and certainly no outflow without sovereignty.

Sovereignty, in other words, can never be sufficiently so. In the case of the contemporary turmoil of the post-sovereign state, this *never enough* is territorially decontained and experienced increasingly without reserve as a nihilism of force that signals therein a fundamental shift in the cross-border and internal patterns of endemic warlike domination over the lowest of the low. For this reason, the *wretched of the earth* both are and are not what they used to be, for in the epoch of the generalized proletarianization of humanity the distances between the highest height of power and the lowliness of the rest (the planetary conditions of mastery and of subordination, in other words) have become utterly immeasurable, never witnessed before in the history of humanity in either scope or scale. Meanwhile, biopolitics strives to conceal that experiential abyss by fortifying the coextensiveness between the production of bourgeois forms of life, bodies, political economy, and naked force. But the fact that biopolitics can never truly saturate existence, in the same way capitalism can never absorb absolutely all meaning into the commodity form, still leaves a door ever so slightly ajar for the stakes of infrapolitical thinking.

In the meantime, it is clear to us that different forms of paramilitary force — different parallel or irregular military state forms, partisan or (counter)hegemonic rogue-state entities — have *always* contributed to the development of modern regimes of production and accumulation, internal imperial and national forms of economic progress, ideological hegemony and counterhegemony, law enforcement, revolution, resistance, and, indeed, processes of stabilization and destabilization. From popular uprisings to private or regional armies of multiple forms, from insurgencies and counterinsurgencies of all kinds to the myriad forms of local and regional telluric defense, it is clear that throughout the histories of the modern it is impossible to disentangle paramilitary violence — armed irregular force and its techniques — from both the exercise of legitimate power and the zone of indistinction between law and the anomic exception, which is the social function of sovereign power without law. In this sense, paramilitary mobilization in its myriad forms has always attested to the fragility and mutability of the law in relation to the history of sovereignty and the sovereign exception, to the history of the forceful expediency and impetus, or the means and ends, of modern commodity fetishism (which has always thrived on the anomie of sovereign exceptionality and extralegality, of course), as well as to the history of popular or subaltern resistance to those means and ends.

There appears to be no state or popular sovereignty without the economized force of an irregular parallel state form working both internally and externally, intrinsically and extrinsically. Again, there can be no sovereignty without a degrounding of its very own foundation. Paramilitary force is an anomic *beyond* of sovereign power that signals sovereignty's limit or finitude and, as such, remains *proper* to classical sovereign mastery to the extent that it occupies the threshold between the *beyond* and the *proper* — between anomie and *nomos* — rendering them indistinguishable but also conditioning and mediating the domain of sovereign decisionism.

Having said that, in the era of the post-katechontic decontainment of force the sovereign function of anomie is shifting beyond all recognition, for the absence of foundation globalizes and makes itself make sense via the infinite subjectification of mastery and inferiority, serving itself and using itself up via the market-state duopoly's desperate and never-ending quest for transnational economization, which is not to suggest that such a quest is, or can be, infinite. We all know this but are apparently incapable of deciding on it *other than* via more subjectification, more technicity, and therefore an ever-greater objectification of the human. Neither is this, however, the end of the world just yet, merely the ongoing and impending consummation and completion of the relation between the technicity of political economy and human existence, of a particular relation of *logos* to *world*, which globalization, as the technification of *world*, strives to cover over and cast into oblivion at all times. That's all.[11]

Historically speaking, there can be no doubt that the zone of indistinction between law and anomie that paramilitary force inhabits works differently in different contexts and at different times. It is never the same thing twice, either spatially or temporally. For instance, it is clear that the phenomenon of Colombian self-defense paramilitary groups from the 1980s to the present has little in common with the narco-paramilitary groups, self-defense organizations, and paramilitary police forces that have come to the fore in Mexico over the last two decades. Sociological discussion of such differences is ultimately of little importance for understanding the question of paramilitary force itself, which is only ever a register of sovereign fragility and force simultaneously — or at least of sovereignty as a relation to anomie — in any historical, geographical, or cultural context. As a result, and despite their obvious differences, what Colombian and Mexican paramilitary forces do share is the fact that they both shed light on the different ways that late neoliberalism, for example, administrates or turns a blind eye to the effects of the forms of violence and accumulation that it has unleashed, continues to release, and strives to veil on a local, regional, national, and transnational scale.

The Colombian "peace process" between the state, the FARC (the Revolutionary Armed Forces of Colombia), and the ELN (the National Liberation Army) is clearly an attempt — via a Hegelian-Weberian desire for the dialectical neutralization of unfettered paramilitary violence — to pacify conflict and orient national territory and institutional power back toward a modern sovereign principle of integrity and immunity. It is therefore an official attempt to orient history and the political back to the state's monopoly over the legitimate use of force — to make force once again the property of the modern state — after half a century of open enmities of varying kinds, including the ideological and the economic. In this sense, the underlying logic of the Colombian peace process is that of the teleological apparatus of modern development and the philosophy of history that anchored it to the Hegelian politics of recognition, even though that apparatus and philosophy are largely being destroyed, forced into a state of continual *perishing*, by the violent de-containment of political space on a global scale.

The wager of the negotiating camps in the "Colombian Peace Process" was that violence may once again be seen to make order possible and that it no longer has to be incommensurate to the legislative calculations and econ-omized power of the nation-state. In this sense, it marked a modern wager for legitimacy against a crisis of the state that has come about to a large extent as a result of the collapse of the principles of political modernity.

It should also be pointed out, however, that this Hegelian-Weberian prin-ciple of sovereign immunization was sent into disarray, left unhinged mo-mentarily, by the democratic process itself, when, on October 2, 2016, the peace process was rejected at the urns, forcing the interests of the right-wing paramilitaries and their political allies back onto center stage. The slightly modified peace accords were finally ratified on November 24, 2016, with oppo-sition from right-wing military sectors. Obviously, it is too early to tell whether the Hegelian neutralization and reorientation of violence toward sovereign reason will bring long-term peace and stability or, for that matter, justice to Colombia. The duopolistic logic of global decontainment indicates, however, that the underlying political reason of the peace process, which appears to be haunted by the specter of the liberal teleology of progress, cannot and will not come into presence in Colombia. Historically speaking, why should it?

In the meantime, Mexico is as far from the principles of collective immu-nity, the dialectical neutralization of violence, or the teleology of progress as it has been since the upheaval of the Mexican Revolution at the begin-ning of the twentieth century. Intimately intertwined with gendered forms of social violence such as that of the notorious Juárez feminicides, the ever-changing rhythms of fully paramilitarized narco-violence have extended and intensified *in the wake of* the decomposition of the Ejido (as a not-so-functional economic and demographic category of rural social organization), the demise of the peasantry as a political force and as a pillar of modern state hegemony, the decomposition of the historical mission of the Institutional Revolutionary Party as a party, the financial collapse of 1982 (caused by the demise of the economic model of import-substitution industrialization and the emergence of new forms of finance-led accumulation), the ratification of the North American Free Trade Agreement (TLC) in 1994, and the struc-tural geoeconomic shifts of the last three decades alongside the generalized state of socioeconomic instability and impunity that has reigned ever since in Mexico.

One way of calculating and territorializing the relation between means and ends (for example, that of the postrevolutionary relation between the state, capital, labor, and culture) has been overrun by the emergence of other (post-sovereign) ways of calculating and acting upon the relation between means and ends, in the twilight and, very often, in the complete absence of those prior forms. In other words, while the decade-long turmoil of the Mexican Revolution inaugurated the closure of the so-called *pax porfiriana* and its reorientation toward the modern PRI state form, contemporary paramilitary and sovereign narco-violence is registering the perishing of the so-called *pax PRIista*, which — uncoincidentally — is now overlapping with and is in the process of being folded fully into the US-led wars on narcotics, "terror," and immigration (all of which fold into one another in rhetorical terms as the contemporary *public enemy*).

While Colombia appears to seek to immunize itself against the ravages of permanent conflict, Mexico is overrun by an endemic principle of ruin. This is a principle of paramilitarized ruin lying at the heart of the social that renders any Hegelian process of dialectical reabsorption mediated by the nation-state unimaginable now and in the immediate future, not least because everyone has known for decades that the state itself has always been a major player in the extension and institutionalization of this ruin.[12]

One thing that is clear is that Mexico's principle of paramilitarized ruin remains constitutive of both the economic and the political realms, to the extent that its decontained, unabsorbable violence — a force that undermines almost entirely the legacy of modern Mexican *civitas*, understood as the strength and unity of common intentions and purpose — keeps the principle of late-neoliberal commodity fetishism, circulation, and accumulation not just alive and kicking but vibrant. This violence — the consummation of the definitive demise of the dialectical politics of recognition between state and People — is a fundamental source of vast illicit and legal economic wealth both within national boundaries and beyond. In short, it is good for business. It is the ontology of the commodity form in full force.

In the pages that follow I will limit myself to addressing not the question of paramilitary force in the modern period but the paramilitary force of contemporary narco-accumulation as a problem concerning the increasingly blurred lines of distinction between war and peace, civilian and military, or between army, police, militia, and civilian. As already observed, this phenomenon of conceptual and institutional destructuration — this twilight of sovereignty — is both internal and essential to the current regime of extractive accumulation, highlighting the centrality of a destructive, or suicidal, violence that is predicated on the duopolistic indistinction between market and state. This an-archic destructuration lies at the heart of the excessiveness of the new violence but also at the heart of both legal and illicit capital itself. As such, a certain sense and experience of ruin is fundamental for the perpetuation of the post-sovereign economics of endemic warfare in contemporary Mexico.

Herein lies not complete chaos but certainly an experience of the abyss, extending itself across contemporary sovereignty, which demands further elucidation. It is this experience of ruin and of the perpetuation of endemic war that accompanies it that obliges us to confront the limitations in our very understanding of the era of the "twilight of sovereignty" in reference to Mexico (but not just Mexico, of course) and, in particular, to reckon with the question of whether our understanding of the limits of the political and of a possible turn therein can only ever be immanent to the brutal perpetuation of techno-economic force, or whether there is available to us an infrapolitical distancing from endemic techno-economic warfare.

In *Janus's Gaze: Essays on Carl Schmitt*, Carlo Galli asks: "Can global war become a constituent conflict? Can the confusion of peace and war, or juridical order and violence, become the origin of a new political form? In philosophical terms: is an image of the World still possible?" (130). While saying this, Galli is also aware that "global war will not turn back into modern war" (133). This question is far from insignificant. Returning to the concerns he had previously registered at the end of *Global War* ("We must find a new 'guiding image' that can reveal to us the concrete possibilities of the new political space we . . . already occupy" [189]), Galli asks whether there might be a new political form available to us through thinking the political still in a relation of immanence to contemporary techno-economic force, or nihilism, on a global scale. What concrete political language, superidealized form of unified representation, worldview, or world picture, Galli asks, could we possibly give to this fundamental shift in the relation between sovereignty, war, and the techno-economic, when sovereignty no longer performs in the name of restraint, that is, in the name of a structuring principle or specific sovereign form capable of functioning as a restraining or dialectical force against the abyss of excessive social violence?[13]

Ultimately, Galli's neo-Schmittian question is whether global war can become a founding violence, dialecticized into a specific veiled or harnessed power, political reason, or system of representation, that is, into a language and form of conceptual containment capable not of reproducing prior forms and limitations but of originating and ordering a new *nomos* of the earth, a new epoch, a new moral law, a new hegemony, and, presumably, a new gathering of the subject that is somehow *different from* the modern metaphysical inheritance that has been surviving solely on the regurgitation of its own collapsing forms for decades, if not for more than a century. Is it possible, Galli asks, to *begin again all over again*, to *refound a founding* violence from within the twilight and consummation of our modern inheritance? Again, here we face the question of the interregnum.

There is a clear quandary lying at the heart of such a desire for a founding violence, however, and that difficulty is not only the explosion in the exacerbated subjectivisms that drive global war but the perpetuation of the nihilist order of the ontology of the subject itself. In the face of so much reactionary, paranoid, nostalgia-driven babble in recent times, in the face of an already cadaveric yet newly branded "again" of an American-dominated interstate *nomos*, or regenerated political theology—a "new" yet already moribund metaphysics of identitarian containment ("Make America Great Again"), the violent rhetoric of which is grounded in the Anglo-nativism of a national container wall constructed in the name of imperial greatness financed (though not really) by the arbitrarily defined racial and/or economic enemies of the one true nation ("America First"), and this extended in conjunction with anti-Black police violence, arbitrary and equally paranoid roundups, "extreme vetting" of Muslim immigrants and nonimmigrants, and deportations of undocumented Central American workers on a massive scale—in the face of all these contemporary onto-theological exorcisms, immunizations, so-called renewals, and already obsolescent *recommencements*, I express caution regarding the possibility of "the new" itself, which strives to safeguard the thinking of our times as an *interregnum* in the history of representation and therefore as a temporary hiatus between concrete past and future sovereign nomic forms as well as between past and future forms of political legitimacy.[14]

I step back from Galli's formulation neither to suggest that it is in any way reactionary nor to imply that *becoming* and *creation* are no longer at stake (for they are absolutely at stake). Rather, I do so in order to open up a slightly different question in relation not to a new *nomos*, origin, founding violence, or will to power rising up from within the nihilistic world of techno-economic force, carrying along within itself, as the dialectical conditions of its own inevitable future betrayal, all its own inherited adversarial counternarratives, ideological and practical barricades, reactionary responses, and warlike postulations. After all, given the essentially modern demand for the new and the teleological conceptualization of temporality that underlies it, this "new" political form could most likely only regale itself—as yet another conjuring act in the wake of that already outlined in Marx's *Eighteenth Brumaire of Louis Bonaparte*—with the borrowed language, names, battle cries, and costumes of prior historical forms that, now in the twilight of sovereignty (and over a century and a half later), have already been brought to their point of complete accomplishment, exhaustion, and post-sovereign ruin.

In the interest of a certain apostasy, then, I suggest a retreat from Galli's neo-Hegelian and neo-Schmittian nomic formulation regarding the possibility of a new "world picture," in such a way as to question whether there is available to us an infrapolitical turn or detour *away* from the unquestioned, silenced, and fully concealed camaraderie and kinship that underlies and determines the teleological relation between endemic techno-economic warfare and the political world of narco-accumulation. In other words, can there be a fully responsible detour, at all times cognizant of Jean Luc Nancy's "unheard-of, inconceivable task," *away* from, rather than toward, the will to power and any *new origin* of the political?

To the extent that "we are seeing the end of the concrete and spatially determined concept of the enemy, brought about not (or at least not only) by technology, nor by a worldwide revolution, but because of globalization" (Galli, *Global War*), it is clear that the phenomenon of paramilitary force holds, if not *the* key, then at least *a* key for understanding not only the relation of facticity between contemporary technics, death, space, and the political but, indeed, for addressing the very possibility of *a register for thinking other than that of a dialectical or legislative political consciousness*. In our post-katechontic epoch, prior patterns of specifically national hegemony collapse, while the subjectivist force of sovereign decisionism becomes privatized, generalized, socialized, corporatized, franchised, and "para-narco-ized" often via hypervertical, *cacique*-style forms of social organization in which the tradition of local or regional kinship relations is transplanted into illicit transnational economic groupings and in which freedom and consent are dictated by the reason of the strongest, experienced on the ground in cruelly simple terms as the freedom to choose between "money or lead."[15]

With this in mind, circumnavigating the not-so-secret filiation between force as the midwife of history, the nihilism of the given, and the practical seductions of a new origin of the political is, it seems to me, a most pressing yet elusive commitment at this time. What remains still unfulfilled is the development of the question of *facticity* in the relation between contemporary force, historicity, and the mode of being of beings and of thinking, which, as already referenced, was first raised almost two decades ago by Moreiras's reading of the exhaustion of difference. Therein lies a discussion that still remains to be extended on the meaningfulness of extreme violence — or of global war in just one of its "regional" manifestations — in the era of post-sovereign decontainment, of the postkatechon that determines contemporary dwelling and estrangement.

## Facticity, or the Question of the Right Name for War

It is at this point that we confront the question of how to determine a path for thinking from within the register of decontainment, as opposed to against it or in spite of it. In the following pages I address what I consider to be the most rigorous sociological scholarship carried out thus far on the contemporary order of narco-accumulation as a particular form of post-katechontic conflict, though neither of the two books I foreground below uses those terms specifically.

I am referring in particular to Dawn Paley's *Drug War Capitalism* (2014) and Guadalupe Correa-Cabrera's *Los Zetas Inc.: Criminal Corporations, Energy, and Civil War in Mexico* (2017). The intention in my approach to these two works is to highlight the question of facticity, that is, the problem they raise regarding the meaning of the mode of violence and, consequently, the meaningfulness of the existence of beings immersed in and subsumed by the extension of global capital in its supposedly illicit forms. This will then allow us to address the conceptual implications of post-katechontic violence in the epoch of the end of epochality.

Dawn Paley's *Drug War Capitalism* is without doubt a committed and extensively researched book. It is also an essential point of departure for highlighting some of the limitations inherent in interpreting contemporary force from within an essentially modern political and cultural matrix. In this work the violence of narco-accumulation is portrayed correctly as an amalgamation of intracapitalist conflicts unleashed from within the context of the generalized collapse of postrevolutionary sovereignty in Mexico. These intracapitalist conflicts owe their existence to the devastating social effects of decades of domestic austerity policies, militarized territorial and commercial control, and foreign financial investment guaranteed and protected by a counterinsurgency-styled social conflict. Since the financial crisis of 1982 and the passage toward the definitive institutionalization of the North American Free Trade Agreement in 1994, all of this has been achieved within a context of formal neoliberal democracy that, in its *legal* framework, supports the cross-border movement of products and goods but, due to US-Mexico transnational military integration and the construction of an increasingly apartheid-like border architecture since 1994, limits the cross-border movement of people.

In its *illegal* framework, however, this very same democracy strives to guarantee the cross-border flow of illicit consumer goods *and* people, in the process ensuring and intensifying the exploitation of migrant proletarians hailing originally from within Mexico, increasingly from Central America, and now even from parts of eastern and sub-Saharan Africa, India, Afghanistan, etc.

"Security" is the watchword for the legitimization of an official language of economic growth and stability, foreign investment, business, and energy development. This same word is also used to lend legitimacy to a (false) relation of equivalence between security and the prosperity of all, in which if we are all "secure" we are all "prosperous." The fallacy is clear for all to see.

Meanwhile, paramilitary security is accompanied by an economy built on the patterns and forms of transnational corporatism, financialization, transportation, and market accessibility. This potent combination is upheld in the *illegal* sector by the collateral violence of hired assassination, taped beheadings, targeted kidnapping, incineration of innocents, hangings in strategic public places, "narco *mantas*," mass disappearances, extortion, trafficking, rape, the imposition of exorbitant property rent payments, and arbitrary territorial taxations. This is also accompanied by rampant resource extraction coordinated in conjunction with the systemic theft of natural resources (oil, gas, coal, iron, etc.) and by a fully socialized violence that uncovers the neoliberal market-state duopoly as a narco-confederation of state and parastate authoritarianisms in which police, army, and narco groups are often rendered indistinguishable as both market co-competitors and *rogue* partners. These are essentially the symptomatic conditions for what Rosanna Reguillo ("De las violencias") has called Mexico's contemporary state of "paralegality," Rita Segato (*La escritura en el cuerpo*) has referred to as the "second state," and Sergio González Rodríguez (*Campo de Guerra*) has called contemporary Mexico's *an-Estado* (or *a-legal State*).

All these formulations are attempts to define the lived institutional and social effect of the post-katechontic condition that precedes and underlies them, that is, the emergence and extension of the post-sovereign market-state duopoly in which *nomos* and anomie, or law and lawlessness, are increasingly indistinguishable and in which this lack of distinction is extremely lucrative for some — indeed, for many — but produces the abandonment, death, brutalization, and immiseration of countless others.[16]

Understandably, Paley is unsure of *how to name* the war that has been unleashed by the advent of the Mexican *market-state duopoly*, or post-sovereign (that is, post-katechontic) state.[17] Paley's ambivalence regarding how to name the war highlights one of her book's most significant dilemmas and also one of its most valuable contributions.

Toward the beginning of the fourth chapter the author observes the following: "The drug war in Mexico can hardly be called a civil war, due to the extent of international involvement in the conflict. . . . The scale of the killing has pushed the conflict far beyond the frame of being a dirty war. In some senses, it is a war with no proper name" (88). Rather than clarifying, Paley's formulation tends to misconceive the stakes, but that misconception is in itself of considerable significance. The author's formulation upholds an outdated yet still commonly held (Platonic) division between civil war (*stasis*) and war between external sovereigns ( *polemos*) via an oversimplified "inside versus outside" spatialization of the relation between modern or contemporary war and the political. As a result, Paley's initial formulation conceals more about the fog of contemporary war than it reveals, for here the presence of external or foreign involvement invalidates the import of internal, internecine, kindred, or interclan conflict (*stasis*). In this Platonic definition of drug war capitalism, Paley oversimplifies contemporary endemic conflict by sustaining an outmoded dichotomy between inside and outside.[18]

By the end of *Drug War Capitalism*, however, Paley has decided that it is in fact necessary to assign the violence of contemporary paramilitary force with a specific name and political value by connecting it definitively to the history and development of the postrevolutionary Mexican nation-state. In her interpretation, however, the violence of narco-accumulation merely becomes the history of modern sovereignty in inverted form:

> In reading information from the U.S. government and the status quo media, one finds a careful reiteration that the war in Mexico is non-political. . . . The war in Mexico is political; it is a counter-revolution, a hundred years late. It is decimating communities and destroying some of the few gains from the Mexican Revolution that remained after NAFTA was signed in 1994. Conceiving cartels as paramilitaries politicizes their actions and creates space through which to have a more informed discussion of the ramifications of drug war violence in Mexico and elsewhere. (188)

Here Paley strives to suture endemic warfare to the sovereign history of "actual politics" in Mexico by assigning it the value of a belated internal counterrevolution. In this assignation the conflict remains a war that understands space — the integral space of sovereign power — in the modern, late-nineteenth-century sense of the term (that is, as "spatial"). Within this essentially Hobbesian, or in fact Porfirian, formulation one can hear the echo of a Hegelian legislative consciousness desirous of neutralizing violence — of dialecticizing and reconverting violence into political reason — in order to forge once again an integral Commonwealth or national state form capable of guaranteeing the return of the metaphysical instantiation of the "People" and of doing so in the name of a new *counter-counterrevolution*, perhaps a new collective subject mobilized against the war of all against all translated back into the heart of the *polis* by the will to power of a new-found militant or revolutionary subjectivity. But this desire is extraneous to contemporary reality.

For this reason, a number of questions immediately come to light. First, as in Paley's initial formulation, this one also differentiates excessively the frontier between internal, or kindred, conflict (*stasis*) and external, or foreign, interstate war ( *polemos*). Once again, the spatial clarity remains unconvincing. Second, the question arises as to whether the violence of narco-accumulation configures space in the modern sense of the term at all, that is, as "spatiality" mediated by the modern national-popular integral nation-state. The answer here is obviously negative, and, in fact, Paley's scholarly work in *Drug War Capitalism* examines the symptoms of this process of dissolution in considerable detail. Third, the question arises as to whether this violence can really be considered a counterrevolution a hundred years late. There would be much to discuss here regarding the historical and conceptual precision of such a formulation given the history of the sovereign exception, the almost continuous political, racial, and sociocultural counterrevolution that characterized so much of the twentieth century in postrevolutionary Mexico, and all of this in conjunction with the levels of foreign economic involvement in modern Mexican society at least since the Porfiriato.[19] One would also have to distinguish between the characteristics of a preconceived conspiratorial counterrevolution a century in the making and a systemic uprising of legal and illicit paramilitary force that remains internal to the geoeconomic shifts of global war in its Mexican vein, since the two, while not unrelated, would generate very different forms of force. The first remains framed within the concentrated spatialization and integral history of the postrevolutionary national-popular, "the People" and "*lo mexicano*." It is therefore katechontic in nature. The second recognizes and gives priority to the delocalized spatiality of global war and requires a rethinking of the limits of the political that Paley falls short of advancing. Indeed, it would probably require a rethinking of the signifier "Mexico" as nation form itself.

In light of these pending questions, perhaps it could be suggested that what is most significant in Paley's formulations is the way that she rejects outright the idea that the war could possibly be "nonpolitical," doing so in order to anchor her analysis to the restraining order of a specifically modern dialectical understanding of political space that is mediated exclusively by the history of nation-state formation, though without accepting the nomenclature of civil war, or *stasis*. Here it is noteworthy that Paley's affirmation lies in contrast to Etienne Balibar's approach to the contemporary topographies of cruelty:

Violence can be "unpolitical" . . . but still form a system or be considered "systematic" if the various forms reinforce each other, if they contribute to creating conditions for their succession and encroachment, if in the end they build a chain of "human(itarian) catastrophes" where actions to prevent the spread of cruelty, extermination etc., or simply limit their effects, are systematically obstructed. ("Outlines of a Topography of Cruelty," 26)

Here Balibar refers to the "unpolitical" nature of contemporary force in terms slightly different from those delineated by Paley, who assures us that "the war in Mexico is political; it is a counter-revolution, a hundred years late" (188). For Balibar, contemporary cruelty is not a counterrevolution but a "preventive counter-revolution" or a "preventive counter-insurrection" (26), a concerted effort to keep revolution and popular mobilization at bay. But this might also benefit from further nuance. The zone of indistinction — the hyphen, or internal split — that underlies, extends, and perpetuates the internal interactions and the constant circulation of the post-sovereign market-state duopoly, in all its myriad forms, ceaselessly produces two simultaneous forces: the circulation of bellicosity and pacification, aggression and neutralization, in a form of total, socialized war that no longer allows for any kind of dialectic between the two. The unceasing simultaneity of previously distinct dialectical forms of force underpins what was first outlined by Gilles Deleuze in the early 1990s as the "society of control." Balibar's formulation of contemporary cruelty as a "preventive counter-revolution" is still essentially modern to the extent that it still places Revolution — the taking over of the modern state form in the name of the emancipation of the proletariat — as the ultimate buttress and object of the political and, indeed, of the contemporary. But it is no longer clear whether Revolution can still be located as the secret kernel of the political, as the subsumed counter-object of the market-state duopoly, or as a potential externality to the means of state power dedicated to its occlusion. The promise of the return of the repressed of proletarian revolution might now be little more than a modern humanist article of faith reserved for devout Hegelians and heartfelt neocommunist affiliations. Contemporary force is a question of the consumption of *security* and, more precisely, a question of the ceaselessly, persistently, unhaltingly generated creation, expansion, and circulation of the feeling of permanent *insecurity*, of turmoil, from within the immanent sense-making of the market-state duopoly, and this for the benefit of the contours and representational forms of biopolitical extraction. Within the contemporary configuration, to consume anything at all is to have already capitulated. The expiration date on revolution, akin to that of the historical avant-gardes, passed some time ago. However, this is a reality that should not be equated with just giving up on freedom.

In the relation between a war "with no proper name," a war characterized as a "counter-revolution, a hundred years late," and cruelty as a "preventive counter-revolution," the shifting sands of contemporary force remain untouched in both conceptual and practical terms. The journalist Ioan Grillo recognizes a similar dilemma of naming in the relation between Mexico's mass graves and the apparent normality of everyday life: "How can we understand this paradox and classify this bloodshed? Is it simply a horrendous crime problem, or is it an actual war? . . . The truth is that the conflict is neither just crime nor civil war, but a new hybrid type of organized violence" ("The Paradox of Mexico's Mass Graves"). Grillo, however, cannot move beyond this initial identification of the question at hand. My contention is that this question, which is a question regarding understanding, cannot be assigned a relation to the truth via merely journalistic, historiographical, juridical, or sociological terms. It can only be grasped truly—in all its *excessive*, unmediated subjectivism and brutal metaphysics—in conceptual (some might even dare to say "theoretical") terms. In this sense, it far surpasses the confines of Mexican national borders and cultural production. It surpasses the very idea of national culture itself.[20]

The significance of Guadalupe Correa-Cabrera's *Los Zetas Inc.: Criminal Corporations, Energy, and Civil War in Mexico* (2017) lies in the fact that she carries the discussion of the extreme violence of illicit globalization toward the terrain of the business model of the market-state duopoly, in particular pursuit of a "new theoretical framework to understand organized crime and violence in Mexico" (1). Concentrating on the Zetas as a transnational criminal organization structured along the lines of a paramilitary-corporate franchise business model—a kind of shadow market-state duopoly—Correa-Cabrera documents with precision the innovative structures and activities that the Zetas have incorporated into their overall warlike posture and the ways this posture, or counterinsurgency-styled "killing industry" (37), has benefited the extractive industries, the transnational financial sector, and private security contractors in particular (12, 258).[21] Given their organizational sophistication and entrepreneurial experience, the author observes, "it is difficult to imagine that organizations of this type have been solely led by men with no business preparation like Miguel Ángel Treviño or Heriberto Lazcano" (75). For Correa-Cabrera the Zetas have essentially created a parallel illicit state form that has enabled them to "take away the state's sole grasp on the means of violence" (95). But, she indicates, it is economic agendas—rather than political ideologies — that drive the conflict in what she calls Mexico's "new civil war" (126), "fourth-generation war" (126), "sui generis civil war" (127), and "modern civil war" (136). In contrast to Paley, then, Correa-Cabrera questions the notion that the war in Mexico is a political war, since she recognizes that the extreme force of narco-accumulation makes a travesty of politics.[22]

Like Paley, Correa-Cabrera raises the question of the specific disclosure and form of meaningfulness that contemporary force assumes in its relation to the ontological ground of the commodity form and to the beings that are forced to survive in and through it. I would suggest, however, that the author still falls short of grappling with the essence of the problem presented in that force. Referring to the violence of narco-accumulation as a modern civil war is closer to the truth than Paley's formulation of it as a "counter-revolution, a hundred years late" (188). But to the extent that the author scarcely touches upon the clarification of the question of civil war itself, *Los Zetas Inc.* still falls short of constituting "a new theoretical framework to understand organized crime and violence" (1). It demonstrates with utmost clarity the history and inner workings of the Zetas as an illicit paramilitary market-state duopoly and brings us convincingly to the conclusion that civil war holds the key to understanding the current conjuncture. However, its overriding sociological framework means that it fails to take that intuition to its ultimate conceptual consequences, which touch upon the history of the political paradigm of the West. For that reason, we still need to move in the direction of the essence of contemporary civil conflict itself.

## Decontainment and *Stasis*

As in the case of the katechon, it is well known and widely commented on that *stasis* refers to the civil discord that tormented the Greek *polis* and helped construct one of the foundational pillars of Western politics. The question, however, is in what way *stasis* is a term that can be considered to be coterminous with contemporary narco-accumulation, or global war in its Mexican vein. In *Stasis: Civil War as a Political Paradigm* (2015), Giorgio Agamben appears to be in general agreement with Carlo Galli, Jacques Derrida, Jean-Luc Nancy, and others when he observes that "the very possibility of distinguishing a war between States and an internecine war appears today to have disappeared" (1). It is from within this context that Agamben examines what he calls the "secret solidarity" between the necessity of civil war, on one hand, and the necessity of its exclusion, on the other, which from ancient Greece to Thomas Hobbes are two oscillating necessities that have structured the foundation of politics in the West (4).[23] These fluctuating dynamics are, he says, "two faces, so to speak, of a single political paradigm" (4). Ancient Greece uncovers the need for, and even the inevitability of, civil war understood as *stasis emphylos*, that is, as the conflict proper to blood kinship that is "inherent to the city" (7–8). The theory of the modern state in Hobbes, however, inscribes the need for the exclusion of filial or internecine conflict (12). As such, *stasis* in Hobbes would become expelled into the *state of nature*, as the metaphorical place of the dissolution of orderly traditional bonds of authority, recognition, and legitimacy and therefore as the site of the war of all against all, the externality of which was designed to immunize the Commonwealth, the modern *polis*, from internal strife but not from external, alien, or foreign conflict (*polemos*). *Stasis* and *polemos* indicate two distinct yet intimately intertwined modalities of violence and social unrest and, as such, two different and dialecticizable means by which to understand the function of turmoil in relation to the political ground of the *polis*. Moreover, at least since Plato these distinct yet related forms, encapsulating two distinctive frames and contents, have been handed down to us in advance as the pillars for every understanding of the relation between force and the means and ends of the political.

The central question Agamben seeks to address in *Stasis: Civil War as a Political Paradigm* is formulated as follows: "Where does the *stasis* 'stand'? What is its proper place?" (14), a question that is subsequently repeated as "Where does the *stasis* 'stand'? What is the proper place of civil war?" (16).[24] The essay is significant, however, precisely because by sticking faithfully to the specific locus of the city, of the *polis*, and therefore of citizenship as the integral concept of political life "in classical Greece, as today" (23), ultimately Agamben fails to reckon with the contemporary shifts in the inherited metaphors regarding political space and even less with the ongoing demise of "the spatial" understood in terms of the Hobbesian geometry of power. Agamben thereby falls short of accounting for the reasons why "the very possibility of distinguishing a war between States and an internecine war appears today to have disappeared" (1). In other words, Agamben identifies the problem of the eclipse of a political paradigm yet upholds the constitutive metaphors of that paradigm as if they were still as functional today as they were in ancient Greece or in seventeenth-century England.

His reading, however, is worthy of further commentary. Agamben retraces Nicole Loraux's classic work on *stasis* in order to provide what he considers to be a corrective. He observes that for Loraux *stasis* was a "revealer" of the *oikos* (11) and civil war a "war within the family," an *oikeios polemos* (13). Why, asks Agamben, would this not present a political mystery for Loraux? Agamben counters what he considers to be Loraux's oversimplification as follows: "Stasis does not have its place within the household, but constitutes a threshold of indifference between the *oikos* and the *polis*, between blood kinship and citizenship" (15). *Stasis* is the "border between the household and the city" (15) that confuses "what pertains to the *oikos* with what is particular to the *polis*, what is intimate with what is foreign" (15), and does so to such an extent that "the effect of the *stasis* is that of rendering the *oikos* and the *polis* indiscernible" (15). This means, Agamben continues, that "*in the system of Greek politics civil war functions as a threshold of politicization and depoliticization, through which the house is exceeded in the city and the city is depoliticized in the family*" (16). In Agamben's proposed rereading of Loraux the metaphors of house, city, and family anchor and mediate the oscillations of the border/threshold for politicization and depoliticization, or *stasis*. Also, in this schema *stasis* determines and mediates between the "polar opposed processes of politicization and depoliticization" (19), for *stasis* is a threshold "through which domestic belonging is politicized into citizenship and, conversely, citizenship is depoliticized into family solidarity" (19). For Agamben, it is as a result of the depoliticization of citizenship (which, let us not forget, is one of the constitutive symptoms of Marramao's "twilight of sovereignty") that global terrorism becomes "the form that civil war acquires when life as such becomes the stakes of politics" (24). In Agamben's formulation, terrorism is globalized life politics in inverted form.

One thing that Agamben proposes in this essay is the need to reinvent "the foundation of Western politics" "from scratch" (11). However, if, as the author says, the tension between politicization and depoliticization is "irresolvable" (23), then it remains unclear how "the foundation of Western politics" can be "rethought from scratch" (11) while in fact remaining faithful to Platonic-Hobbesian metaphors of gathering and containment such as "domestic belonging," "citizenship," "house," "family," "the city," "the *polis*," etc. After all, a project grounded in the maintenance of those metaphors could not formulate a way of thinking "from scratch" at all. It would be just another chapter in the political realignment of the foundational and modern metaphors of Western metaphysics, as already given.

Having said that, Agamben ends his essay on *stasis* by observing, perhaps unsurprisingly, that in global war "the sole form in which life as such can be politicized is its unconditional exposure to death — that is, bare life" (24). But if bare life were to be the basis of a repoliticization and therefore of an inevitable return to the realm of representation, it would have to turn its back on the aporetic limit between life and death, reenter the realm of given history, and once again become the basis not of exposure to death but of a turning away from death — from the thrownness of *ek-sistence* — in the name of a measurable index for political reason. The purpose of the dialectical mediation of history would once again be the sublimation of death to life, the sublimation of the cadaver to the indexing of the political or the aesthetic, when what in fact should never be set aside is "the simple fact that the general future of mankind has nothing to offer to individual life, whose only certain future is death" (Arendt, *Crises of the Republic*, 128). This abyss between finitude and the political probably explains why the question of *life*—as a "means by which to escape from the equality before death into a distinction assuring some measure of deathlessness" (165)—should always be questioned, rather than reinstated as an objective or as a means to an end.[25]

Something here does not quite add up in relation to Agamben's opening remark on global civil war. It is fundamental, for example, that in this essay the spatial is in fact a conceptual and historical given. *Stasis* is certainly the disclosure of a threshold, or limit experience, but herein the city, the *polis*, the house, family, solidarity, and citizenship all consolidate the tradition of given categories that remain internal to the legally defined space of the *polis* as the classical and modern inheritance. In contrast, however, the problem of contemporary turmoil runs deeper. We would do well to recognize that "it is no longer possible to identify either a city that would be 'The City'— as Rome was for so long—or an orb that would provide the contour of a world extended around this city. . . . The city spreads and extends all the way to the point where, while it tends to cover the entire orb of the planet, it loses its properties as a city" (Nancy, *The Creation of the World or Globalization*, 33). Along with the loss of the city as the metaphorical and conceptual ground of the political—as the very space of socialization of the history of *logos* and of the *zoon politikon*—the idea of locus and of everything that was previously considered to be "inherent to the city" (such as the Aristotelian *good life*) declines and fades away, including the city's foundational political concepts and figures such as the *koinon*, the common, or, for that matter, the professional philosopher, the double bind of the family-city (the list is endless).[26]

If globalization signals the disintegration of the history and question of the city as *the* foundation of the philosophy of history, then the structural principle of the public enemy—which establishes the distinction between *polemos*, or of war "strictly speaking," and *stasis*—is also in a state of disarray. This dissolution of metaphor precedes, underlies, and haunts the current twilight of sovereignty, and it cannot be ignored, subsumed, or dialecticized. Its loss—the ongoing *perishing*, the disclosedness of the demise of the conceptual history of the city—is the basic sociological meaningfulness of the closure of metaphysics and of the post-sovereign order of decontainment, or of post-katechontic turmoil.

While in Agamben there is still a "secret solidarity" between the necessity of civil war, on one hand, and the necessity of its exclusion, on the other, with both necessities representing the "two faces, so to speak, of a single political paradigm" (4), now we are becoming aware of the fact that that entire political paradigm — the political paradigm of inclusion and exclusion, indeed, of *the very West itself* — is, if not entirely moribund, then most certainly in a state of irreparable collapse at least in part because there is no longer any specific locus — no *polis*, no Commonwealth — from which to exclude *stasis* and, as such, from which to consolidate order. It is not by chance, after all, that in late neoliberalism so many want to "Build That Wall!": This is the reactionary expression of a modern desire for the concrete borders of the integral nation-state, of the homeland. It is the expression of nostalgia for forms of spatial and political meaningfulness that have already run their course.

Ultimately, what we are experiencing is the exhaustion of a political paradigm that has created itself on the factical differentiation between *polemos* and *stasis*, as two different yet intimately connected ways of gathering (that is, of geometrically spacing), and therefore of categorizing upheaval, unrest, and war as "a mode of being-there of factical life" (Heidegger, *Facticity*, 66). The modern history and theory of sovereignty orient both *stasis* and *polemos* in the direction of differential yet interrelated relations internal to *logos*. Agamben emphasizes differentiation by upholding the foundational metaphors of gathering (home, city, etc.) as the specific *arche* from which internecine conflict confronts its outer limit, or threshold, and consequently crosses over into *stasis*. In such a formulation, in contrast to *stasis*, *polemos* guarantees synthesis and unity. Through *polemos*, in other words, we approach the co-belonging of reason and confrontation as the uneliminable metaphysical foundation of the political understood as unification, gathering, or the synthesizing of the given: "Confrontation neither divides nor destroys unity. It constructs unity; it is logos. Polemos and logos are the same thing" (Heidegger, "On the Grammar and Etymology of the Word 'Being,'" 65).[27] In *The Gift of Death*, Derrida builds on this characterization of *polemos*: "Polemos unifies adversaries; it brings together those who are in opposition . . . as if they were intertwined by means of the extreme proximity of a face-to-face" (19). *Polemos* brings Being to light in the discord between gods and human beings, uncovering their difference in unity. It anchors beings in the metaphysics of the immanent and the transcendent, of the here below and the beyond, of appearance and reality. As such, in sociological terms it anchors the place of the state as an organized political entity *against*, for example, the chaos of the state of nature. It produces filiation at origin and birth, the familiarity of the family, the proximity of the neighbor, etc. And through its metaphysical gathering into proximity and domesticity, *polemos* becomes the metaphysical translation of divine personification, or the worldly ground of social conflict and equilibrium. Within this process the will to sacrifice is measured in the metaphysical difference between gods and beings and, by extension, between sovereign power and the People. *Polemos*, in other words, is the anchoring of common interests and common frameworks of language and dialogue (*logos*) via the consolidation of perspective, or the One.

As Carl Schmitt observes, however, *stasis* uncovers the underlying hostility that never ceases to undermine the unification of adversaries, splitting and undermining "standpoint": "The One—*to Hen*—is always in uproar—*stasiazon*—against itself—*pros heauton*" (*Political Theology*, 122). Schmitt continues with the question of uproar at the heart of the One in the following terms: "*Stasis* means in the first place quiescence, tranquility, standpoint, status; its antonym is *kinesis*, movement. But *stasis* also means, in the second place, (political) *unrest*, movement, uproar and civil war" (123). The root image of *stasis*, as Kostas Kalimtzis notes, is that of the disease (the turmoil and fratricidal strife of *nosos*) that overtakes *logos* (and therefore the common frameworks of *polemos*) when there is "a reprioritization of values that no longer respond to common interests and, hence, have no need for a common framework of dialogue" (*Aristotle on Political Enmity and Disease*, 10).[28] The vanishing of common interests is responsible for a "demise in logos—a corruption in both speech and rational calculation" (10), at which point the rhetoric of *stasis* takes over, assaults *logos*, and leads to "the elimination of the primary regulatory function of friendship (*philia*)" (11). This produces a breakdown of law, the destruction of a *polis*'s internal structure and constitution (23), and a generalized perception of injustice (33) resulting from the unbinding of unity and the unleashing of social discord as a "pathology resulting from injustice" (15). *Stasis*, then, is not the cause but the effect of a dissolution that "begins only when a split in values occurs in the ranks of the rulers, whereby some of them make wealth, rather than honor, the principal value of the constitution" (29). *Stasis* in its classical sense is the setting in motion of this split and of the inequality and injustice that inscribes separation and uproar at the heart of the gathering metaphors of the One.

Nicole Loraux observes that what we understand as *stasis*, or civil war, in contrast to adversarial unification (*polemos*) is actually a Platonic misnomer for *diastásis*, that is, for mere separation, or perhaps for the pathological split that is prior to and underlies the formation of the common and therefore of the political community itself. In a footnote to *The Politics of Friendship* Derrida turns to Nicole Loraux, whom he references in the following terms:

Recalling that Plato shares with all his contemporaries the "logic" of the opposition of complementarity between *pólemos* and *stásis*, Nicole Loraux adds, by way of drawing interesting consequences, the following point: "But the insistence on emphasizing that, in the case of civil war, stasis as a name is especially Platonic. Only a name: a simple appellation, indeed, as a passage from *Laws* suggests, an inaccurate appellation. Defining 'the worst scourge for a city,' the Athenian-nomothete is at great pains to contest the pertinence of the standard appellation of civil war, 'whose right name would indeed be rather *diastasis* than *stásis*.'" (134)[29]

We are left to wonder about the interesting consequences and nuance of this reference to *separation*. Stasis and *polemos* clearly uncover the legacy of two substantivized historical objects of, and forms for, knowledge regarding war, upheaval, or the private-public enemy distinction passed down to us from Plato as the political tradition of the West. However, Loraux appears to indicate that *diastasis*—mere separation, or, in its modern usage, the pathological splitting and opening up of cartilage from bone, or, physiologically, the concluding pulsation from one instant to another in the movement of a heartbeat (that is, in the arrival and passage of blood and therefore of the timing of life itself)—denotes an originary, infrapolitical separating movement or momentary lapsus prior to and beneath all force. Perhaps this allows for the coming into perception of the *with* of every *being-with*; that is to say, it brings *publicness* itself, including that of the intimacy of the *oikos*, into the realm of disclosedness for experience, and therefore for facticity.[30]

Is what we understand as *stasis* the substantivized (and therefore subsequent, second, doubled) mark and effect of an infrapolitical *diastasis* indicating the very question of *being-with*? If this is the case, then what is at stake in *diastasis* is therefore the question of *relation as such*, thereby indicating that gathering is always already split from within as much as it brings together. *Diastasis* would be the originary, infrapolitical splitting that remains at all times prior to each and every form of conflict or dialectical politics of recognition, which as such never succumbs to the extension of knowledge, value, representation, or politics. Indeed, to the extent that *stasis* can in fact be brought into the signifier for representation (for example, as the representation of the political relation between the human and the ontology of the commodity form itself, or as "narco-culture"), by definition it would also be the active concealment and oblivion of the infrapolitical separation inherent to the question of *being-with* that underlies ontological disclosedness. Diastasis would be the infrapolitical movement of spatial and temporal separation that ungrounds common-sense understandings (the representedness) of the public as the common.

In the age of the postkatechon, perhaps it is ongoing *diastasis* — decontained and decontaining splitting at the heart of the *stasis-polemos* relation — that nullifies the clarity of the spatial arrangements (inside-outside, *polis*, city, home, Nation, etc.), thereby rendering impossible the dialecticization of any new epoch. Now that the city has spread and extended all the way to the point where it loses its properties (its internal structure and historical constitution) as a city — thereby marking, and extending the mark of, the topographical collapse of the spatial relation itself — *diastasis*, this infrapolitical splitting that is internal to both the disclosedness and perception of *publicness* as well as to the disintegration and destruction of the *polis*, remains and extends its aporetic mutability in such a way as to distance political theology from the question of the state, which leads the latter to lose its monopoly not only on violence but on the modern concept of the political.

Herein lies a terrible conundrum and an opportunity for thinking. This double loss we refer to here as *decontainment,* a term that certainly carries the splits and divisions of *stasis* along with it but does so in the context of global post-katechontic, or post-territorial, endemic war, discloses the originary, infrapolitical separation that underlies the *diastasis-polemos/stasis* relation and the force it generates. This uncontained form of infrapolitical *diastasis* (or of a splitting internal to a body now without a specific "standing" or "proper place," though certainly indicating an ever-shifting frontier and uprising between depoliticization and the political across national boundaries and spatial limitations) can no longer be actively forgotten, amnestied, or reconciled in the name of the "political duty" and peaceful order of the city (Agamben, *Stasis*, 21). After all, who, or what entity, can amnesty a constant infrapolitical *diastasis* that is itself globalizing the problem of *relationality as such*, beneath the market-state duopoly, the extraction of relative surplus value, exacerbated subjectivism, and the order of the demetaphorization of modern order, all at the same time?

Along with the *interregnum*, it appears that no such thing as amnesty or reconciliation is available to us anymore. It is too late. Moreover, since *diastasis* has no proper place or particular standing in globalization, it is everywhere and nowhere in particular. The *stasis* it leads to — the visibly violent mark of a splitting, cutting, separating, or bordering given over to discord — is decontained licit and illicit force in the pursuit of domination and value extraction and also the state of separation and of riot that shadows it. If, as Giorgio Agamben maintains, the political project of our times is the reinvention of the metaphysical tradition "from scratch," then perhaps it could be suggested that *diastasis*—the uncovering of the *with* in *being-with*—rather than the Platonic distinction between *polemos* and *stasis*, which has determined the thinking of the entire political paradigm of modernity, is an infrapolitical point of inflection that exists prior to and runs beneath the entire Western tradition of war and of civil war thinking.

It is a question of the body: the pathological separation of cartilage from bone, or the final impetus of a heartbeat, and therefore of the relation between time and existence, or of the passage of life toward its existential limit. As such, if "The One—*to Hen*—is always in uproar—*stasiazon*—against itself—*pros heauton*," as Schmitt observed, and if the city no longer has the properties of the city, then the gathering of the One—that is, all historically given forms of the common—just might be little more than a reaction against "the empty place of the common good, and the empty place of the common as a good" (Nancy, "War, Right, Sovereignty—*Techne*," 137).

Globalization is, in other words, a dreadful hollowing out of the Platonic and Schmittian distinction between *polemos* and *stasis*. It is the increasingly boundless abyss and fury that is the incommensurable nonplace of the exhaustion of difference (Moreiras), the twilight of the metaphysics of "the West" rather than the framing of a particular object of knowledge, the specificity of its represented forms, and its potential relegislation in the name of the political.[31] *Diastasis* is the separating, infrapolitical *wherefrom* that raises the question of and underlies *being-with* as such.

Within this context, if indeed we are referring to the force of narco-accumulation neither as a counter-Revolution (Paley) nor as a preemptive counter-Revolution (Balibar) (since both formulations remain sociologically unconvincing) but as a phenomenon that does exist within the overall register of global civil war (Agamben), though not in the sense of recuperating either *bare life* or the reinvention of Western metaphysics "from scratch," and certainly not as an example of "modern civil war" (Correa-Cabrera), then we have to confront the fact that it is a civil war, but not necessarily in the (classic) Platonic or (modern) Schmittian sense. It is the continual splitting within, and of, the disclosedness—of the very *being-there*—of *relation as such*. It is not political in the legislative, biopolitical sense of that term, and it is never enough to say that it is *either stasis or polemos*.

The despatializing killing industry that is narco-accumulation makes a mockery of war, the political, and the representation of their inherited categories. For this very reason, narco-accumulation is not only a case of bare life or of necropolitics, understood as the monstrous underside of biopolitical regulation. It is the uprising of a question of *facticity* that occurs in the infrapolitical distance to and from the realm of politics. For this reason, within the (dis)order of the postkatechon, in order for there to be a thinking, it is incumbent upon us to account for never-ending separation, *being-with*, or relation *as such*, and therefore for the very question of facticity, or meaningfulness, itself.

## Theater of Conflict I: "Here There Is No Choosing"

Toward the end of Cormac McCarthy's screenplay *The Counselor*, the eponymous main character, played in the film by Michael Fassbender, finally realizes — but only when it is too late — that he is up to his neck not in the modern state's legal monopoly of force (of which he, as a narco-lawyer, is a corrupt representative but a representative nevertheless) but in narco-accumulation's extralegal monopoly on the sovereign decision to kill or let live. Without realizing it, the Counselor is floundering in the everyday mandates and collateral damage circulated by the market-state duopoly. In the scene in question, which made it only partially into the film's final cut, the Counselor confronts the logical outcome of his free choice to invest in the transnational contraband transport business. Here the Counselor crosses the line from the economic world of corruption and self-interest to slowly come face to face with the unknown and the singular: death and mourning.

In a desperate phone conversation, the Counselor beseeches "Jefe" (Rubén Blades in the film) to spare the life of his kidnapped partner, Laura (Penélope Cruz in the final production), who will be sacrificed on account of the Counselor's sin of investing in and organizing a shipment of cocaine from Mexico that has not been delivered successfully to its final destination in the United States. The Counselor hopes beyond hope to negotiate the freedom of his lover, or simply to petition "Jefe" — this anonymous narco-sovereign, or contemporary mortal God — for a humane solution. He hopes, in other words, for a "gentleman's understanding," for a humanist way out.

"Jefe," however, merely explains to the Counselor the cold, burdensome simplicity — the incommensurable pain, grief, and mourning — of his remaining time on earth. Here the Counselor is brought to the realization that an invisible limit has been crossed and that he cannot renegotiate the duty that binds him to "Jefe." He can only take responsibility for his decision to invest, in the same way "Jefe" had also been forced to take responsibility two years before in the murder of his own sixteen-year-old son (145), perhaps indicating that in this world, when a certain invisible line is crossed, there is no specific front between responsibility and irresponsibility "but only between different appropriations of the same sacrifice" (Derrida, *The Gift of Death*, 70).

In the agonizing singularity of his situation, in which he will have to become a willing participant in the execution of the death penalty that now applies to his lover, the Counselor's only available ethical decision is to sacrifice Laura and to bear witness for the rest of his days to that decision. For this reason, "Jefe" tells the Counselor that absolute renunciation is his only path:

> I would urge you to see the truth of your situation, Counselor. . . .
> The world in which you seek to undo your mistakes is not the world
> in which they were made. You are at a cross in the road and here you
> think to choose. But here there is no choosing. There is only accept-
> ing. The choosing was done long ago. . . . I don't mean to upset you,
> but reflective men often find themselves at a certain remove from the
> realities of life. In any case, to prepare a place in our lives for the trag-
> edies to come is an economy few wish to practice. . . . There is no rule
> of exchange here, you see. Grief transcends every value. A man would
> give whole nations to lift it from his heart. And yet with it you can buy
> nothing. . . . You may dedicate your life to grief or not. The choice is
> yours. (145)

As the beyond of the material, grief does no work and suspends every economy, observes "Jefe." For this reason, it is only ever infrapolitical. The time for self-delusion has passed, "Jefe" seems to tell the Counselor, for in this death penalty the protagonist has entered a domain in which he can no longer tell himself stories about economic value, social privilege, or the preservation of life. This is the point at which the only thing he can do is wake up to and assume full responsibility for the truth of his condition: finitude rather than salvation, that is, attunement to the understanding that death be permitted to linger in its own way, making itself felt for the rest of his days, or not. This is the only choice available.

What is truly exceptional about this brief scene from Cormac McCarthy's screenplay is that it is one of the very few moments in the entire corpus of literary and filmic production on both sides of the Mexico-US border oriented toward the representation of narco-accumulation, in which *tragedy*— the thematization of the incommensurable relation between law, freedom, desire, death, grief, and mourning, "in the face of a powerful enemy, in the face of a sublime hardship, in the face of a horrible problem" (Nietzsche, *Twilight of the Idols*, 205)—takes precedent over the almost complete subordination of language and image to the clichés of the genre's largely costumbrist complacency. In a cultural corpus dedicated to the representation and history of extreme violence or to analogous phenomena such as Central American and Mexican migration, just for the briefest of moments Cormac McCarthy "raises the drink of sweetest cruelty" (Nietzsche, *Twilight of the Idols*, 205) to the existential question and thematization of mortality and suffering, that is, to the absolute singularity of finitude, to the experience of grief, to the responsibility of bearing witness to death, and, as such, to the time of existence itself.[32]

Along the fragile line of communication that joins and separates them, "Jefe" essentially points out to the Counselor that from this moment in time, no one and nothing can take Laura's inevitable death from her, in the same way no one and nothing can take away the Counselor's initial decision from him, or the burden of the grief that will consume him for the rest of his life. In other words, for the first time the cruelty of what can occur when a certain limit has been passed forces the Counselor to confront the basic existential fact that no one "can take the Other's dying away from him" (Heidegger, *Being and Time*, 284). Everything else is just the will to power of the law of the *I* that endures, but only for a while, in the guise of *life*. As such, in the conversation between the Counselor and "Jefe" Cormac McCarthy invites us to contemplate, through the imposition of the law of sacrifice, the significance of the ontological difference between *beings* and *Being*, the differential register that unifies and separates the ontic to and from the ontological.

The Counselor's Achilles' heel, the source of his tragic destiny, is the arrogant assertion of his self-certainty: He has actually believed and misunderstood that even existence is negotiable and that a rationalization of responsibility — a common ethical ground, a new law forged between him and "Jefe," for example — could suffice to change the underlying conditions of his and Laura's situation. He still seems to think his is merely a social and economic problem, when in fact it is existential. As such, the Counselor's tragedy is also to enter into the realization that finitude is not negotiable, for Jefe's lesson is that there is no generalized substitution of conditions available. The death penalty announced and guaranteed in this world has only given the Counselor the complete irreplaceability of Laura's and his own predicament and of their cruelly different experiences of it.

It is at this point that the Counselor is forced into an awareness he has never safeguarded, can no longer conceal, abide, or make sense of, but will suffer through to his final breath: the knowledge that the imminence of a disappearance "seals the union of the possible and the impossible, of fear and desire, and of mortality and immortality, in being-to-death" (Derrida, *Aporias*, 4). Laura is murdered, her body dumped on a landfill, and a video recording presumably of her torture, rape, and death is mailed to the Counselor. In the end, he is left to confront in his absolute solitude the incommensurable price he will pay on account of his (mis)calculations regarding the relation between time, the everyday profits and losses enabled and guaranteed by vanity, and mortality.

If the accession to facticity is the hermeneutic relation of the mortal to an approaching death, an approach to death gifted only by death, then we have to say that Cormac McCarthy has penned a screenplay on one level like so many other narco-narratives, in which there is an abundance of deaths produced but no thematization and making sense of finitude itself, or even of the aporetic threshold that confronts it. On one level there is in *The Counselor* a clichéd concealment of the question of finitude and no facticity available at all. On the other hand, we also have to recognize the exceptionality of this brief moment in the screenplay, in which McCarthy undermines the laws of the genre of narco-narrative. Suddenly through the foil of the death penalty this communication between "Jefe" and the Counselor announces the singular significance of the question of existence, which momentarily punctures a hole in the self-concealments of the lives represented in the film as well as in the very *style* that has become the dominant mode of *narco-narrative*, a style that amasses representations of the cruelty of death-giving as a social reality while at all times concealing the existential question and thematization of finitude itself.[33]

This fundamental concealment is predetermined. For example, McCarthy's attunement to the existential predicament in *The Counselor* gestures only in the direction of the enduring traces of Christian metaphysics, since "Jefe" is obviously a fallen stand-in for the Abrahamic God of the Commandments. He is a quasi-transcendental figure *acting like* God at the heart of the closure of metaphysics. It is not that the biblical morality of Christian onto-theology reigns supreme in this story of narco-accumulation but that narco-accumulation is itself a fully economized and technologized, fallen monotheism dominated by the principles of means, ends, and origin (*arche*). This is what the Counselor has not understood, what brings Laura to her death, what leaves the main character grieving in its wake, and what allows Cormac McCarthy to thematize death in such a way as to probe momentarily into the disclosure of meaning, at least at the level of the individual.[34] At no point, in other words, does the Counselor turn toward the possibility of a sense-making *other than* that of Christian sacrifice. Similarly, while *The Counselor* gestures, in the interaction between "Jefe" and the Counselor, toward the question of *being* from within its approach to ontological difference, the screenplay itself is not attuned to the possibility of dislodging the fully constituted Christian representation and technicity of subjective force.

It is for this reason that the screenplay's representational form falls short of actually moving in the direction of a differential grasping of *techne*, finality, ending, perishing, and *being*. By remaining in the subjectivist order of death-giving *The Counselor* closes off the infrapolitical question for the *beingness of being*, or for the intelligibility of its meaning, which is the only horizon of questioning that could now, as ever, not just shake but destroy the Christian ontology of subjectivity and its relation to the commodity form, or to the ontic mode-of-being of what is at hand. For this reason, there is no transformed or transformative claim of presence either in the screenplay or in the film. Rather, it momentarily presents an infrapolitical problematic, only to conceal it again in the somnambulistic path of the main character and the screenplay's overriding humanism.

As a result, to the extent that "mortality and first-order ἑρμηνεία [under-standing] are two sides of the same human coin," that "mortality lets us make sense of . . . and in fact *requires* us to do so if we don't want to die," and that "the facticity of thrown-ness into meaning becomes utterly serious when we realize that meaning-making — our very way of staying alive — is possible only because we are mortal; and our mortality is the groundless ground for why we have to make sense" (Sheehan, "Facticity and Ereignis," 47), we begin to discern that in order to approach a turn to existence in narco-accumulation, accounting for the internal limitations of *The Counselor*'s representational form and content necessitates the circumvention of the technicity of the *narco*-determinations, of the very force that provides the genre with its origins and cultural corpus.

## Theater of Conflict II: 2666, or the Novel of Force

Simone Weil penned her essay "The Iliad, or the Poem of Force" in response to the Nazi invasion of France in the spring of 1940 and the demise of the Spanish Republic just months before. When considered in the light of cur-rent global conditions, Weil's essay on force and the epic form is rendered mute before an overall contemporary warlike posture that Weil did not have any reason to address. That warlike posture is the effect and extension of the exhaustion of the model and sovereign structures of national and imperial territorialization that emerged in the relation between two world wars and the collapse of the Cold War. Times have changed, in other words, and the modality of war that Weil is striving to comprehend and counter in 1940 — which in the end is a modality sutured directly to the myths and histories of territorialized sovereignty ( *polemos*) — has been overrun by a generalization of war that her essay simply could not register. But what is the meaningfulness of this limitation?

In her reading of *The Iliad* the theater of cruelty, the picture of uniform and impersonal horror that gives poetic language to the siege of Troy and that Weil reads in order to shed light on her most immediate past and desperate present, is interspersed with what she calls "luminous moments, scattered here and there throughout the poem, those brief celestial moments in which man possesses his soul. The soul that awakens then, to live for an instant only to be lost at once in force's vast kingdom, awakes pure and whole; it contains no ambiguities, nothing complicated or turbid; it has no room for anything but courage and love" (23). These luminous moments, she indicates, underscore the enduring tradition of hospitality—the Greek "apprenticeship of virtue" (14)—that persists and dispels the blindness of war from within the *poiesis* of Homer's epic. Weil seeks to recuperate the Greek apprenticeship of virtue in 1940 in order to suggest that Europe cease "to admire force, not hate the enemy, no[r] scorn the unfortunate" (30). For Weil it is not cruelty but the humanist apprenticeship of virtue that makes us human and thereby presumably distinguishes the human from the animal. But her recuperation of the humanist tradition of hospitality and virtue that is still at the heart of her reading of war in 1940, that is, before Auschwitz, Hiroshima, Nagasaki, Vietnam, and post-9/11 globalization, is insufficient for our times, for it does not take into consideration the sheer coldness of capital's mechanisms of reproduction and industrial slaughter. This, however, is not to say that her reading is entirely worthless; far from it.

Weil opens her essay on "the only true epic the Occident possesses" (27) with the following words, which immediately displace the human as the subject of history:

> The true hero, the true subject, the center of the *Iliad* is force. Force employed by man, force that enslaves man, force before which man's flesh shrinks away. In this work, at all times, the human spirit is shown as modified by its relations with force, as swept away, blinded by the very force it imagined it could handle, as deformed by the weight of the force it submits to. For those dreamers who considered that force, thanks to progress, would soon be a thing of the past, the *Iliad* could appear as an historical document; for others, whose powers of recognition are more acute and who perceive force, today as yesterday, at the very center of human history, the *Iliad* is the purest and the loveliest of mirrors.
>
> To define force—it is that *x* that turns anybody who is subjected to it into a thing. Exercised to the limit, it turns man into a thing in the most literal sense: it makes a corpse out of him. Somebody was here,

and the next minute there is nobody here at all; this is a spectacle the *Iliad* never wearies of showing us. (6)

Weil calls force that impersonal *x* that turns anybody subjected to it into a thing, making a corpse out of him or her. In this sense she refers to force as *techne*, as the simultaneous positing of the human as both subject and object. But for Weil *The Iliad* is not only a poem about force — not only about the impersonal exercise of force at the heart of war — but also a poem about the repeated recalibration of force, via its self-duplication into justice, for "those who have force on loan from fate count on it too much and are destroyed" (14). Force duplicates itself as its own intimate justice, and it is in this sense both exception (excess, cruelty) and Law. This retribution, she says, "has a geometrical rigor which operates automatically to penalize the abuse of force," and it is the geometrical rigor of retribution that "was the main subject of Greek thought. It is the soul of the epic" (14). In this sense, in Weil's reading of *The Iliad* impunity is not absolute and never extends fully throughout the world of mortals. Justice is always extended by a geometrical causality that is internal to the existence and exercise of force and technicity; in this sense, Law and exceptionality (excessive cruelty, evil, brutality, turmoil, uproar) co-belong in their echo and duplication, and force (in order to be force) simultaneously makes itself just, a retribution, and the Law (and therefore the law of recognition and representation, the very positing of humanity in the world). Force is incommensurately excessive and simultaneously proper to the realm of the just.

In Weil, then, vengeance or justice, for here they are synonyms, can still be constituted within a regime of representation and, as such, within a horizon of metaphorization as a geometrical bringing-forth of retribution and balance. And this reliance on metaphorization is the underlying idealism and humanism of Weil's essay. It is her establishment of an imaginary relation to the Law, even when her real conditions (the Nazi occupation of France) have at least momentarily suspended that relation, that still outlines her act of faith in a humanist resolution for, or turn in, the relation between human and world.

For Weil, what goes around always comes around in and thanks to force. Everyone who acts in rage or cruelty will always get their comeuppance from fate, and the experience of the turns of justice will always be translatable, can always be metaphorized, and, indeed, are only available to humanity via poetic metaphorization. For Weil in 1940 the world had not yet succumbed to the absolute rule of calculation via the instrumentalization of capital on a global scale. In other words, the cold instrumentalism of technological warfare could still be met with the poetic truth of *The Iliad*—indeed, with the uncovering of the virtue of its exemplarity—which for the author still lay in the equilibrium of the Greek word *Technikon*.[35]

Roberto Bolaño's *2666* is the hollowing out of Weil's residual faith in the poietic metaphorization and humanist uncovering of *techne*. Of course, this is not the same as saying that Bolaño's writing is not poietic, which would be an unreasonable thing to suggest. But it is a *poiesis* that empties out its own humanist grounding, or, rather, it is humanist grounding both presented and undermined for almost one thousand pages. *2666* is the writing of a horizon of repeated demetaphorization of the relation between humanist truth and revelation, between exceptionality and Law. It is the written inscription of a horizon in which we face the destruction of metaphoricity itself, while in the process confronting the cruelty and devastation imposed by the instrumentalist calculations of post-sovereign capital.

But let us not abandon Weil's text entirely, for there is more to the essay than faith in the humanist apparatus and its regimes of metaphorization in the years before the Shoah and everything that followed. For example, in *The Origin of Politics: Hannah Arendt or Simone Weil?* Roberto Esposito highlights the double origin of the political that is at stake in Weil's thinking. In this book, the Italian philosopher refers to the co-belonging of reason and evil as the unelim inable foundation of the political: "At its core, politics is nothing more than war transferred into the city; *polemos* translated into *stasis*. It is in this sense, and only in this sense, that Troy is located at the beginning of our political history: for it is the first of an infinite series of cities invaded and destroyed by war" (51). Force—the originary, impersonal $x$ that splits and marks a difference—always becomes a question of translation and therefore not just a question of physicality but of the limits of language and facticity. The $x$ marks permanent upheaval—the continuous placing of the human as a particular value, and object, within the order of *techne*—as the status quo of politics' foundation and marks the political as the attempt to translate force into the common, while at the same time shepherding the latter toward the reason and language of subjective power. No politics without reason (logos) and no reason without force, with a ceaselessly imperfect translation of one into the other at origin and end, at the foundation and the destruction, of the city. For this reason, force for Esposito "is not the wound destined to heal into the regularity of politics" (50). On the contrary, it is the uneliminable and most intimate wound of the political, situated at the very heart of (indeed, *as*) that which is always and only ever prior to and beneath the political itself. As Weil puts it:

Force is as pitiless to the man who possesses it, or who thinks he does, as it is to its victims; the second it crushes, the first it intoxicates. The truth is, nobody really possesses it. The human race is not divided up, in the *Iliad*, into conquered persons, slaves, suppliants, on the one hand, and conquerors and chiefs on the other. In this poem there is not a single man who does not at one time or another have to bow his neck to force. (11)

Here we have to recognize that for Weil force is both poiesis (unconcealment) *and* metaphorization (which, following Heidegger, we can understand as the oblivion of Being itself). For Weil force is immutable, impersonal, and, as such, present in the same form throughout history (from the origins of the Western tradition to 1940). And perhaps it is this — the absence of a consideration of time — that overdetermines Weil's residual humanist metaphysics in this essay, as she confronts the technological slaughter of industrialized warfare in 1940.

Moreover, perhaps this is where Roberto Bolaño's 2004 novel *2666* might be said to gesture toward the need for a detour, for a historically and materially determined deviation away from humanist metaphysics, no matter how residual, in the name of an alternative pathway toward questioning. At the heart of this turn toward a potential difference lies the question of the split, the cut (*diastasis*), that marks the disclosedness of *publicness* and the form it assumes in the novel. Clearly, in a work comprising around a thousand pages — or perhaps it would be better to say that in this imperfect suture of five different novels into one — the question of the originary split is equally the question of the bind between stasis and form. This is not something that can be treated exhaustively. In what follows, then, I will simply try to shed partial light on force understood as *diastasis*, on the form that limitless splitting takes in the novel, and on its relation to content in *2666*.

Brett Levinson's 2009 essay on *2666*, "Case Closed: Madness and Dissociation in *2666*," is to my mind the most accomplished reading of the novel as form, as a form that continually strives to traverse but always stumbles up against the co-belonging of reason and the upheaval-equilibrium of *splitting* (*diastasis*) as the uneliminable cruelty underlying history and the political. In this essay, Levinson approaches the relation between language, form, and *diastasis* as follows:

Bolaño's narrative evolves as the accretion of disparate tales, each bound to the next by a common and continuous form. The reader therefore encounters no fragments in *2666*, appearances notwithstanding. . . . This "nature," which is the novel's form, holds *2666* together

in such a fashion that one can hardly imagine it otherwise. Form . . .
serves as the binding . . . that contains the sharp deviations, disruptions
and disappearances that drive through the content. (177)

As a result, virtually any content will do in 2666. This leads Levinson to
note in reference to characters such as Fate or Amalfitano, but also in reference to the novel's readers, that "the subject who associates, who draws links,
is himself de-arranged by the very effort to unify, to produce a narrative" (182).
As such, translation de(ar)ranges rather than orients or establishes meaning,
and the novel is well aware of this. For example (and such a gesture of exemplarity is always insufficient, of course), there is a moment in *La parte de Fate*
in which Rosa Méndez describes to Rosa Amalfitano what the difference is
between having sex with a policeman and having sex with a narco. Rosa is
utterly bewildered by Méndez's metaphorization of experience, which makes
a mockery of metaphorization itself: "So," concluded Rosa Amalfitano, "if a
cop fucks you it's like being fucked by a mountain inside the mountain itself,
and if a narco fucks you it's like being fucked by the desert air." "Right on,
sister, if a narco fucks you it's always out in the open" (415). The problem of
the entire novel is contained in this unexceptional interaction, for 2666 is
the unfolding in language, the (de)grounding, or the chiasm underlying the
incommensurable relation between experience and metaphor. 2666 is this
(de)grounding, this chiasm that expresses the horizon of intelligibility — the
novel's facticity, the novel as facticity — through the unintelligibility of the
*perishing* of metaphor.

Levinson takes into consideration the experiential untranslatability of *diastasis* by describing the effect that continual de(ar)rangement has on the
relation between content and form in the novel, on the act of understanding,
and therefore on the question of facticity:

In all cases, the subject is dissociated from the narrative *by* narrative;
removed, he takes with him the correlation of events. The result appears as dissociated narratives, or narratives joined by their dissociation.
It is not the subject (Fate, the critics) as *character* who withdraws from
the tale. What dissolves is the subject as principle of unity. Narrative
explodes not events but their relationship: meaning. Thus, a given
atrocity in 2666 cannot be interpreted as the figure of another: the
Juárez murders or the [literary critics'] racist assault of the [Pakistani]
chauffeur cannot be explained according to the Holocaust as metaphor. The episodes, that is, cannot be understood in terms of the
Holocaust, as "little Holocausts," "post-Holocausts," or even "fascism,"
though Nazism is the central theme of the text's final portion, tempt-

ing the reader to analyze the novel as a meditation on the persistence of Nazism or fascism in the contemporary world. No atrocity in 2666 serves as the example or ground of atrocity as such. Rather, each functions as one more atrocity in a disconnected but repeating series. (182)

At this point, Levinson initiates a subtle shift away from the ontology of the subject and begins to consider the narrative form of dissociation and repetition as time and temporalization. The times and rhythms of boredom and suspense in the novel are the adhesive that bonds narratives and displaces chronology through the experience of repetition (185). In a novel in which "time is form as separation, as presence without representation . . . form without an idiom or narrative" (184), "only the form of repetition remains" (185).

Here we begin to see that the technique of repetition is "the true master" in 2666. Repetition is the *force in action*—the novel's impersonal protagonist— that "suspends the subject from his own work. Assuming the subject's role as the site of coherence, repetition murders (the subject)" (189). This—the automaticity or technicity of the repetition of atrocity that traverses the novel in its entirety but that comes to a head in *La parte de los crímenes*—"discloses the great enigma of the times, our times" (190), as Levinson puts it, as each act of brutality is nothing but the repetition of other such acts that are (in) different in and of themselves as well as to each other. Repetition anchors and stabilizes the permanent upheaval of atrocity and evil:

> The accounts pile detail upon detail, name upon name, so as to materialize as an incomplete heap, unfinished not because more victims will be found (although this is true), nor because the true murderer cannot be located (this too is true), but because the relationship of reports can always be reordered, thus converting one case into an alternative event, distinct from this particular case. The one stack, potentially, is an infinite permutation of rearrangements. . . . The possible combination of events multiplies accordingly. This is why each case must be closed without resolution: *se cerró el caso*. The "stop" is the rhythm of murder that binds one assassination to another, or, to all the others. (190)

I have indulged in a brief detour through Levinson's reading of 2666 in order to get to this point: "The accounts pile detail upon detail, name upon name, so as to materialize as an incomplete heap, unfinished. . . . The one stack, potentially, is an infinite permutation of rearrangements." In the *potentially infinite permutation of rearrangements*, Levinson says, "it is not the victims that lack a name: in 2666 they are precisely named. Missing an appellation is the closure itself, which relates the fictitious universe of 2666 to itself and to other universes, real and imaginary, cutting the whole thing apart, again and again" (190–91).

In Levinson's important formulation, he signals that what is missing is the form of the contiguity, or what we might call the "prostheticity," that frames, binds, and anchors the piling up of accounts, detail upon detail, name upon name, repetition after repetition, splitting after splitting. This is very different from the immutable eternity that grounds the humanist essence of Simone Weil's reflection on force in 1940. In 2666's *The Part about the Crimes* there is no metaphysical anchor or definitive perspective available to us because the detective, that mundane embodiment of the metaphysical anchor of sovereign Law, of *Logos*, is as ineffective as the reader. As such, there is no specific ground and therefore no measure from which to judge and account for the precise relation between the repetition of force and the instrumental reason that arbitrarily closes down around it: "Case Closed."

When we have closure without legibility, there is no containment of horror and no place from which to comprehend it. The instrumental reason constitutive of the closure is equally constitutive of the horror, which is akin to namelessness. In this regard there is no interruption and nothing revelatory in closure, because it fails to interrupt the co-belonging of reason and cruelty that lies at the heart of the public sphere. It is via repetition in the relation between the symbolic and the horror it strives yet fails to name (and therefore represent, delimit, restrain, and contain) that we begin to see the emergence of the real in 2666. The novel narrates the insufficiency of the signifier and the signifier as insufficiency in its relation to and split from horror. It is only via the repetition of the signifier's inability to signify and via the absolute arbitrariness of its closure from, or circumscription of, horror that we glimpse the workings of the real as the undermining of the symbolic order and as the unsymbolizable placeholder of the truth of 2666, which is that repetition inscribes namelessness as the experience of decontained horror.[36]

In the meantime, metaphoric language in the novel is constantly and repeatedly exhausted from within the internal unfolding of demetaphorization. As Barry Seaman, one of the co-founders of the Black Panthers in *The Part about Fate* declares from his Detroit pulpit: "Metaphors are our way of losing ourselves in semblances or treading water in a sea of seeming. In that sense a metaphor is like a life jacket. And remember, there are life jackets that float and others that sink to the bottom like lead" (322–23). In 2666 it seems that we cannot measure the difference between treading water and sinking to the bottom like lead. Indeed, this exposure to the incommensurable experience of the language of splitting — of language as the $x$ that both creates and splits, that creates via the splitting that is publicness — is both communication and the crisis of communicability.

Supplementing Levinson's question regarding the serial repetition and immeasurable closure of *The Part about the Crimes*, it seems that we are abandoned to wonder what light at all can be shed on the relationship between the infinite permutation of atrocious rearrangements in the novel and the question of "the times, our times." This is where the question of force, which, as already suggested, is only ever intertwined with the repeated question of form in the novel, comes back into view.

In 2666 war is the underlying foundation of everyday experience throughout. The novel's form simultaneously extends both the orientation and the absolute disorientation of that experience. As such, the novel's creativity and destruction are absolutely (in)different to each other. *Diastasis* plays itself out as form at the level of the individual characters but also at the level of the novel's language, taken in its broadest sense not as the writing *of* the threshold of horror but writing — the signifier itself — as *the* threshold of horror.

Even though we could think of *The Part about the Critics* as the novel's communal moment, we also have to recognize that it is a coming-of-age tale situated firmly in the wake of the fall of the Berlin Wall, in which the male members of this new transnational professional bourgeoisie (and I say "new"' because their community seems to move for the first time across national boundaries through environments devoid of all resistance) struggle from within their intimate and professional "friendship" for competitive advantage over the body of Liz Norton. She is in turn a substitute for and a displacement of their true desire: that is, to acquire the legitimate and exclusive claim to private property over the life and persona of the German author Benno von Archimboldi, who is the absent cause and metaphysical anchor of their entire world. What they want, in other words, is to overcome lack and stake a claim over the Sovereign, for them to become one with the Other, the master signifier of their world. Through the critics, the friend-enemy relation is sublimated into nonpolitical experience — into the world of sentimental melodrama, for example (and, as such, into the love triangle between Espinoza, Pelletier, and Norton) — while in this depoliticized world of violence the body of Liz Norton is transfigured into the surface of a sexual war between male friends and enemies that for the most part remains *in potentia* but emerges in displaced form in the racist and highly sexualized beating of the Pakistani taxi driver after their having just driven past the Imperial War Museum in London. In the wake of the beating "it was as if they had finally had their *ménage à trois.* . . . Pelletier felt like he had come. With some differences and nuances Espinoza felt the same way. Norton, who stared at them without seeing them in the dark, seemed to have experienced multiple orgasms" (103). It is only when the European literary critics encounter no longer the sublimated game of war, which they refer to as love and friendship, but the blood of open force in the low-intensity conflict between taxi drivers and doormen in the northern Mexican city of Santa Teresa, that their jouissance is definitively interrupted and their model of communal sublimation slowly begins to fall apart. They split and separate.

At this point we could begin to accumulate example after example after example in the novel, but this would not in fact take us anywhere. We could follow Simone Weil's example and try to account for the sheer proliferation of words in the novel that are used in order to substantiate the word *force* (for example, anal and vaginal rape, multiple stab wounds, case closed, hurricane, wind, sea, fury, painting, television, literary criticism, racism, mental asylum, Black Panthers, murder, drug trafficking, dictatorship, boxing, Nazism, communism, pornography, ventriloquism, World War I, the Treaty of Maastricht, silence, fear, World War II, danger, prison, border, wage labor, full employment, the Cold War, maquiladora, Holocaust, desert, Santa Teresa). Again, the list is interminable; their relations, and of course there are many, remain wholly incommensurable, beyond all orientation, translation, or specific metaphorization.

So where does force, this impersonal, all-pervasive character of 2666 that Bolaño has translated into literary form, "stand," as Giorgio Agamben puts it, in reference to *stasis* and the paradigm of global civil war? Quite simply, it has no specific beginning and no end (which is one of the reasons why The Part about Fate begins with the black maternal cadaver and with its simultaneous displacement into the death of her neighbor, Miss Holly, both deaths occurring in conjunction with the unanswerable question of origin: "When did it all begin? . . . When did I go under?" [295]). As Esposito puts it in his reading of Weil's essay on The Iliad, force's beginning can only be seen to lie in the retreat of every beginning, which is what we see in this double cadaver that opens the story of Oscar Fate. Force is deployed and extended as the originary void that exists only ever in retreat while only ever leaving a trace—an impersonal $x$—in its wake. In this sense, what Levinson refers to as 2666's potentially infinite permutation of rearrangements refers to time itself as the anonymous, infinite rearranging of the originary void that produces the relation between force and the real.

How does 2666 strive to give language to this originary and constitutive void we refer to as the temporalization of the real? Again, the proliferation of images used in the novel as a means of substantiating the *void* is noteworthy. In his 1947 "Letter on Humanism" Martin Heidegger had observed that the essence of evil consisted not "in the mere baseness of human action, but rather in the malice of rage" (272). In 2666 the exiled Chilean philosopher Amalfitano gives the European literary critics a neo-Heideggerian theory of the relation of Mexican intellectuals to the state, in which intellectual language in the age of *techne* has always already succumbed to oblivion and concealment. As such, Mexican intellectuals are incapable of giving language to the sound and malice of rage, even though it is constitutive of their relation to public life. On the contrary, they translate rage into rhetoric, eloquence, and discipline:

> The stage per se is a proscenium and upstage there is an enormous tube, something like a mine shaft or the entrance to a mine of gigantic proportions. Let's call it a cave. But we can also say that it's a mine. From the mouth of the mine come unintelligible noises. Onomatopoeic noises, ferocious or seductive, or seductively ferocious, phonemes or maybe just murmurs and whispers and moans. The point is, no one sees, really sees, the mouth of the mine. . . . They only hear the sounds that come from deep in the mine. And they translate or reinterpret or re-create them. Their work, it goes without saying, is very poor indeed. They employ rhetoric where they sense a hurricane, they try to be eloquent where they sense fury unleashed, they strive to maintain the discipline of meter where there's only a deafening and useless silence. They say cheep cheep, bowwow, meow meow, because they're incapable of imagining an animal of colossal proportions, or the absence of that animal. (162–63)

Humanist knowledge makes a mockery of the murmurs, whispers, moans, and useless silence that signal the infrapolitical abyss — the unthinkable nonplace at which the real encounters itself in its own lack (Copjec, *Read My Desire*, 122) — that underlies the Mexican intellectuals' rhetorical relation to state power. In *The Part about the Crimes* the aging visionary Florita Almada goes into a trance on a local Santa Teresa TV show accompanied by a ventriloquist, who is just another translator. Witnessing her trance — her abandonment into the void that is the real — the ventriloquist fears the danger of a possible truth uncovered:

> She was afraid to close her eyes, since it was precisely when they were closed that she saw what the possessing spirit saw, so Florita kept her eyes open. . . . The ventriloquist looked at her and his puppet, as if he could not understand anything though he could smell the danger, the moment of revelation that flashes by and leaves us with only the

certainty of a void, a void that very quickly escapes even the word that contains it. . . . She closed her eyes. . . . "Women are being killed there. They're killing my daughters. My daughters! My daughters!" she screamed, . . . "The fucking police do nothing, they just watch, but what are they watching? What are they watching?" (546–47)

Just a few pages later a misogynist Mexican cop talks to the private detective Harry Magaña about what they—these two male officers of the male law, one public, the other private, one from one side of the border and the other from the other—see: "Ramírez talked about women. Women with their legs spread open. Wide open. What do you see? What do you see? For Christ's sake, this wasn't dinner conversation. A fucking hole. A fucking eye. A fucking gash, like the crack in the earth's crust they have in California, the San Bernardino fault, I think it's called" (552–53).

In 1940 Simone Weil positioned European humanity in a relation of lack to what she called the "luminous moments" of Homer's epic, "those brief celestial moments in which man possesses his soul. The soul that awakens then . . . awakes pure and whole; it contains no ambiguities, nothing complicated or turbid; it has no room for anything but courage and love" (23). This, she says, is the enduring tradition of hospitality that persists at the heart of the *polis*, momentarily dispelling the blindness and cruelty of war from within poetic language. Through this notion of lack—a lack that is absolutely necessary for Weil to anchor her discourse of life and hope in relation to the symbolic Other (that is, to Homer, Greece, the epic, the city)—Weil wants to suggest that Europe can still cease "to admire force, not hate the enemy, no[r] scorn the unfortunate" (30). As such, for Weil the era of industrialized warfare can still be salvaged ethically and politically thanks to its relation of lack to its symbolic Other, that is, to the Greek "apprenticeship of virtue" extended in the name of the *polis* (14).

But in 2666 there is nothing lacking in relation to the symbolic Other, for it is patently clear that the symbolic Other is the metaphysical covering over of the abyss, a covering that in 2666 is perishing from novel to novel, from repetition to repetition, from page to page, indeed, from signifier to signifier. It is true that at the start of 2666 the literary critics establish their common affinities in relation to Archimboldi in much the same way Simone Weil forges her relation to Homer's epic poem. But in Santa Teresa, Bolaño's literary critics fail miserably in their metaphysical quest, and by the time the reader enters the cold and cruel monotony of the Santa Teresa feminicide we are faced with the impossibility of sustaining a language in relation to the virtue of the commons, of the *polis*. On the contrary, we are confronted by the void, the abyss that is internal to a limitless war conducted nevertheless in the context of almost full employment. Here there are no "brief celestial moments in which man possesses his soul," no pure and whole awakening, only the brutality of the impersonal splitting that is *publicness* itself.

In 2666 politics is no longer war ( *polemos*) translated and transferred into the city, as Esposito put it. Now what reigns is *diastasis* — splitting — transferred across all borders, lives, psyches, bodies, and images. There is no container, no katechon. The desert is now the notion of place rendered strangely out of place, as the condition and experience of the postkatechon. With the city (Law, *polis*) rendered politically inoperative and "place" rendered obsolete, in the desert we are left without legibility, for now the subject becomes a prisoner not of the Other that exists in its absence but of the absolute void. The era of the "infinite permutation of rearrangements," or the era of "generalized metonymization" (Sumic) — an era that 2666 translates into form — is a world in which, as Lacan put it in 1975, "there is but one social symptom: every individual is in effect a proletarian, that is to say that no discourse is at the disposal of the individual by means of which a social bond can be established" (Lacan, "La troisième," qtd. in Sumic, "Politics in the Era of the Inexistent Other," 10). For this reason, *The Part about the Critics* can end only with the architecture of "a bunker holding a corpse" (207).

Perhaps, then, the unmeasurable, generalized metonymization of form (who knows what it could be called!?) embodies the demise of the idea that literature (or art in general) can open up the possibility for a new aesthetic, epoch, politics, or ethics. Perhaps in the world of decontained force aesthetic contingency no longer matters. Contingency (along with its modernist aesthetic sidekicks irruption, rupture, crisis, and interruption) just might be banal in the era of the generalized metonymization of perennial splitting, or *diastasis*. Jacques Derrida, of course, observed in his early reading of Foucault that there are "crises of reason in strange complicity with what the world calls crises of madness" (Derrida, "Cogito and the History of Madness," 62–63). But 2666 is the realization set in motion — as extended form — that we are living in times in which the modern (for example, the avant-garde) complicity between reason and madness, that is, the historical social bond between modern reason and its outer limits, has itself run its course, or at least has run *a* course, and we are in its wake without a hermeneutic at our disposal and without a figuration or metaphorization of madness available to us to challenge and interrupt it. The exhaustion of prior significations brings with it the exhaustion of prior attachments to the externality of madness. We can no longer say "War is madness!!" or "Give Peace a Chance!" or, as the Futurist Manifesto put it a century ago, "We want to glorify war — the only cure for the world — militarism, patriotism, the destructive gesture of the anarchists, the beautiful ideas which kill, and contempt for woman." We cannot say any of that and expect it to transform the banality of the everyday experience of *techne* (largely because it already reinforces that given world). On the other hand, 2666 inscribes the demetaphorization of such gestures in the face of limitless *diastasis*. But it also inscribes the horizon of non-metaphor—the horizon of destruction, the desert, the corpse—starting from which one might be able to address, in the wake of romanticism and the avant-garde, in the wake of the Cold War and the full saturation of what Sergio González Rodríguez has referred to as the contemporary *battlefield*, the problem of metaphoricity itself.

Perhaps the destruction that lies at the heart of 2666 is, if not the actual uncovering of the impossible upon whose shoulders the possible can be considered once again, then at least the writing of a recognition that such a thing is more necessary than ever.[37] If this is the case, then in 2666 there might be no room for pessimism, because the journalist Guadalupe Roncal or whoever it was who said "No one pays attention to these killings, but the secret of the world is hidden in them" just might have been right. As Heidegger noted at the end of "The Question concerning Technology": "The closer we come to the danger, the more brightly do the ways into the saving power begin to shine, and the more questioning we become" (35). The problem, of course, is that the task of reading and questioning has only just begun, for in the face of Bolaño's novel of force we are still very much in our conceptual infancy.

Like the figure of Lotte Hass at the end of the novel (Hass is Archimboldi's long-lost younger sister and the mother of Klauss Hass, imprisoned in Santa Teresa), we are before the abyss, before the absent ground that opens up at the limit of language: "'I don't understand anything and the little I do understand frightens me. Nothing makes sense,' said Lotte . . . 'Will you take care of it all?' . . . 'Will you take care of it all?'" [1115–16]). In the face of the novel's measureless overabundance of instrumentalized and calculated force, danger, fear, cruelty, and impunity—all of which is written in the narrative form of *diastasis*, the constant splitting that marks the demetaphorization of historicism, of any philosophy of history, and the abyss of meaningfulness itself—is there a language available to us for the saving power of safekeeping? What would it take to talk of a change in direction? What would it take to effect a detour in thought? A withdrawal? What would it take to take care of it all?

If such a thing were possible, it would clear a way for a moment of freedom and difference. In the end, and quite literally at the very end of absolutely everything for Bolaño, this is the author's hospitality, his call or hailing on the threshold of his own death: Will you take care of it all? And in the silent expanse that follows the question, we can only lend an ear to what, one can

conjecture, underlies the question: "Because I have failed, for *I*—the constitutive ground of every humanism—*is* the site of failure (repeatedly, inevitably,
enduringly)."[38]

On the contrary, the accession to facticity is the hermeneutic relation of the
mortal to an approaching death, to an approach to death, gifted only by death
(Derrida, *The Gift of Death*, 52). It is this accession to the incommensurability
of responsibility in the impersonal face of finitude that marks and extends, to
an extent at least, the singular writing we call *2666*. But it is also this accession
that leads us to determine that if the freeing of the regime of metaphor that we
inherit grants presence to the clearing of a possible transformation or turning
toward the impersonal, then *2666* ends with the demand for a clearing but
fails to provide it itself. This is not necessarily its failure. On the contrary, to
the extent that *2666* eschews the moralizing tendencies of beauty and aesthet-
ics and, rather, "suffers from life" (Nietzsche, *Twilight of the Idols*, 93), it is the
novel's, indeed, Bolaño's, historical and artistic merit. For this reason alone,
there is no *beyond Bolaño* (Hoyos, *Beyond Bolaño*, 2015), merely an infrapolitical dwelling on the finality—on the exhaustion of significations—that
his thinking obliges us to attempt to traverse for the rest of our days. It is not
by chance that the novel opens at the beginning of the end ("The Critics")
and ends at the beginning ("Archimboldi"), traversing the time of the twentieth century handed down as that of industrial development and war, for in
that gesture the novel leaves us only with the problem of passage through our
inherited and by now our only ever tired, tardy, and toppling metaphors of
subjectivity. For in the face of death it is always too late for more subjectivity.

## Toward the Void

As already noted, if politics is predicated on the dialectical negation of violence, as it is in the modern Hegelian-Marxist tradition, then the active
forgetting of *stasis* would be, in Giorgio Agamben's formulation, "a political
duty" (21). However, as also mentioned previously, there is clearly no positively amnesic political duty available to us in Mexico or elsewhere in Latin
America or, for that matter, in the world (though, as already indicated, the
Colombian peace process is certainly an attempt to stage, reinstate, and nor-
malize the forgetting of *stasis* via the logics of sovereign immunization, and
look how that's turning out). Contemporary paramilitary conflict renders the
threshold between peace, war, and civil conflict—or between peace, *polemos*, *stasis*, and *diastasis*—indistinguishable. It does so in such a way that the
*oikos* is increasingly scattered everywhere, thereby rendering the *polis*, or the
question of *dwelling*, increasingly nowhere to be seen, despite all claims to

nationalism, patriotism, "our America," etc.[39] For this reason, current para-military violence is in fact political *in appearance alone*. Perhaps it would be better to suggest that it is the nihilistic splitting force that, in its extensive and excessive socialization, destructures the historically given political conditions of the *polis* (Balibar). It is the exacerbated post-sovereign decontainment and simultaneous consummation of the historicity of the *polis*—a historicity of both colonial and postcolonial subjectivity—in progress.

In light of the intensification of post-katechontic uproar, the joint US-Mexican administration and intensification of militarized force is an utterly ineffective way of countering, or of bringing to a close, the nihilistic realities of narco-accumulation (unless, of course, the reabsorption of violence into political reason is not actually its goal, despite all claims to the contrary). In light of this problem—that is, in light of the militarized deterritorialization of Mexican sovereignty (*nomos*) since 1994—in 2014 the journalist Sergio González Rodríguez examined Mexico's technological absorption into the US military-security apparatus, as exemplified in the legal ratification in 2008 of the Mérida Initiative, or Plan México, which in the last decade alone has led to over $2.5 billion in military and security appropriations destined for the Mexican state.

In *Campo de Guerra* González Rodríguez strives to examine social turmoil at a time in which the Mexican state itself comes increasingly into focus as one of the prime perpetrators of the non-neutralization of narco-violence (Ayotzinapa being a fundamental chapter, of which there are surely many more, and even more to come).[40] González Rodríguez speculates that the *absorption* of Mexican sovereignty by the US military apparatus indicates that the extreme, unabsorbable violence of the last decade on Mexican soil is itself already being reconverted into new forms of political reason and securitized domination in the sphere of the economic and political elites of the North. This process of post-katechontic reconversion of Mexican sovereignty into the US military-security complex, states González Rodríguez, ultimately upholds the sovereign performance of the Leviathan but locates its restraining force exclusively in the United States' intelligence and military apparatus (the Drug Enforcement Agency, Federal Bureau of Investigation, Pentagon, Central Intelligence Agency, National Security Agency, Department of Homeland Security, etc.).

While it is still too premature to consider the military-technological absorption of Mexican sovereignty into the US military-security apparatus as a definitive, unquestionable historical process of katechontic realignment of hemispheric proportions, it is certainly the case that when we look beyond the US-Mexico border—toward the joint US-Mexico militarization and securitization of Mexico's *southern* border with Guatemala and Belize (as can be seen in the National Migration Institute's inauguration of Programa Frontera Sur [2014]) — we can glimpse the absorption of Mexican national territory into the living extension southward of the northern Mexico-US border architecture as a military and paramilitarized zone of containment, security, and self-defense beyond the boundaries of the US state proper, designed to extend the unique interests of the United States.[41] This southern geographical arrangement of homeland security establishes a military and paramilitary territory of fixed and mobile immigration checkpoints from Chiapas and Tabasco to Oaxaca, Veracruz, and beyond, via the installation of a security network characterized by formal and informal patterns of surveillance, espionage, intimidation, fear, harassment, racism, physical abuse, and extortion, as well as by new protocols for the illicit, increasingly sophisticated and cut-throat enterprise of drug and human trafficking from Central America to the southern states of the United States.

Programa Frontera Sur is in rhetorical terms a humanitarian program that nevertheless extends the security-intelligence agendas of the DEA and US immigration, customs, and border protection all the way down to the Mexico-Guatemala border (and even further into Honduras and El Salvador). In the process it transforms Mexican territory into the place of execution of US homeland security by essentially converting national territory into a buffer zone, a military architectural network for mass arrest and deportation.[42] What was previously sovereign national territory is reconverted into the ritualized performance, living geography, and paramilitary endgame of post-katechontic force, thereby realigning Mexico's military-economic relation to the North while also redefining and intensifying Mexican paramilitary force's relation of dominance over the impoverished political spaces of, and the migrant bodies that flee from the social violence in, the South. The national territory of Mexico becomes the new border, the tomb of the proper, the negation of space by space. If spatialization requires a line — such as a border or a wall, or both — and the line itself negates the indetermination that constitutes it, thereby constituting a territory, then the shifting of the conditions of the line thousands of kilometers southward, via "securitization" or "humanitarian" policies, uncovers the fact that the combination of postnational spatial extension and homeland security no longer negates the indetermination that constitutes space. Rather it circulates, institutes, economizes, and militarizes the utter indifference of the relation between the spatial and despatialization. It is for this reason that by definition President Trump's border wall serves no purpose beyond the affirmation of a fully racialized nationalism.

On the other hand, President Peña Nieto's (and now President López

Obrador's) Programa Frontera Sur inaugurates the pure *techne* of a new form of Mexican post-katechontic non-sovereignty, or active and willful sovereign abdication, which puts into doubt the very word "Mexican" itself while at the same time shining a cold spotlight on the (in)humanity of humans and on "the globalness of the world" (Nancy, "War, Right, Sovereignty — *Techne*," 138). With this, I wish to indicate that this recent "humanitarian" program highlights a fundamental double shift in the relation between the principle of sovereignty, post-territorial dominium, and the standing reserve. Upon becoming absorbed by US security agendas, Mexican sovereignty relinquishes authority yet, in the renunciation itself, increases its regional military and paramilitary strength over Central America under the banner of non-sovereignty (indicating therefore that this is not a war between sovereigns). To the extent that narco-accumulation has established the US-Mexican a-legal and post-sovereign market-state duopoly as a business venture of transnational proportions, the systemic antimigrant "humanitarianism" and violence that subtends Programa Frontera Sur can be understood as a long-term strategy designed to guarantee and sustain the market-state duopoly as a doubling with, as a shadowing, and as an obscuring of what used to be called the "official" (postrevolutionary PRI) Mexican state apparatus and its national territory.[43]

Obviously, Dawn Paley's idea of a "counter-revolution, a hundred years late" fails to account for the complex, long-term effects of these geoeconomic shifts in the technologies of war, sovereignty, and the everyday life of global capital. Guadalupe Correa-Cabrera comes closer but falls short before the question of civil war. Indeed, perhaps we could even say that there is no ideological certainty, political actuality, subject position, legal apparatus, or identitarian configuration that can account for, or counter, such shifts, all of which uncover the truth that paramilitary force — endemic turmoil in the epoch of the twilight of sovereignty — is a model of executive and finitive *techne* in process: It is "that x that turns anybody who is subjected to it into a thing. Exercised to the limit, it turns man into a thing in the most literal sense: it makes a corpse out of him," as Simone Weil defined the impersonal nature of force in 1940.[44]

The "durable disorder" (Galli, *Political Spaces and Global War*, 163) of post-katechontic paramilitary force allows for, extends, and guarantees conflict. It is an end, a technological non-sovereign finality in itself, which exceeds conceptual representation and experiential capture while at the same time inaugurating "the great suspension of the historicity by which we have been carried along" (Nancy, "War, Right, Sovereignty — *Techne*," 129). This great suspension of the modern historicity of the social bond and of the "natural" origin of the nation-state accomplishes the closure of the historically given metaphysics of containment (as seen in the historicity of the subject, the Nation, modern sovereignty, and the time of development). However, it is also the most reactionary exacerbation, intensification, and reinstantiation of the violent nihilism of that historicity. It is that historicity reconverted into the active fury of decontained *diastasis*: the very splitting across borders of *publicness* itself. There is no longer any constitutive outside available for sublimation and renewal, and the question of the enemy is now understood as humanity, or as the human as standing reserve, as general equivalence in the face of *techne*, or nothing at all. It is too late for the subject. Too late for hegemony.

If narco-accumulation is just one of the means by which to evoke the urgent need for a facticity of the closure of metaphysics, then once again this raises the question of how to proceed. What does this closure open out onto, if it is not to a constitutive, dialectical outside?

The *post-sovereign market-state duopoly*, *post-katechontic* state, *a-legal state*, *post-state* state, or *global civil war* in its regional/Mexican vein are all nomenclatures that are indicative of the modern nation-state form having succumbed already to the nothingness — the *nihil*, the nonfoundation — that underlies the law (*nomos*). Therefore, the paramilitary force of narco-accumulation installs and extends, socializes and economizes, indeed *is*, the nothing of the law's foundation fully exposed for all to see and to experience as a fully decontained and unmediated *killing* and *accumulation* industry. This *nihil* cannot be grasped, restrained, and administered into inexistence by a modern sovereign state form or by the contemporary market-state duopoly that displaces it, since the latter is no longer interested in the fabrication of functional sutures between state and population but in their perennial splitting, differentiation, and positing as subjects and objects. Hence the perpetual atomization and technologization of the public and of everything that comes with it, along with the extension and viciousness of the ontology of the subject and of the reason of the strongest that legitimizes and naturalizes it.

"Culture" can no longer compensate or provide meaning in the face of the general equivalence of so much humanity and so much inhumaneness. Having said that, since in contemporary Mexico turmoil keeps things economically and socially alive via war; impunity; the greasing of palms; necro-work; land theft; resource theft; criminalization; extortion; rape; trafficking of arms, drugs, and people; prostitution; ghettoization; mass migration; mass incarceration; deportability and deportation; etc., then like all forms of turmoil this one must also exist in light of "some invisible and spectral sur-vival" (Derrida, "Faith and Knowledge," 87). It must remain open to something "other and more than itself: the other, the future, death, freedom, the coming of love or of the other, the space and time of a spectralizing messianicity beyond any messianism" (79–80).

By this I wish to indicate that with the contemporary collapse of the Hegelian dialectical reconversion of force (anomie) into a political reason grounded in anything other than domination, or into a fully harnessed legislative power, and with war's reconversion into the daily economic life of extreme competition and excessive force that characterizes Mexican–Central American–US globalizations, then the advent of the other, the future, freedom, and the coming of love or dignity are extremely difficult, if not impossible, to contemplate or even to imagine at this time, at least from within the confines of the "actually" political.

Therefore, the question emerges as to whether, against all odds, narco-paramilitarization — this mark of the end of a particular understanding of history as dialectical progression, progress, and development, this epoch of the end of epochality itself (Schürmann)—can in fact be a prism through which the symptoms of technological and subjectivist rule can be reoriented toward what Jean-Luc Nancy has referred to as a still-unheard-of, inconceivable task for thinking.

Such a conjecture would no longer entail reconstructing or revitalizing, in the name of a specific "new" politics of the subject, the open space of publicness already left devastated by the market-state duopoly and the technics of its extreme subjectivism. It would entail, rather, bringing to light the hidden nonpolitical or infrapolitical undercurrent that has always been there and that remains in spite of the spatio-political devastation wreaked on modern political space by global war in its US–Mexican–Central American vein.

While it is true that coercion and subjectivist force found, protect, and expand political space, it is also true that political space is never fully saturated by or fully reducible to the actions of coercion and subjectivist force. It is in this subtle yet fundamental threshold at the heart of the permanently violent splitting that *is* the market-state duopoly and its nonpolitical extension of endemic conflict, or post-katechontic *diastasis*, that the infrapolitical can be seen to operate and to leave its indelible existential mark. It is finally toward this existential mark that we can now turn, as the final move in the passage toward the infrapolitical.

## The Migrant's Hand, or the Infrapolitical Turn to Existence

Time and mortality in the midst of death-giving — which is not, of course, the same as *perishing*— indicate a task for thinking that remains pending in the context of the deterritorializing movements of narco-accumulation, analogous social phenomena such as migration, and their cultural representations. It is for this reason that Diego Quemada Díez's film *La jaula de oro* (*The Golden Cage*, 2013) might be of singular interest.[45] I would conjecture that this film is alone in its presentation and exploration of the uncovering of meaning and understanding in the sociohistorical context of contemporary Central American migration from beyond the Suchiate River on the Guatemala-Mexico border, northward through the territories of Plan Frontera Sur, through Tapachula and up the coast to the notorious La Arrocera, Arriaga, through Oaxaca up to the US-Mexico military border complex and ultimately into *el otro lado*.

It is clear that *The Golden Cage* follows the faux-documentary conventions of the contemporary "migration movie," as the camera follows its characters along the migrant trail and registers the brutal civil turmoil that accompanies and sustains it:

> It is the story of three youngsters—Juan, Sara, and Chauk—who accompany one another atop the Beast. The viewer in turn follows them for a period of roughly a month, acquiring an idea of the variety of dangers, harassment, and attacks that a migrant is subjected to on their way to the United States. Apart from the risk of falling onto the tracks or of succumbing to the climate, hunger, or thirst, *The Golden Cage* presents encounters with predators lying in wait for the train: migration police officers with the ethics of an assailant, civilians who intercept the train with the complicity of the engine driver, gangs interested only in grabbing women, kidnappers who extort money from the migrants' contacts in the United States, and, on the northern border, the legendary Minute Men: civilian snipers who save the Migra the work of deportation. (Solórzano, "La jaula de oro")[46]

There is, of course, more to it than that. The film opens with a double gesture toward a certain difference that resides at the heart of publicness: The self-appointed leader of the adolescent group, Juan, leaves his home and strides forcefully out into a militarized and impoverished public sphere in which the local garbage dump is the only source of employment. Behind the closed door of a public bathroom, Sara conceals her gender in order to become "Osvaldo," presumably in an attempt to avoid rape and sexual exploitation on what will become the migrant trail. Sara opens the bathroom door and steps out as a young male, and the relation between publicness and the demand for concealment in the name of masculinity immediately begins to take shape. Along with Samuel, with whom Juan meets up at the garbage dump, the gathering of three begins its journey. We know nothing of their past or circumstances other than the poverty they come from, which determines them entirely, and from here they launch themselves into a present that can only be the vanishing point of all things past. Presumably, their collective mind is made up *to split*, though their *splitting* can only ever raise the question of, rather than solve or define, any freedom of choice. In the wake of such an irresolvable dilemma they merely throw themselves out and forward, devoid of dwelling and history, but certainly as a provisional gathering, a mobile form of coexistence of sorts.

Upon crossing the Suchiate River into Chiapas the group encounters Chauk, a young indigenous tsotsil speaker who attaches himself to the group and tags along. Chauk has no past and speaks no Spanish, and the film offers no translation of his tsotsil. Juan, the pale-skinned racist, despises Chauk hovering on the edges of the group, and against Sara and Samuel's wishes is insistent on actively excluding him from their community. The mestiza Sara is more hospitable to Chauk, tries to understand him, and treats him as an equal, thereby initiating a belligerent rivalry between the two young males for Sara's attention and desire. In the end, it is only when Sara/Osvaldo threatens to go alone without them that their physical duel dissipates. After being deported back to Guatemala from Chiapas, Samuel decides to remain in Guatemala; Sara, Chauk, and Juan return to the migrant trail, hitching a ride atop the Beast. The train, however, is accosted by a criminal gang looking to kidnap migrant women, presumably for sexual exploitation. "Osvaldo" is outed as Sara and is swiftly kidnapped, never to be seen again except by Chauk, just for a split-second in spectral form in a migrant hostel further up the trail in Arriaga, on the border between Chiapas and Oaxaca. Chauk helps Juan convalesce from his injuries suffered at the hands of the (most likely Zeta-affiliated) criminal gang, and Juan later reciprocates Chauk's selflessness by saving him from the clutches of a kidnapping and ransom operation led by a Guatemalan from "Zona 3."

Sara has become the absent source of their newfound sense of duty to each other, and the two young men begin to bond as equals and continue the journey north in her absence, finally entering the United States after helping smuggle sacks of marijuana through the US-Mexico military border complex. As they walk cross-country northward into the United States, however, the indigenous Chauk is immediately picked off by a sniper in a minor reenactment of an entire history of indigenous extermination. Now a solitary and silent figure, Juan continues alone into the United States and finally finds employment not in a garbage dump but in a meatpacking plant, cleaning up the animal debris from the factory floor.

It is clear from this account that, on one level at least, Quemada Díez's film obeys the basic form and causalities of the Hollywoodian *"central conflict,"* or "industrial narrative paradigm." As such, it actively rejects the inhabitual from within the cinematic image itself. In his work on the Chilean-French filmmaker Raúl Ruiz, Willy Thayer defines *"central conflict* theory" and the "industrial narrative paradigm" in the following terms:

> The theory of central conflict is a system of ideas that subsumes every other idea, circumlocution, digression, or virtuality capable of delaying, displacing, relativizing, withdrawing, or interrupting narrative coherence to its diegetic unity of action and causality. Beneath its agglutinating axis, digressions, hyperbolic sequences, and special effects can be included and will form part of the plot only to the extent that they can be integrated without detours into the fluidity and necessary concatenation, adding cohesion and tension to the narrative movement of the storyline, its unity, its tension, subtensions, and governed *pathos.* . . . The "industrial narrative" paradigm is constituted as a pluridialectical governance of the image and of life, a versatile plasticity of containment that spreads throughout the bends and folds of immanence like a more or less open system of judgments and prejudices of a taste for the *ready-made* or for the *ready to wear.* (Thayer, "Raúl Ruiz," 21–23)

The industrial narrative paradigm offers a *positive anthropology* in image form. Tiqqun refers to the molding of a positive anthropology as the creation of an "amniotic environment" (*Introduction to Civil War*, 11), characterized by "an irenic, slightly vacuous and gently pious conception of human nature" in which "the *struggle for life* plays a reassuring role, for it still offers some practicable convictions concerning the essence of man" (12). With this in mind, it is not just that *The Golden Cage* is a sociological re-presentation, via the use of nonprofessional actors and actual migrants, of the trials and tribulations of the migrant experience, or of "the sad product of the time of multitudes" (227) already documented extensively by Oscar Martínez in *The Beast: Riding the Rails and Dodging Narcos on the Migrant Trail* (2014). It is that, like the genre of the migration film in general, *The Golden Cage* is profoundly Aristotelian in its unifying structuration of easily memorable actions, events, and names, in which the image itself governs the unalterable ordering of what is necessary and plausible (Thayer, "Raúl Ruiz," 27). As in Aristotle's *Poetics*, in *The Golden Cage* "narrative *diegesis* precedes and governs the production of the image in such a way that before, during, and after being produced it is, above all else, a narration, a *diegesis* subordinated to a 'saying' (*logos*). The image always says something, narrates something, is the image of something" (Thayer, "Raúl Ruiz," 28). For this reason alone, *The Golden Cage*'s "documentary realism" is conformist and generic, for the image is, on the whole, only ever allowed to err on the side of what can be calculated as recognizable, knowable, and possible. The lives of its protagonists are plausible, representable, and therefore immediately understandable within the everyday context of precarity and bare life.

But there is more to it than this, for in the film there is also an insistence on the return to and repetition of certain images that do not frame or mold the gathering of events, actions, characters, or causalities in space or time. Rather, they produce a non-narrative *diegesis*, a distance from *diegesis* in which what takes place is the momentary pause and withdrawal from — the abandonment or letting go of — the frame, space, time, and movement of the industrial narrative paradigm. In these fleeting moments, the film's central narrative paradigm is momentarily displaced in favor of something — an impossible experience, or the experience of the impossible — that, while at all times internal to the overall *diegesis*, withdraws from the unity of the film's central action, which gathers inevitably around the characters' collective and individual life trajectories.

The consequences of these fleeting moments are, nevertheless, significant, since in distinction to the central conflict or industrial narrative paradigm that gives the film its dominant structure and storytelling form, there is therein "something that shows itself as something that shows itself," giving "no directive to a definite domain of subject matter" (Heidegger, *Ontology*, 53). These moments withdraw from the order of representation and of subjectivity forged by the central storytelling. In other words, in these images something comes to presence in a self-giving that is free of covering-up, thereby allowing a certain clearing to be discerned. Hence there is something in the storytelling of the "golden cage" that strives to circumnavigate the contours of its own industrial storytelling paradigm, proposing an opening out onto an *other* attunement to perceiving and questioning, a differential grasp in relation to *world*, rather than merely in relation to the calculations of means and ends that remain internal to the ontological domination of the commodity form, its humanist conventions, and its tales of the dignity, suffering, and victimization of the contemporary migrant standing reserve.

This second order of imagery — this accumulation of essentially posthegemonic, infrapolitical instantiations of the image in *The Golden Cage* — is conformed around the question of what is immediately at hand but also around questions of time, mortality, and therefore of a certain gesture in the direction of meaningfulness and the limits of sense-making (that is, of facticity). The film, then, is certainly about the collective experience of the migrant trail. However, it also raises the question of the preparation of the path that remains to be traveled in relation to the possibility of a turn in the ontology of the commodity form and of globalization as the continual positing of humanity as means alone, rather than as an end unto itself.

In his summer 1923 lectures *Ontology—The Hermeneutics of Facticity*, Martin Heidegger asks: "What does 'world' as the 'wherein' of being mean?" (65). He responds that "the world is something being encountered" and then asks: "As what and how is it being encountered?" (65). Heidegger observes that *world* as the wherein of being is encountered in attunement and care for the meaningfulness, the sense-making, the facticity of the *wherefrom, the out of which* that thinking uncovers in its coming to presence:

> What we are concerned about and attend to shows itself as that *wherefrom, out of which*, and *on the basis of which* factical life is lived. Explicated in such a manner, this wherefrom, out-of-which, and on-the-basis-of-which will provide the phenomenological basis for understanding being "*in*" a world, i.e., for a primordial interpretation of the phenomenon of factical spatiality turning up there and the phenomenon of being "*in*" it. The how of this being-"*in*" ["*in*"-*Sein*] as a living *from out* of the world as what is being encountered in concern shows itself as *caring*. (65–66)

Heidegger continues this early reflection on *caring, facticity*, and *world*, observing that *world* is encountered in what we attend to in the everydayness of the "environing world." This attentiveness to the everydayness of the environing world clears a "factical spatiality," as the "wherefrom" or "out-of-which" of perception and meaningfulness itself, "out of which and on the basis of which the space of nature and geometrical space originally arise by means of a certain shift in our way of looking" (66). What is at stake for Heidegger, in other words, is how to look at and care for everydayness in its originarity, that is, at a distance from the technical calculations of geometrical, technological, or given sovereign spacing. Care is exercised in thinking in regard not just to the beings living in *world* but to Being itself as the clearing of a factical spatiality, as the uncovering of the anticipation and meaningfulness of death that makes existence possible in the first place.

For this reason, "what is first needed," states Heidegger, "is a straightforward presentation of *what* the world is encountered *as*" (66). This is a question that is close to the heart of Diego Quemada Díez's attunement to the infrapolitical image in *The Golden Cage*, which both establishes and withdraws from positive anthropology in such a way as to suggest care for a possible clearing of factical spatiality, as the framing of what the world is encountered *as*, and of how the being of beings comes to presence in relation to the meaningfulness of being-toward-death.

In *The Golden Cage* there are three imagistic registers to be emphasized (beyond the positively anthropological "storyline"). These three registers function in relation to what Heidegger calls the "straightforward presentation of *what* the world is encountered *as*."

True to the insight that "the hand cannot be spoken about without speaking of technics" (Derrida, "Geschlecht II," 169), the first register is most evident in its reiterated portrayal of the migrant body, and of the male hand in particular, as the marking of a mode of presence, of a specific "there," in relation to its encounter with the environs of the migrant trail. These fleeting frames, which traverse the entire film, emphasize touch, grasping, and the dominant technicity of the world at hand. In these brief encounters with a world commandeered by equipment (*techne*), migrant manual labor — that is, the already instrumentalized positing of the human as subject and object of poverty and labor — bears silent witness to the limits imposed upon it in the journey forward and in its attempted abandonment of the past, traversing the technological geographies of anomie and lawlessness (Figures 1–9).

Life on the migrant trail in these images is predetermined by the nonfreedom generated from within geometrical (sovereign) social space, or *extensio*, and by the migrants' absolutely necessary movement across and through those imposed limitations. In this register, the positive anthropology of the industrial narrative paradigm — the "grand, one-dimensional game of identities and differences" (Tiqqun, *Introduction to Civil War*, 127) — begins to expose the idea and reality of community to existential solitude (to the fact that "no one can take the Other's dying away from him," as Heidegger put it in *Being and Time*) and therefore to the constitutive limit of significance of the common

Figure 1. Equipment: Chauk lays a hand on an abandoned train carriage.

Figure 2. Equipment: Juan grasps the Beast.

Figure 3. Equipment: Measuring the passage through "La Frontera Sur."

Figure 4. Equipment: The Beast beyond.

Figure 5. Equipment: Border Wall.

Figure 6. Equipment: Subterranean Passage.

Figure 7. Equipment: Production in the wake of friendship.

Figure 8. Equipment: Production, Nationalism, and Solitude.

Figure 9. Equipment: Indistinction between Labor, Human, Meat, and Death.

itself. For this reason, this order of the image emphasizes the fact that in a world saturated by the ontology of the commodity form, "world" is concealed in and dominated by the principle of production, of *techne*, and as such by what Jean-Luc Nancy calls the *un-world* of globalization (*The Creation of the World or Globalization*). The migrant trail is a journey traversing the differential conditions of the standing reserve from subordination to subordination, from will to power to will to power, across the hemispheric geographies of *diastasis* and the given order of nihilist reproduction. But there is no freedom or difference to be found there. This register of the image in *The Golden Cage* is fully consummated in the meatpacking factory at the end of the film, in which the hands of mainly, though by no means exclusively, male migrant laborers are rendered part-objects, now supplemented and guided by the prosthetic equipment of industrialized labor, that is, by the handiwork and handling of death in technical form via the hooks, knives, and meat cleavers that calculatingly split animal meat for mass human consumption and on behalf of the utilitarian taste for profit. Human being herein, in this ontic gesture in the direction of hands following the technical requirement of their prostheses, splits, cuts, separates.[47]

The second register in *The Golden Cage*'s "straightforward presentation of *what* the world is encountered *as*" signals the reiterated portrayal of a natural spacing in the migrant's movement through geometrical sovereign space. This second spacing — which, in an echo of Juan Rulfo's *Pedro Páramo* or of the wisdom of the ancient Greek seer Tiresias, offers empty skies traversed by birds of ill omen — stands in a direct symbolic relation to the accumulation of past and future deaths. It therefore offers an allegorical support for the industrial narrative paradigm and, as such, folds nature into the order of representational means to an end, echoing the very symbolization and representation of disappearance and death by means of which living beings are portrayed as objects. What is most significant in the portrayal of its everydayness is that this imagistic register emphasizes the fleeting, ungraspable character of death that it points toward in reference to both past and future (Figures 10–14).

The third register is the most significant, for herein the film points to an incommensurable distance from the technical calculations of geometrical, or social, space that are designed for exclusion and exploitation. This register uncovers the anticipation and meaningfulness — the forehaving — of death that makes the facticity of existence possible in the first place. This third — infrapolitical — register in the film's attunement to the "straightforward presentation of *what* the world is encountered *as*" emphasizes the *signifier*, and therefore language itself, as the uncanny, anxiety-laden place-holder of Being, understanding the latter as "Being toward death, that is, the visiting card by which a

Figure 10. Death as Point of Departure.

Figure 11. In the wake of Sara.

Figure 12. Chauk and Juan elude, and move in the direction of, death.

Figure 13. Border Wall. Death Foretold.

Figure 14. US Border Patrol.

signifier represents a subject for another signifier. . . . This visiting card never arrives at the right destination, the reason being that for it to bear the address of death, the card has to be torn up" (Lacan, *The Other Side of Psychoanalysis*, 180). Obviously, there is nothing new here. But its significance in *The Golden Cage* lies in the fact that it opens the presentation of *what* the world is encountered *as* to the question of the "*how* of being of beings" (Heidegger, "On the Essence of Ground," 112).

Ultimately, what is at stake in this register is a differential grasp on — indeed, the unveiling of an ungraspable grasp in relation to — the signifier *world* itself. And it is the tsotsil signifier *teiv* that offers the key to a certain ungraspability, of a belonging without belonging, or of a letting go of belonging that comes to the fore in the film. *Teiv* is the axis of a single signifier around which meaningfulness itself appears to turn in the film. In an exclusively Spanish-speaking film, the monolingual tsotsil-speaking Chauk, who remains without translation into Spanish throughout, unveils a particular stance or standing in reference to what the world is encountered *as*.[48] Here the relation between Sara and Chauk, and in particular the relation between concealment and un-concealment that they convey, comes to the fore. We have already highlighted the gender concealment that Sara is forced to undergo on the migrant trail as a tactic of survival that, in the end, fails her. Her self-concealment is an attempt to veil the technicity of social value that is immediately, thoughtlessly, assigned to her body as a woman, object, and sexual commodity. In the end it is the sexualized ontology of the commodity form itself — and, of course, its male enforcers — that unveil her value as an object and immediately drag her away against her will.

In a slightly different play of concealment and unconcealment, the first

Figure 15. Teiv.

time we encounter the tsotsil signifier *teiv* is in Chiapas, when Juan, Sara, and Samuel gather together in order to choose backdrops for the photographic images they want to have taken of them as souvenirs of their coming journey northward. They are, at this point, at origin, already looking forward to Mnemosyne, and, as such, immediately anticipating the past. From outside the close gathering of the three Guatemalan friends, and concealed behind Sara/Osvaldo's body, Chauk's hand stretches out and points to one of the photographic images as he announces for the first time the tsotsil signifier "teiv" (Figure 15).

Juan immediately elbows him out of the communal gathering. Just for a second, the tsotsil signifier has disrupted the fraternal order of Spanish-speaking Guatemalan migrants. In a foreshadowing of his assassination at the hands of a sniper in the US border region, Chauk chooses to be photographed before a wintry backdrop sporting a Native American headdress (Figure 16). When he sees the photographic image, Juan fails to comprehend the indigenous deterritorialization of what being-there might indicate in Chauk's attunement to and staging of the enigma of the uncanny three-way relationship (Mexico–United States–Guatemala), or *teiv*. Whereas Chauk gestures toward an imaginary amalgamation of collective indigenous histories that existed prior to the nationalisms that subordinated and exterminated them, Juan merely refers to the tsotsil speaker as a pinche indio and pushes him to the ground. Retroactively, the spectator encounters in teiv an unveiling of past genocide and the anticipation of death that makes the question of existence possible in the first place, both in the film and, indeed, in the history of the Americas.

However, it is only now that the viewer also realizes that this is not the first encounter the film has established with *teiv*. Retroactively, it first comes to the fore as snowflakes falling from the spaciousness of an empty black sky, in the

Figure 16. Teiv: Death Foretold.

Figure 17. Teiv.

formlessness of an ungraspable void, as Chauk sleeps on the Beast. But at this point it comes to light as a state of mind open to the groundlessness — to the ex nihilo — of world and of world as the incommensurable withdrawal into the *ex-scription* of home, subjectivity, dwelling, abode, origin, nation, identity, etc. (Figure 17).[49]

The image offers the trace of a clearing toward world as simply that which is inexplicably unconcealed, as that which unconceals itself apparently for no particular reason as a quasi-transcendence (merely as a wherefrom of falling snowflakes). This image of the spaciousness of an empty black sky — perhaps of absolute distance, proximity, or difference, or of a state of mind — punctuates the film throughout but becomes particularly significant in its final sequences. As such, teiv does not conform to "all those significations of 'future,' 'past,' and 'Present' which thrust themselves upon us from the ordinary conception of time" (Heidegger, *Being and Time*, 374). It does something else; it takes on the status of the trace of a parergonal existentiality that signals an overall environment of facticity.

Within the film's dominant storyline, however, the second time we encounter the signifier *teiv*, it assumes a different disposition. This is an interaction between Osvaldo/Sara and Chauk, in which they teach each other Spanish and tsotsil vocabulary about nature and the body. "Osvaldo" finally reveals his true self to be in fact Sara, and Chauk immediately raises both hands upward and slowly lowers them, moving his fingers as they fall, in a gesture that appears to indicate a mysterious spatiality beyond translation. He accompanies this gesture with the word "teiv." But Sara merely says, "I don't know. I don't understand" (Figure 18).

Herein signifier and hand appear to provide a bearing upon understanding, as rooted in a certain thinking. But something here remains beyond representation, and Sara cannot grasp the significance of the deterritorializing tsotsil signifier spoken and gestured in the wake of the unconcealment of her name and gender, a mysterious physical gesture that, retroactively, stands in stark contrast to the men's grasping hands that will force Sara's disappearance into brutal sexual commodification and almost inevitable rape and death, in a world in which there is absolutely no room for sexual difference, only for subordination. It is also a gesture that retroactively lies in stark contrast to the industrial "handling" of dead animal tissue that generates the profits for the US meatpacking plant in the film's final scenes. If the hand is a tool of tools, as Aristotle put it, in this gesture its instrumentality is momentarily suspended in the name of something that remains beyond comprehension, that is, quite literally, beyond, or other than, "grasp."

It is only after Sara's kidnapping and disappearance that we experience

Figure 18. Teiv: Un-concealment and Grasplessness.

the third encounter with the tsotsil signifier *teiv*. Chauk and Juan are on the border but have not yet crossed over into the United States. A miniature train set—the inversion of the experience of the Beast—comes into frame as artificial snow falls around the mountainous terrain in the represented world through which it passes (Figure 19).

Chauk and Juan's hands press on the store window, and the two adolescents are entranced by the childlike vision they have before them, a vision that is, nevertheless, a fully objectified nature, a completed metaphysics, the effect of a "world picture," a represented object-world whose technicity posits them, as observers, as its external objects. Before the miniaturized spectacle of an artificial nature and industry intertwined and represented—that is, of a fully enclosed techne—Chauk merely says "teiv." For the first time Juan gets it: "That means snow, right?" Chauk nods and smiles (Figure 20).

Understanding in Spanish is predicated on the subordination of the tsotsil

Figure 19. Techne: Object-World.

Figure 20. Techne: Subject-Object-World.

signifier to the technicity of representation and metaphor, on the passage from mere sound to sense-making. Without the Other of technicity and its signifier, and without the loss of the tsotsil voice in the translation, for Juan there can be no sense-making, no common sense, and no gathering across grammars. The film registers but does not dwell on the not-so-minor details of the history of Western metaphysics. Rather, it keeps moving beneath it.

It could be said that after this technological enframing and representation, there can be only death for Chauk and the solitude of alienated labor for Juan, which in this instance would merely assign *teiv* the value of an end to innocence. But this would require paying no heed to the relation between mortality and time that the film, via the signifier itself, has carried along within itself since the beginning. There is more to this than an end to innocence or to *teiv* as the signifier of Chauk and Juan's thwarted American Dream. *Teiv* is not the signifier of a completed and regurgitated metaphysics. Rather, it names the anticipation of death that points in the direction of the *how* of being of beings, as both the subject posited from the beginning as an object by *techne*, but also, and more significantly, as the ungraspable thrownness of being-toward-death, of what it means to dwell in proximity to death.

The film's final sequences are particularly significant in this regard since they take us from the manufactured dead objects and materials of labor — the noise and alienation that constitutes the industrialized production of the meatpacking factory, of its systemic cruelty, in a world dominated by *techne* — to the withdrawn, and withdrawing, spaciousness opened up in relation to the tsotsil signifier *teiv*. Herein lies the passage from the nihilism of materialism (the cruelty and solitude of the factory floor) to the ex nihilo of world. Whereas the meatpacking plant reduces the world to the reign of technology (to meat and the worker's body as common objects of death), *teiv* obliges an encounter with the unfathomability that unites sense-making and meaningfulness to an opening to the nothing that gives mortality.

After his shift at the meatpacking plant, Juan walks out of the darkness and snow and looks skyward (Figures 21–22). The frame cuts to the figure of an abandoned, homeless, and solitary Juan at a distance, with his back now turned to us. When we contrast this image with the force of the film's opening frames of Juan striding out into the public sphere, we see that a turn has quite literally been effected (Figure 23). At the film's commencement he is leaving behind everything that has come before in pursuit of a distant and unimaginable future. Now, the anxiety of the racist Juan has been transferred elsewhere — it has become deweaponized — and he is bereft of all *ready-to-wear* understandings of time itself. In stark contrast to the primacy of the future that, up to this point, has given a specific orientation to the forward trajectory

Figure 21. Teiv.

Figure 22. Teiv: Mnemosyne.

Figure 23. Teiv: A Turn.

Figure 24. Teiv: Care for World, in Memoriam.

of the film's central conflict and faithful adherence to the industrial narrative paradigm, now we begin to glimpse retroactively that the constitutive primacy of the future falls away before the average everydayness — an everydayness that is now brought to the light — of what has happened already and has come to pass as the "wherein" of a life lived in proximity to death. What comes to the light is merely that which has always been *there*, most proximally, yet concealed, that is, mortality in its concern for world.

The frame cuts again to align with the turn, which is *what* the world in the end is encountered *as* in *The Golden Cage*: the signifier *teiv* in its relation to world (Figure 24).

The encounter in this image is with an immeasurable spaciousness, which, in retrospect, has always been ahead of itself, beyond itself throughout the film, from the very beginning. This ahead of itself — this echo and figure of dissociation, unbinding (one could say diastasis), thrownness, dispersion, and therefore of migration — has always been the concern that only now is disclosed as such. Therein, the signifier — language itself — is the placeless, thrown placeholder of the meaningfulness and understanding (the very facticity) of having always dwelled in proximity to death.[50] Here precisely storytelling comes to an end, and care — the this-worldly horizon of nonmetaphor, or death — comes to light as an "ahead-of-itself-Being-already-in (the world) as Being-alongside entities which we encounter (within-the-world)" (Heidegger, *Being and Time*, 293).[51]

From within the cruel topographies of narco-accumulation and the global civil war that extends it, at the end of *The Golden Cage* we encounter *teiv* as exposure to the migrant environment of a worldhood in which "the nothing becomes present as being. The nothing is being itself" (Axelos, 2015, 89). At an unfathomable retreat from the modern political spaces of containment and of post-katechontic decontainment, both of which determine our access to the *un-world* (Nancy, *The Creation of the World or Globalization*), understood as the global domination of the calculation of means and ends, *The Golden Cage* ends in a (dis)encounter with environmentality — with the worldhood of world — as factic spaciousness and therefore as "the grasp of (and by) Being," which is a differential "grasp of no entity, of *nothing* that is" (Nancy, "The Decision of Existence," 91).[52]

In the end, the signifier *teiv* clears a path toward — it makes room for — the glimpse of a manifold area of concern and zone of caring in relation to *being-with* as the migrant estrangement of subjectity. It unconceals the possibility of understanding being "*in*" a world as a living *from out* of meaningfulness, as the *wherefrom* of world, as the appearance of mortality's shared environmentality, or spaciousness.[53] This indicates that the problematic of the modern legacy and inheritance of space, understood as *extensio*, or as "political space," is turned in such a way as to insinuate the potentiality of finitude (of mortality), and therefore of *Being* in general, as the effectuation of a potential turn away from the ontological domination of the calculations inherent in the commodity form and the market-state duopoly that generates its technical and technological domination.[54]

The factical understanding that *The Golden Cage* unveils, and which is where its primary concern dwells, is in the infrapolitical attunement to and *caring* for an ontological ground *other than* that of the narco-accumulation that perpetuates brutal, excessive force (the constant *splitting* that is global civil war), along with the subjectivist (sociological, anthropological, costumbrist) stories that accompany and reinstate its metaphoricity. It is profoundly intertwined with the everyday manifestations of narco-accumulation's brutality. But it is also hospitable to the possibility of a differential conceptual and existential grasp on *world*.

In factical understanding, it comes to light that the only basic infrapolitical necessity is freedom. But freedom here "is not what disposes of given possibilities. It is the disclosedness by which the groundless Being of existence exposes itself, in the anxiety and joy of being without ground, of being in the world" (Nancy, "The Decision of Existence," 109). Once again, against the primacy of the future (and therefore of the Hegelian tradition upon which modern "progress" and "development" is construed), *The Golden Cage* moves in the direction of that which is always already out of grasp and which can only be left to be *as such*, as promise. The actuality of the sociological and anthropological politics of both Right and Left can only aspire to conceal or contain this freedom in the biopolitical calculation of means and ends, in the name of the status quo of the Christian metaphysics of salvation and sacrifice, or in the humanist Promethean — that is, thetic — underpinnings of the Enlightenment tradition.

In contrast, if the epoch of the end of epochality is to be encountered factically, that is, in a relation to the hypothesis of meaningfulness, it can only be done so in the infrapolitical expression of a differential grasp on *world*. If, as Jean-Luc Nancy puts it, "There is nothing on the horizon except for an unheard-of, inconceivable task — or war" ("War, Right, Sovereignty — *Techne*," 41), then the infrapolitical register in thinking marks the possibility of a turn toward that unheard-of, inconceivable task. Against the forceful regional ontologies of global civil war and narco-accumulation, the infrapolitical is in this regard the sole opportunity for the elucidation of world-being in withdrawal from the histories of the modern katechon, and therefore from God, its imperial humanisms and spatial extensions, or the recurrent claims to the extension of a Global South that offers nothing more than another world picture, or *Weltanschauung*, oriented fully by subjectivity, the domination of its orders of representation (and therefore, once again, of world as object), together with the nihilism that rationalizes them.

While the katechon elucidated in Passage I is the Christian (imperial) metaphysics of the postponement of death transposed into the realm of the political, and while the postkatechon is its ongoing decontainment extended both at the level of the closure of metaphysics and at that of the concomitant collapse of the tradition of political modernity, *world* is the *ex nihilo* that is neither given nor posited in advance and that *ex-scribes* the diminished world of *techne*, representation, and subjectivity (Nancy, *The Creation of the World or Globalization*, 71). Always at a distance from the work of the philosophies of *the subject* — which are only ever attuned to the biopolitical principles and calculations of masterful decision making and its subordinations, and therefore also to the metaphysics of our excessive contemporary death-giving — the infrapolitical turn to existence is the a-principial care for the freedom and worldhood whose only *wherefrom, out of which,* and *on the basis of which* is the ownlessness that underlies *being-with* itself. Anything else is just the nihilism of the global battleground for the extraction of value and, as such, for individual or collective ownership over the anthropo-sociological stories it tells itself in the name of *separating words* (Badiou, *The Rebirth of History*, 77) such as humanism, culture, identity, representation, race, private property, subjectivity, *techne*, politics, and the biopolitical *forms of life* that "real politics" imposes and seeks to legislate and naturalize.

In contrast, *The Golden Cage* moves via its underlying subject matter toward the imagistic opening of an *other* (ecstatic) spaciousness endowed with the passage of the earth around the sun, with the cold and dark descending movement of the unhurried passing of time before dawn, and with the singularity and solitude of an existence that remains at a distance (in a relation of expropriation) from every gathering.[55]

If the katechon signals the inheritance of an imperial-national spatialization of a political and cultural imagination grounded in the perpetuation of empire, and if the post-katechontic marks the active decomposition of that modern legacy of political and cultural metaphoricity — its ongoing post-sovereign *perishing* — then what we glimpse in *The Golden Cage*'s final existential gesture, or potential clearing — its opening to the Open — unveils the fact that the somnambulist forms of everyday institutionalized humanism framed by the modern Cartesian-Hegelian metaphors of the "I think," self-consciousness, and subjectivity — all those metaphors of presence — do not and never will "set the *humanitas* of the human being high enough" (Heidegger, "Letter on Humanism," 251).

For this reason, it is only in the infrapolitical turn to existence, which in the case of *The Golden Cage* and, indeed, of this book emerges via the trace of the forcelessness and homelessness of the tsotsil signifier *teiv*, that *being-with* can be understood in the terms of an opening toward *being-toward-death*, in which the human "belongs to being and yet, amidst beings, remains a stranger" (Heidegger, "The Age of the World Picture," 72). It is here that an overall environment for questioning, for a potential infrapolitical inception in thinking in the wake of the humanist metaphysics of the subject, can be posited. This positing of ontological difference bestows in the relation between the signifier and the singular mourning the unhomeliness of the having-been (without shelter, property, ownership, *patria*, homeland, or longing), and it stirs our thinking in a direction other than that of the "industrial narrative paradigm" of biopolitical storytelling. Indeed, it does this in such a way as to move just a little closer toward an attunement to *being-with*, to what it means to be human — to be — in the absence of nationalism, and therefore of a "People."

In the end, future historicity, the trace of any possible dawn in the dark, might depend on such an infrapolitical stir within the relation between thinking and acting, that is, on a movement toward the silent vigilance that we encounter in Jean-Luc Nancy's identification of a hyphen lying between an "unheard-of, inconceivable task — or war." The latter installs the ontological ground and murderous madness of biopolitical subjectivism and, as such, of ongoing oblivion and perishing, while the former indicates attunement to the decision of existence, that is, to Being's knowledge before all else that it will die. Finally, within that silence or infraexcess withdrawn momentarily from representation, endowed by the unhomeliness of finitude and estrangement, and therefore also by the previously inapparent question of *relation as such*—what is it to be?

Perhaps in the face of post-katechontic, post-sovereign force and estrangement it is still not too late for the advent of the infrapolitical decision of existence. For the alternative is just more subjectivist biopolitics striving to naturalize and conceal what Percy Bysshe Shelley, in his 1816 poem "The Daemon of the World," deemed our murderous inheritance of "mitres, and crowns, and brazen/chariots stained/With blood, and scrolls of mystic wickedness,/The sanguine codes of venerable/crime." In the shadow of such an inhumane inheritance, what is it to be? The violent ontological determinations of incessant subjectivism or the infrapolitical clearing toward the decision of existence?

Sabarís, Val Miñor, September 2018–August 2019
Ann Arbor, September 2019–July 2020

# Notes

## Exordium: Extinction and Everyday Infrapolitics

1. This illustration of the intimate relation between infrapolitics and the everyday language of contemporary turmoil is offered in anticipation of this work's Introduction, in which I propose a more detailed and systematic assessment of the origins and critical deliberations lying at the heart of infrapolitical thinking from 2006 to the present. In his Seminar X, *Anxiety*, Jacques Lacan makes direct etymological reference to the question of turmoil: "*Emoi, turmoil*, is trouble, the fall of might. . . . *Turmoil* is trouble, *to become troubled* as such, to be as deeply troubled as one can be in the dimension of movement" (13–14). In response, A. R. Price, the translator to English of *L'angoisse*, observes in a note that the English word "turmoil" is of uncertain origin, although one etymological hypothesis suggests that it contains the words "turn" and "moil" (or drudgery) (n4, 340). Herein lie the basic question and challenge for thinking registered in the title of this work: *Infrapolitical Passage* as the troubling dimension of movement internal to contemporary endemic force, and *turmoil* as the grinding slog of contemporary experience.

2. "*Parrhesia*, the act of truth, requires . . . a challenge to the bond between the two interlocutors . . . it involves some form of courage, the minimal form of which consists in the parrhesiast taking the risk of breaking and ending the relationship to the other person which was precisely what made his discourse possible. . . . This is very clear in *parrhesia* as spiritual guidance, for example, which can only exist if there is friendship, and where the employment of truth . . . is precisely in danger of bringing to question and breaking the relationship of friendship which made this discourse of truth possible" (Foucault, *The Courage of Truth*, 11–12).

3. Indeed, it can be said that the Chilean uprising and enduring resistance of 2019 is precisely this: a massive and sustained uprising, beyond the calculations of the neoliberal political order, against the translation of every aspect of daily life into

the social codes of commodification. The Right responds with crude, naked force and the neofascist rhetoric of war, the Left with the hope of a juridical redistribution of force in the name of a new constitution. But the uprising itself is directed against everything that undermines the right to a life worthy of being lived. In order to speak of such a revolt as "infrapolitical," however, one would first have to elucidate the distinction between life, presence, survival, and existence as being-toward-death, that is, as finitude. If the specifically existential were not elucidated, the signifier "infrapolitics" would reflect the mere instrumentalization of a sociology of revolt. Rather than another Hegelianism, however, the infrapolitical signals that for which the dialectic cannot account. It moves in a direction other than that of Spirit.

4. Of particular note in this regard are Derrida (1989); Derrida, Gadamer, and Lacoue-Labarthe (*Heidegger, Philosophy, and Politics*); Lacoue-Labarthe (*Heidegger, Art, and Politics*); and Fried ("A Letter to Emmanuel Faye"). Fried observes that "the issue is not preserving Heidegger's reputation — he was a sorry specimen as a person, no doubt; the issue is how Nazism was part of *our* history, as a Western 'civilization,' and how it *remains* a threat, wearing many masks, both familiar and unfamiliar, in our world today. Its potential is still part of who we are, and we are fools if we refuse to confront the fact that fascism grows from within our most venerated traditions, not from some alien infection . . . what Heidegger represents, beyond his own character and person, is the inevitability of the confrontation with our planetary politics. Not he but his questions are unavoidable, alas. I return to the conviction that we must confront this kind of argument, even if its source is deplorable, because it arises from a crisis that is inherent to the human condition today" (244–46).

5. Here Derrida is highlighting a fundamental question of translation, and therefore a problem of representation and orderability, in the distinction between the English term *globalization* and the French *mondialisation*. The first reflects the extension of the subjectivist power of instrumentalism, calculation, and concealment (globalization, that is, as the oblivion of world via representation). The second echoes the possible inoperativity of the first via the unconcealment — the coming to presence — of *world*. This question of translation and inoperativity between globalization and the question of *world* has been taken up more consistently by Jean-Luc Nancy in *The Creation of the World or Globalization* (2007). It is also a tension that underlies this work throughout.

## Introduction

1. Badiou expresses particular interest in defending his thinking against detractors (Antonio Negri in particular) who allege he is a non-Marxist communist. In response, Badiou's diagnosis of the contemporary takes the form of a Marxist interpretation of globalization (see *The Rebirth of History*, 9–10, also 13). It is here, however, that Badiou also defines Marxism as a doctrine of militant action, calling it "the organized knowledge of the political means required to undo existing society and finally realize an egalitarian, rational figure of collective organization for which

the name is 'communism'" (8–9). If this is, in fact, the case, then there is an abyss between Marxism, understood as a doctrine of the subject, and the ontological premise of the first volume of Marx's *Capital*. The true subject of *Capital*, says Felipe Martínez Marzoa (*La filosofía de El Capital*, 132), is modern Western *techne*, with *value* as the ground through which Marx approaches the complexity of the question of what *being* means in the epoch of the commodity. However, not only does this fundamental point appear to be of no concern to Badiou, but his thinking appears to be always already subsumed under the exigencies of *techne* as the simultaneous positing of the subject-object relation in the necessary *manufacturing* of a new history. In Badiou's *The Rebirth of History*, as elsewhere, the ontological ground of commodity fetishism itself remains intact. "Communism," in this light, refers only to the willing of the will to power of the militant subject.

2. Immediate riot is "blindly progressive or blindly reactionary" on the grounds that "things as they are must be regarded as unacceptable" (*The Rebirth of History*, 21). "Latent riot" uncovers "a latent riot subjectivity" that "attests to the fact that circumstances can extract from our apathy an unforeseeable life beyond our lethal 'democracies'" (31–32). "Historical riot" is the result of "the transformation of an immediate riot, more nihilistic than political, into a pre-political riot" (33). Here Badiou is reapplying to the uprisings of 2011 his formulation of the underlying movement of the event and the communist hypothesis.

3. "In a world structured by exploitation and oppression masses of people have, strictly speaking, no existence. They count for nothing. In today's world nearly all Africans, for example, count for nothing. . . . This is exactly what people in the popular rallies in Egypt were saying and are still saying: we used not to exist, but now we exist. . . . This rising is the rising of existence itself. . . . What has occurred is restitution of the existence of the inexistent . . . it is what people are saying in the here and now" (*The Rebirth of History*, 56–57). It should be noted that existence here is coterminous with the plenitude of the subject in its self-saying, in the here and now, and with its supposedly full sociological presence via subjectivation.

4. Here we can say that Badiou thinks transcendence as *overcoming* and therefore as the underlying ground of speculative dialectics. What does "overcoming" mean? We can turn here to Martin Heidegger: "To overcome signifies: to bring something under oneself, and at the same time to put what is thus placed under oneself behind one as something that will henceforth have no determining power. Even if overcoming does not aim at sheer removal, it remains an attack against something" (*Nietzsche*, 4:223). What remains unthought throughout Badiou, however, is the reign of the *oneself*. It is this forgetting—which uncovers a certain constitutive acquiescence before the legacies of both Descartes and Hegel—that places value on overcoming while elevating subjectivity to the highest and ultimate principle. In this regard, also see Villalobos-Ruminott: "'Overcoming' itself reinstalls the constitutive mechanism of nihilism articulated by the figures of affirmation, expiration, victory and value" ("El poema," 118).

5. Again, we can turn to Martin Heidegger to shed further light on the point

made here by Lacan: "Since Descartes, reason has been conceived as *cogitatio*. Reason is the faculty of 'principles,' a faculty that represents in advance what defines everything representable in its representedness, to wit, the Being of beings. Reason would then be the faculty of the differentiation of Being and beings. And, because reason characterizes the essence of man, while according to modern thought man is the subject, the differentiation of Being and beings as well as the faculty for the differentiation is revealed as a property and perhaps the basic constituent of subjectivity. For the essence of that particular *subiectum* which is distinguished at the beginning of modern metaphysics is representation itself in its full essence: 'reason' (*ratio*) is merely another name for *cogitatio*" (*Nietzsche*, 4:186).

6. See Lacan, *Anxiety*, 334. In this light, also see Moreiras ("A Conversation," 151–53), in which he proposes *savage moralism*—a "savage step back with regards to the ethico-political relation" (152)—as a differential thinking after the crumbling of Ideality. In reference to Heidegger's "Letter on Humanism," Moreiras observes that "for metaphysical humanism, which is the master ideology that lives through us, the subjectivity of the subject is the only horizon for thought and action. Thus, ethics has to be understood necessarily as a rule of subjectivity or a field of subjective expression" (151). However, he continues, "Ethics, in our time, and without entering into what it might have been in other epochs, is either farce, pretense and deceit (in so far as it is based on by now untenable faiths) or it is just pragmatic opportunism (a series of rules that it is convenient to follow in order to get along with friends, at work, or in the street)" (153).

7. Also see Jorge Alemán: "Marx's great work can be understood, along with its truth regarding the law that structures the modern economy, as a discourse that did not lead to a politics constructed from upon the very premises of his critique. . . . So-called historical and dialectical materialism could not rise to the challenge of what he himself unraveled; it was pre-Marxist in relation to *Capital*" (*En la frontera*, 59).

8. See Derrida, *Specters of Marx*, 70–79.

9. See Moreiras, "Línea de sombra: Hacia la infrapolítica," 191–238. For an evaluation of the subalternist turn in thinking in the Latin American cultural studies paradigm of the 1990s, see Williams, "The Subalternist Turn."

10. Jorge Álvarez Yáguez informs us that "the term 'infrapolitics' is not new and has been utilized systematically on other occasions by the American anthropologist James C. Scott, in reference to a variety of gestures, conducts and practices of dissimulation designed to resist institutional domination and the means of repression of any given order" ("Crisis," 22–24). In this anthropological case, which references Scott's *Domination and Arts of Resistance* (1990), the infrapolitical refers to the quality of specific actions that weaken power (23). In the usage of the term under discussion here, however, infrapolitics refers to the necessity of a renewal of thinking from within, rather than against or in spite of, the closure of metaphysics and the total subsumption wrought by global capitalist technicity. In this regard, also see Cerrato: "Nietzsche leads philosophy to its end, earns the final closure of philosophy as metaphysical thinking, but does not achieve the transition to another beginning.

The conquest of the transition, the displacement of the thinking into the passage to another beginning, is the privilege of a deconstructive an-archic thought that dwells in the metaphysical closure" ("Infrapolitics," 83).

11. These are questions that Hardt and Negri's second volume, *Multitude* (2004), essentially fell short of remedying or reorienting. For biopolitics, see Foucault, *"Society Must Be Defended,"* and *The Birth of Biopolitics.*

12. As such, what Moreiras presents is essentially "a passage, to be sure, and thus by definition a transitory moment, but whose transition comes, if one can say that, from the future. It has its provenance in what, by essence, has not yet come-from [*provenu*], still less come about, and which therefore remains to come. The passage of this time of the present comes from the future to go toward the past, toward the going of the gone" (Derrida, *Specters*, 28). The name of the to-come is the infrapolitical.

13. "Fulfilled nihilism definitively shuts itself off from the possibility of ever being able to think and to know the essence of nihilism" (Heidegger, *Nietzsche*, 4:203). The essence of nihilism is the *nihil*, the unthought, the nothing itself, which is avoided at all cost in fulfilled nihilism.

14. For anecdotal accounts of the different forms of discussion that have been oriented toward infrapolitics in recent years, see Moreiras, "Project," 10). Also see his "Infrapolítica y política," 54; Cerrato, "Infrapolitics and Shibumi,", 105n11; and Villalobos-Ruminott, "El poema," 121n4. In particular, see the work and archive of the Infrapolitical Deconstruction Collective (https://infrapolitica.com/about/).

15. Also see Rodríguez-Matos, "Nihilism," 36–51.

16. For the first paradigm, see Rodríguez-Matos, *Writing of the Formless*, 100–4; for the second, see 104–11.

17. Similar questions are addressed in *Passage I* of this work. In this regard also see Williams, "Los límites de la hegemonía."

18. It is precisely for this reason that infrapolitical reflection has been described as a "sustained attempt at working out the sub-ceding passage from politics into a region of existence [that] politics occludes" (Moreiras, "Project," 16). It carries this out in the name of "an alternative conception of the political. . . . Infrapolitical reflection abandons power as principial force . . . for the sake of an an-archy whose foundations can be traced back to Heidegger" (16–18). In Kant and, as such, in the modern period in general, consciousness is elevated to the point of the ultimate *arché* of both subject and experience itself. However, as Reiner Schürmann shows in *Broken Hegemonies*, we are now situated not in the age of the experience of consciousness but in the civilizational expiration of each and every *arché*. This is the epoch of the closure of metaphysics. In this regard also see Álvarez Yágüez, "Crisis epocal," 9–28.

19. "Left-Heideggerianism is meant to designate those thinkers for whom the work of Heidegger is a fundamental point of departure, but who ultimately assume that in Heidegger there is no answer to the question: 'What is to be done?'" (Rodríguez-Matos, *Writing of the Formless*, 108).

20. Hence this work has begun in its Exordium with the language of exodus that lies at the heart of Extinction Rebellion.

21. In this regard also see Moreiras, "Infrapolítica y política de la infrapolítica," 53–72, in which he observes that "infrapolitics inhabits the difference from the political" (56). The problem of *distance* therefore lies at the heart of infrapolitics. In a recent discussion of Felipe Martínez Marzoa, Heidegger, and *Antigone* (*Manual de infrapolítica*, unpublished manuscript), Moreiras nods in the direction of the passage from subaltern studies to infrapolitics over the last twenty years. In 1988 Gayatri Spivak had defined the subaltern not as a subject but as "the absolute limit of the place where history is narrativized into logic" ("Subaltern Studies," 16). This definition was in fact central to my own approach to subalternity in *The Other Side of the Popular* (2002). In 2019 Moreiras defines the infrapolitical distance from the political in the following productive shift away from the subaltern studies legacy: "Infrapolitical distance, the absolute limit of the place where politics is narrativized, has to do with, or is uncovered in, the difference between the *polis* and politics. Infrapolitical distance invokes a proximity to something without which life would be unlivable" (*Manual de infrapolítica*, 82–83).

22. In this regard see in particular Moreiras, from "El segundo giro de la deconstrucción" ("To de-metaphorize is to deconstruct, and to deconstruct is to accede to the possible thinking of being in its difference" [135]) to "Exergo: Sobre *Clamor*, de Jacques Derrida (Un posible segundo momento de la deconstrucción)," in *Manual de infrapolítica*, 5–15. In this regard, also see Cerrato, "Infrapolitics and Shibumi," 98.

23. For the relation between clearing and freedom we turn to Martin Heidegger's notion of *lichtung* (or clearing/lighting): "*To be free* is not to be released from something but to be led forth to something. Not to be free from, but to become free *for something*—for the light. . . . Compare Schiller: 'Bright as day the night is lit.' The night is permeable, something like a forest clearing free of trees, so that it allows a view through it. Light liberates, it sets free a passage, an opening, an overview; it clears. The dark is cleared, goes over into the light" (*Being and Truth*, 124–25); "Freedom is that which conceals in a way that opens to light, in whose clearing there shimmers that veil that covers what comes to presence of all truth and lets the veil appear as what veils. Freedom is the realm of the destining that at any given time starts a revealing upon its way" ("The Question Concerning Technology," 25); "To think against values therefore does not mean to beat the drum for the valuelessness and nullity of beings. It means rather to bring the clearing of the truth of being before thinking, as against subjectivizing beings into mere objects" ("Letter on Humanism," 265); "In the midst of beings as a whole an open place occurs. There is a clearing, a lighting. . . . That which is can only be, as a being, if it stands within and stands out within what is lighted in this clearing. Only this clearing grants and guarantees to us humans a passage to those beings that we ourselves are not, and access to the being that we ourselves are" ("The Origin of the Work of Art," 53).

24. We understand the *decision of existence* in the following terms: "At most,

thought elucidates the fact that *we* decide and that we reach *our* decision, in the anxiety and the joy of existing on vanishing ground. But for such an elucidation, thought must, each time, in this text or the next, bring its own decision of existence into *action*. This is its responsibility as thought, a responsibility that is not simply thought about or left floating in thought. It engages and exposes itself in the mode of existing that is thinking and writing. But this mode can decide nothing for the other modes of existing. Rather, it must recognize just how fully the decision of existence belongs to itself and comes about only from itself, the event of an own-making that is each time singular and each time singularly modalized. Thought abandons itself to its own opening and thus reaches its decision, when it does justice to this singularity that exceeds it, exceeding it even in itself, even in its own existence and decision of thought" (Jean-Luc Nancy, "The Decision of Existence," 108).

25. For necropolitics, see Mbembe. For the discussion of the distance underlying politics and life, in the context of the distinction between the impolitical and the infrapolitical, see Moreiras, *La diferencia absoluta*.

26. Throughout this work I draw on the term "market-state duopoly," first advanced by Brett Levinson in *Market and Thought* (2004), as the underlying basis of both the contemporary late-neoliberal post-sovereign state and the recent reactions against it in the form of neofascist nationalism and myriad forms of racialized nativism. Levinson frames the market-state duopoly in the following terms: "Consensual postdemocracy is a very potent site, a powerful duality or duopoly. . . . We live today in a state/market dyad in which relativism and absolutism, contingency and necessity, deregulation and law, circulation (a key topos of the market form) and production (a fundament of the state form), unfixity and fixity, work together to form our social, political, cultural, and intellectual domains" (15). The market-state duopoly feeds off and circulates the *constitutively conflictual* nature of the state form internal to contemporary globalization. Therein we witness a relation of functional and circulating indifference between the state form and the self-realization of capital. It is this functional and circulating indifference, an indifference that is itself the direct consequence of the violent history of neoliberalism, that provides the basis for understanding the extreme violence of the post-sovereign market-state duopoly. The logic of the market-state duopoly is not far removed from what Bernard Harcourt has referred to as the new *doppelgänger* logic of the digital age. In this new logic, "the idea is to find our *doppelgänger* and then model that person's behavior to know ours, and vice versa, in the process shaping each other's desires reciprocally . . . this means the control of all our intimate information, wants, and desires. . . . It deploys a new rationality of similitude, of matching, without regard for the causal link. The goal, the aspiration, the object is to find that second identical person . . . not the unique individual, perhaps, but rather the matched *duodividual*" (*Exposed*, 145–57). What Harcourt identifies as the underlying logic of the digital age can also be located at the heart of the late-neoliberal state form. As such, in contrast to the extensive political science and sociology literature on the post-sovereign state, which tends to refer primarily to

the constitutional pluralism and political forms of the contemporary European state system, in this work I prefer to think in alignment with notions of post-Westphalian sovereignty outlined in Levinson, *Market and Thought*; Brown, *Walled States, Waning Sovereignty*; Cabezas, *Postsoberanía*; Villalobos-Ruminott, *Soberanías en suspenso*; and others.

## Passage I. Contemporary Turmoil: Posthegemonic Epochality, or Why Bother with the Infrapolitical?

1. In the context of the Latin American humanities and social sciences, the first work to give an extended orientation to such questions and to the responsibility of such questioning was Alberto Moreiras's *Tercer espacio: Literatura y duelo en América Latina* (1999).

2. There is no outside to capital. Our understandings and lived experience of concepts such as the political, community, the common, gathering, identity, difference, genus, species, episteme, race, gender, ethnicity, etc. are all Western in origin and in the historical extension of their metaphysics. For this reason, the critique of Eurocentrism as the affirmation of an outside is essentially the call for a diversity that already lies at the constitutive heart of humanism and of Eurocentrism in the first place. There is no greater logocentric gesture than to "provincialize Europe" or to "decolonize the curriculum" in the name of identity and difference, because the "epistemologies of the south" remain at all times internal to Eurocentrism, since they depend upon it for their basic claim to legitimacy.

3. See Schürmann, *Broken*, 12.

4. Martínez Marzoa puts it in the following terms: "Following the concept of revolution, there has to be a negatively defined point at which the categories used to conceive of modern society are no longer worthy. An *other* situation cannot be conceived; only modern society can be conceived; but to conceive something is to conceive it in its finitude. There is no other way of conceiving anything" (*La filosofía de El Capital*, 247). It is precisely in this form of finitude that we can see the metaphysical structure of Marx's thinking.

5. For the doctrine of containment, see Kennan, "Long Telegram to George Marshall." The historical watershed in the doctrine of containment was the aerial war waged by the United States on the basis of "kill ratios" and "body count" in Vietnam (1955–1975). In this context, Hannah Arendt clarified the historical significance of a changing paradigm of war (see *Crises*, 111). Now *drone warfare* marks the entrance of aerial warfare and surveillance into the zone of a fully decontained and legally unconstrained global *anomie*.

6. Globalization is in this sense the disarticulation and destruction of the history of the relation between average labor power and value. Take as an example the advent of *cryptocurrency* as the dawn of completely incommensurable value disconnected from the social metabolism of necessary social labor time and of money as the materiality of general equivalence. Cryptocurrency is the active

dislodging of the relation between material money as absolute commodity, commodity price, and value. If metal money is the signifier of the universal equivalence of value, cryptocurrency is money value without substance, materiality, weight, or obsolescence. It is universal equivalence reconverted into an absolute virtuality devoid of social content and separated, in appearance at least, from the direct extraction of value from the body of the worker. Cryptocurrency has its roots in accumulated wealth, benefiting the techno-savvy and the extremely wealthy, as can be seen by the fact that (a) fewer than two thousand people working full-time in the global cryptocurrency industry have generated wealth of up to the value of $27 billion (Hileman and Rauchs, "Global Cryptocurrency Benchmarking Study," 10); (b) 94 percent of all publicly known cryptocurrency ATMs are based in North America and Europe, while Africa, Latin America, and the Middle East host less than 1 percent of worldwide cryptocurrency ATMs (108); (c) financial interactions and transfers are for the most part free of institutional oversight, confiscation, or censor (106); (d) currency-transfer fees are based not on the amount transferred but on the transaction size measured in bytes, essentially meaning that a multimillion dollar transaction can be processed for the same fee as a $1 transaction. The concrete, "material" vocabulary of bitcoin signals the fact that cryptocurrency extracts terms from a prior stage in the mode of production and applies them to previously unrecognizable forms, functions, and applications. Bitcoin is the ultimate techno-economic horizon in the wake of the demetalization of the economy that originated in the early 1970s, when the dollar was taken off the gold standard. Its value stems not from the M–C–M relation in Marx, which has gold and the amount of gold in reserve and in circulation as its material anchor, but the mathematical algorithm that allows for the supersession of the M–C–M relation in the name of an M–M relation. Bitcoin is not money per se to the extent that it has not developed from within the territorialized history of legislated bullion. Rather, it is a supplementary technological metamoney that feeds off the preexisting fictive nature of the notions of value generated by the global economy, without which it would cease to exist. For this reason, cryptocurrency is incommensurable parasitical value in motion.

7. "The question of what being consists of in the field of modern society coincides with the appearance of the 'economic law' of movement of modern society, with the discovery of what is called the 'economic base.' . . . Ontology is the very definition of the field, because the analysis of the commodity is the principle within which the constructive process is developed that brings about the ideal genesis of the economic categories" (Martínez Marzoa, *La filosofía de El Capital*, 46).

8. "Because Marx by experiencing estrangement attains an essential dimension of history, the Marxist view of history is superior to that of other historical accounts. But since neither Husserl nor — so far as I have seen till now — Sartre recognizes the essential importance of the historical in being, neither phenomenology nor existentialism enters that dimension within which a productive dialogue with Marxism first becomes possible" (Heidegger, "Letter on Humanism," 259).

9. "*Fundamental ontology*, from which alone all other ontologies can take their rise, must be sought in the *existential analytic of Dasein*. . . . Dasein is an entity whose Being is the determinate character of existence. The second priority is an *ontological* one: Dasein is itself 'ontological,' because existence is thus determinative for it. . . . But the roots of the existential analytics, on its part, are ultimately *existentiell*, that is, *ontical*. Only if the inquiry of philosophical research is itself seized upon in an existentiell manner as a possibility of the Being of each existing Dasein, does it become at all possible to disclose the existentiality of existence and to undertake an adequately founded ontological problematic" (Heidegger, *Being and Time*, 34).

10. Also see Heidegger's *Parmenides*, from the same period, which coincided with the slaughter of the Battle of Stalingrad.

11. "The consequences are far reaching. By breaking down the boundaries, the aspiration to any liberal limits, or checks and balances, evaporates as well. The liberal ideal — that there could be a projected realm of individual autonomy — no longer has traction in a world in which commerce cannot be distinguished from governing or policing or surveillance or just simply living privately. . . . It begins to shape us, at least many of us, into marketized subjects — or rather subject objects who are nothing more than watched, tracked, followed, profiled at will and who in turn do nothing more than watch and observe others" (Harcourt, *Exposed*, 26).

12. Prometheus is the mythical apostle of technology and therefore of all human instrumentalism. Upon his originary theft of fire from the Gods Prometheus becomes the rebel who submits to no authority and pays the price for his insurgency with his own body. His rebellion against the Gods is the uncovering of a new, specifically human, nature and of a new, specifically human, demand to work for the benefit of society and therefore on behalf of the advancement of culture (see Braunstein, *El Inconsciente*, 107). It should be understood that in Shelley's modern *Prometheus* there is an active obliteration of the Greek understanding of the tragic tradition. For the Greeks "the figure of Prometheus (to be found, for example, in Heidegger's Rectorate Discourse) *makes no sense by itself*. It is only consistent as a result of its doubling with Epimetheus, who in turn doubles up on himself" as "the very quality of reflectivity, knowledge, wisdom, and of the quite different figure of remembering, experience" (Stiegler, *Technics and Time I*, 186). In contrast, Shelley simply casts Epimetheus into oblivion, thereby anchoring Promethean individualism to the modern humanist ideology of progress over and against the ontological question of time — of foresight and retrospection — and therefore of the being of historicity. Shelley's Prometheus is unbound from the past and is thereby rendered the humanist *spirit* of the revolutionary Age. In Shelley the myth of Prometheus is rendered a tool of modern Hegelianism.

13. "Understood in an essential way, 'world picture' does not mean 'picture of the world,' but rather, the world grasped as picture. Beings as a whole are now taken in such a way that a being is first and only in being insofar as it is set in place by

representing-producing [*vorstellend-herstellenden*] humanity. . . . In order fully to grasp the modern essence of representedness we must scent out the original naming power of that worn-out word and concept 'to represent': to put forth and relate to oneself. It is through this that the being comes to stand as an object and so first receives the seal of being. That the world becomes picture is one and the same process whereby, in the midst of beings, man becomes subject" (Heidegger, "The Age of the World Picture," 67–69).

14. This extended exploration of Shelley's poem is designed to shed light on the underlying logics of some of the dominant intellectual and political paradigms of both Left and Right Enlightenment thinking, such as those of historical materialism, the multitude (or counterempire), neocommunism, Trumpism, populism, *decoloniality*, and the *epistemologies of the South*, all of which generally confuse *doxa* with *episteme* (knowledge, understanding, acquaintance) in order to affirm thetic, humanist moralism as if it offered a new order and value of the political. They are all paradigms grounded in modern Promethean metaphysics, striving to resituate secular humanity as a prosthetic divinity.

15. "With the beginnings of the battle for mastery of the earth, the age of subjectity presses to its completion. . . . To make something conscious is a necessary instrument of the will that wills out of the will to power. It occurs, as regards the objectifying, in the form of planning. It occurs in the region of man's uprising into self-willing through the continuing analysis of the historical situation. Thought metaphysically, the situation is always the station for the action of the subject. Whether it knows it or not, each analysis of the situation is grounded on the metaphysics of subjectity" (Heidegger, "The Word of Nietzsche," 192).

16. I refer the reader once again to the exodus from biopolitics elaborated in Moreiras, *Línea de sombra*, 191–238.

17. The *katechon* is not a political concept per se. Rather, it is the projection of an onto-theological, spatializing drive in which the prepolitical or the nonpolitical becomes the basis of normative measures for political action and thinking.

18. Herein lies the modern heterogenesis, via the Master-Slave dialectic, of the confrontation with and sublimation of death as the power of history: "It's the game with which you are very familiar: mastery as the slavery of the slave, slavery as mastery of mastery, mediation through labor, and so forth. . . . This mediation of death comes down, despite this great Hegelian revolution, to thinking death within the horizon of the infinite and the parousia of absolute knowledge, which is pure *life*, life with itself of consciousness, just as, generally, consciousness . . . is only a mediation of Spirit and of God reflecting on himself, and so on" (Derrida, *Heidegger*, 200). Derrida later cites Nietzsche's fundamental formulation with regard to the tradition of Hegelianism in *Untimely Meditations*: "History understood in this Hegelian fashion has been mockingly called God's sojourn on earth, though the god referred to has been created only by history. This god, however, became transparent and comprehensible to himself within the Hegelian craniums and has already

ascended all the dialectically possible steps of his evolution up to this self-revelation: so that for Hegel the climax and terminus of the world-process coincided with his own existence in Berlin" (220).

19. It is not by chance, for example, that for both Tertullian and Saint Augustine the Roman Empire was the embodiment of the Latin-Romanic *katechon* as the restraining force against the coming of lawlessness. Cacciari (*Europe and Empire*) provides an extensive bibliographical archive of the history of writings on the *katechon*.

20. I refer the reader once again to Alberto Moreiras's denarrativization of the multitude as counterempire in Hardt and Negri's *Empire*, in specific reference to the Spanish Inquisition (*Línea de sombra*, 191–238). The comparison of St. Paul to Lenin outlined by Budgen, Kouvelakis, and Žižek in *Lenin Reloaded* neglects to address the question and legacy of the Paulist katechon for the history of the communist Left. For Alain Badiou the "communist hypothesis" is essentially a katechontic affair grounded in the militant subject (*Saint Paul*, 2). The communist hypothesis, or the reactivation of the militant figure, offers the restaging of the ontology of the subject as a sustained relation of subordination to the persistent theological order of the Idols (first the Christian God and then the secular militant Man). It is Promethean, thetic thinking in action. It pursues an ontology of the subject grounded in Christian-Aristotelian *courage*, a courage that remains concomitant with the Latin-Romanic virtue of *fortitudo* in the face of impossible odds. This faith in the performative expansion of an identity grounded in one of the four cardinal virtues is constructed via fidelity to a communist invariant that is said to underlie history since antiquity and that in modernity emerges as a dual historical sequence: (1) the sequence that goes from the French Revolution to the defeat of the Paris Commune in 1871 and (2) the sequence that goes from the Bolshevik Revolution of 1917 to the death of Mao and the end of the Cultural Revolution in 1976. The communist hypothesis is an affirmation of virtue based on fidelity to a normative genealogy and an invariant subjectification traversing universal history. For this reason, it offers the certainty of a metaphysical fable of fraternization for the sufficiently militant restrainers of capitalist decontainment.

21. See Pullella, "Pope Rails against 'Dictatorship of the Economy,' Urges Reform."

22. By "integral nation-state" we understand the history of the dialectical unity of political society, or State, and civil society, that is, the integration of the subordinated classes into the expansive project of historical development of the leading social group that came to the fore in the last decades of the nineteenth century (Thomas, *The Gramscian Moment*, 143). Antonio Gramsci classified the integral state as follows: "The modern state abolishes many autonomies of the subaltern classes — it abolishes the state as a federation of classes — but certain forms of the internal life of the subaltern classes are reborn as parties, trade unions, cultural associations. The modern dictatorship abolishes these forms of class autonomy as well, and it tries hard to incorporate them into the activity of the state: in other words, the centralization

of the whole life of the nation in the hands of the ruling class becomes frenetic and all-consuming" (*Prison Notebooks*, 2: PN. 3, #21, 25).

23. See Lupher, *Romans in a New World*.

24. Julia Hell, for whom the "*katechon* is first and foremost a function of imperial logic" (*The Conquest of Ruins*, 410), observes that the Tertullian-inspired Schmitt "begins to theorize the concept in the early 1940s in a series of articles on the war and in his *Land und Meer: Eine weltgeschichtliche Betrachtung* (*Land and Sea: World-Historical Reflections* [1942]). Hell later notes that "after 1939, Schmitt was first and foremost a theorist of empire. . . . In 1947, Schmitt wrote: 'To me the katechon represents the only possibility of understanding history as a Christian and finding it meaningful'" (410). Schmitt's recurrence to the figure of the katechon is the result of his witnessing the demise of British empire and the question of its possible successor in the 1930s (419).

25. See Schmitt, *Nomos*, 214–322. Giovanni Arrighi identifies three imperial cycles that oversaw the evolution of the imperial system of states that Schmitt referred to as the *jus publicum Europaeum* (1994, 231). The fourth cycle — "a US cycle, from the late nineteenth through the latest financial expansion" — signals the crisis of hegemony of the European-led interstate system of capitalist accumulation (274). For the crisis of US military Keynesianism, see Arrighi, *Adam Smith in Beijing*, 309. For contemporary Keynesianism, see Moreiras: "The Marxian prophecy upheld since the *Manifesto of the Communist Party* that the end of capitalism leads necessarily to communism is no longer taken into consideration. The sense is that the neo-Keynesian *katechon*, if such a thing were to be consolidated, would sustain the world not against an alternative order but against the absence of any order whatsoever. In the final instance, this is Carl Schmitt's nomic concern" ("Keynes y el Katechon," 159).

26. See Arendt's polemic with Jean-Paul Sartre regarding the Third World national liberation movements: "To think . . . that there is such a thing as a 'Unity of the Third World,' to which one could address the new slogan in the era of decolonization 'Natives of all underdeveloped countries unite' (Sartre) is to repeat Marx's worst illusions on a greatly enlarged scale and with considerably less justification. The Third World is not a reality but an ideology" (*Crises of the Republic*, 123). In the twenty-first century one can say that the so-called Global South — Gramsci's "Southern Question" extended into a planetary metaphor, alongside the entire project of *decoloniality* (Dussel etc.) — is even more of an ideological projection than the "Third World" ever was.

27. Despite not situating the September 11, 1973, military coup in Chile as a prime entry point into the neoliberal era, through Davidson we do gain a historical appreciation of the fact that the history of modernity is the history of the inability to create an alternative hegemonic process to that of the bourgeoisie, a state of crisis that has now devolved into the international bourgeoisie's turn to neoliberalism and its classic political economy in order to conceal the crisis of legitimacy of bourgeois hegemony itself. That project has failed already in terms of its legitimacy

but not in terms of its ability to guarantee accumulation. The numerous historical sequences reflected in Davidson's book confirm that bourgeois hegemony is only ever contingent, weak, and unnatural. Likewise, chapters 6 and 7 of volume 1 of *Capital* demonstrate the sheer contingency of Marx's formulations regarding the mode of production, the ways that capital and its class power, the bourgeoisie, adapt to circumstances in order to guarantee the ultimate goal, which is the pursuit and acquisition of surplus value. Marx is fully aware that it is the sheer flexibility of capital in its historical processes that escapes definitive understanding. Clearly, this section of *Capital* makes a mockery of the idea of a specifically Marxist philosophy of history, or "historical materialism." Louis Althusser's "aleatory materialism" attempted to circumvent the positivist philosophy of history underlying historical materialist representation. Althusser provided a theory of *encounter* emphasizing history as the unremitting transformation of impermanent forms via new, indecipherable, and unforeseen conditions and events. Aleatory materialism is an attempt to think *actuality* at a distance from law and representation. It does so, however, by sidestepping the fact that as soon as logic purports to think actuality it devours that which cannot be devoured, which is contingency, thereby unwillingly bringing the unrepresentable back into the laws of grammar, configured as historicity. Aleatory materialism emphasizes metonymy over metaphor and therefore the signifier over the signified, but the primary ontological subject is still *techne*, with terms such as the *encounter* and *multitemporality* serving as sociological predicates of that primary subject. The ontological transformation desired via aleatory materialism remains elusive, since it remains essentially *unattuned* to the question of fundamental ontology — the ontological difference — itself.

28. See Kissinger, *World Order*, 89, 286.

29. Donald Trump's electoral victory in 2016 is the market-state duopoly converted into dramatic and political representation, borderline circus act, and neonativist exceptionalism. Trump's victory was built on reinforcing ongoing global resource extraction and economic austerity (oil, coal, gas, finance, Russia, Ukraine, health care "reform," corporate tax breaks), while couching that work in the rhetorical rejection, via the language of "economic nationalism," of the very duopoly that he, his cabinet, and his family entourage are and have been for decades. Trump does not care about the state as a juridical order, became president on that basis, and acts, speaks, and tweets accordingly. However, since in the market-state duopoly caring for corporate well-being above all else is itself already and only ever caring for the state, Trump can actually say one thing and do the opposite without necessarily contradicting the dogma of the reigning economic regime. Meanwhile, the racialist rhetoric of constructing a US-Mexico border wall or of separating Central American families at the border is the expression that Mexicans, Mexican-Americans, Central Americans, and Anglo-Americans (which include the defenders of the racist Confederacy, of course) have thoroughly incompatible cultural and economic values. In what is essentially a case of classic reactionary, vertical populism, by loving their man — the utterly fallible king and thoroughly inarticulate

billionaire—Trump supporters can both love themselves in, and rail against, their own subservience a little more than before. This, coupled with the nostalgia for a time of "greatness" prior to the supposedly calamitous imperial and moral descent experienced in the present, creates the conditions for an extreme conservatism built on the ritualism of a reparative religion. Trump is no anomaly. Trump's anti-Black, anti-Muslim and anti-Hispanic/Latino nativism, while confirming much of Gustave Le Bon's 1895 definition regarding the group mind's thirst for obedience, or its extreme passion for authority taken up later by Freud in *Group Psychology and the Analysis of the Ego*, echoes many of the ideas found not only on the alt-Right but also in Samuel Huntington's Harvard-sanctioned and widely commented-on *The Clash of Civilizations* (1994) and *Who Are We?* (2004). In these works, the Harvard political scientist's language of white, protestant cultural nationalism legitimizes itself on the basis of displacing historical biological racism in the name of cultural "values," "tradition," and "identity."

30. When Galli addresses the exhaustion of Hobbesian-Schmittian political space he does so necessarily from within an essentially bourgeois understanding of space and power as sovereign *extensio*. The globalized market-state duopoly, in which the spatialization of the inside and the outside of capital implode, is the site of collapse of that understanding. "Global war" is the work of collapse and the work against collapse simultaneously.

31. "Total Mobilization" refers to the development of *the power of the state* in the advancement of *war*. In this regard, "since war is the recognized form of the struggle for power when the competitors are States, every increase in the State's grip on economic life has the effect of orienting industrial life yet a little farther towards preparation for war" (Weil, *Oppression and Liberty*, 116). The contemporary avatar of war, then, is total mobilization in its fully decontained, globalizing form within, beyond, and often in the absence of the state. It is the market-state duopoly in action.

32. By "standing reserve" I refer to Martin Heidegger's definition of the world dominated by *techne*: "Everywhere everything is ordered to stand by, to be immediately at hand, indeed to stand there just so it may be on call for a further ordering. Whatever is ordered about in this way has its own standing. We call it the standing-reserve" ("The Question concerning Technology," 17). Herein lies a fundamentally critical stance in relation to what Michel Foucault called *biopolitics* (which he recuperated and developed in reference to the bourgeois extension of the sphere of politics as fully coextensive with the production of the sphere of life). Echoing the Marxian notion of alienation while also questioning the notion of equality bequeathed by the Enlightenment tradition, in *The Gift of Death* Jacques Derrida references the question of the modern standing reserve, highlighting the concealment upon which it is constructed: "The individualism of technological civilization relies precisely on a misunderstanding of the unique self. It is the individualism of a *role* and not of a *person*. . . . Equality for all, the slogan of bourgeois revolution, becomes the objective or quantifiable equality of roles, not of persons" (37). In a slightly different though intimately related register, Jean-Luc

Nancy develops the notion of "general equivalence" beyond the specific money form, as global capital saturates humanity: "If globalization has thus a necessity — the necessity that Marx designated as the 'historical performance' of capital and that consists in nothing other than the creation by the market of the global dimension as such — it is because, through the interdependence of the exchange of value in its merchandise-form (which is the form of general equivalency, money), the interconnection of everyone in the production of humanity as such comes into view" (*The Creation of the World or Globalization*, 37). If biopolitics is the technological production of life that "places life in the state of producing itself as a whole, and of re-appropriating the exteriority of domination in a common auto-production or auto-creation whose vitality reabsorbs and accomplishes, in itself, any politics" (95), then clearly Heidegger, Derrida, and Nancy are not thinkers *of* biopolitics — thinkers, that is, *of* the *standing* within life that is sutured to capital in such a way as to precondition every subsequent subordination, or hegemony. Rather, they are thinkers *at a distance from* biopolitics, in the name of freedom from the standing reserve that every biopolitics, or productionism, presupposes and naturalizes via the subjectification of the subject (bourgeois, socialist, or communist). As outlined in the Introduction to this work, it is this distance that fuels the infrapolitical thinking that constitutes a renewal of the project of deconstruction (see Moreiras, *Línea de sombra* and *Infrapolítica*).

33. "Capital is both master and coin of the realm, except there is no realm, no global polity, governance, or society, and neither are there boundaries or territory that delimit capital's domain. Rather, today, we face increasingly faltering theological political sovereignty, on the one hand, and capital as global power, on the other. This makes for a strange inversion and paradox. While weakening nation-state sovereigns yoke their fate and legitimacy to God, capital, that most desacralizing of forces, becomes God-like: almighty, limitless, and uncontrollable. In what should be the final and complete triumph of secularism, there is only theology. This is how the post-Westphalian decontainment of the theological and the economic rhetorically echo each other, even as they move along different trajectories" (Brown, *Walled States*, 66). In this formulation, Carl Schmitt's secularization of the Paulist onto-theological *katechon* is falling apart. It is not dead but systemically moribund. Later Brown adds: "If in a Westphalian order the state is the container for the nation and political sovereignty contributes the hard metal of this container, then it is unsurprising that contemporary nationalisms issue demands for rearticulated state sovereignty through visible signs of its containing powers. Settled and intact state sovereignty does not require such signs. . . . Waning state sovereignty loses these capacities to contain the nation and the subject" (118).

34. It should be noted in reference to the phenomenon of "Trumpism" that Trump's promise to "Make America Great Again" upholds the rhetoric of fake epoch-making. This fake epoch-making is the only essential truth of the politics of the Trump administration and, indeed, of the international resurgence of neo-fascism in general.

35. See Braunstein, *El inconsciente*, 125–28.

36. It will be said no doubt that I am cynical, but this would be imprecise. In ancient Greece the cynics preached renunciation as the exercise of free will and as an affirmation of moral superiority. But there is no longer any room for cynical renunciation, because there is no longer an outside to the social, to the city, or to capital. A different register of renunciation from that of classical cynicism is required for thinking. As already referenced in the Introduction to this work, for Ángel Octavio Álvarez Solís ("On a Newly Arisen Infrapolitical Tone," 123–41), infrapolitics inaugurs "a change in the orientation of thought, a change in the fragile conceptual structure of theory, a change in the way in which discursive practices admit new horizons of experience. . . . The politics of tone indicate a dispute regarding open ears" (124–27).

37. In a 2017 essay titled "Left and Right: Why They Still Make Sense," Carlo Galli calls for a revamped Enlightenment populism of the Left capable of administering an "equality of dignity" that is neither identitarian nor constructive of antagonisms. In this privileging of praxis, or of the centrality of the subject, Galli appears to advocate the active concealment of one of the essential determinations of our times: that is, "the epistemological crisis of subjectivity." Galli advocates, in the wake of crisis, and against crisis, the concealment of crisis in the name of leftist populism. This is a short circuit that is created by still emphasizing the sociological primacy of politics over existence.

38. It is not by chance, for example, that in the context of the Chilean uprising of 2019 the imagination of the parties of the Left immediately moved in the direction of the constitution as the only realistic and politically expedient conduit for a limitless and unrelenting reservoir of discontent that far surpassed anything the Left or the government could represent, capture, and control, other than via naked brutality.

39. We should recognize that for a good part of the Marxist tradition deconstruction does not even present a valid basis for a conversation. Take, for example, the case of Enrique Dussel and the proposition of "decolonization." For Dussel the Latin American Marxist Left is the embodiment of the coming and will to power of the Messiah-People as the salvific name of a new epoch. This new epoch is predicated essentially on decolonization from the historical determinations inherited from colonialism. In particular it is predicated on the victims of colonialism reclaiming their presence in the present and past. For this reason, decolonization is a project to refill (with subjectivity) the absence left in the wake of the disappearance, or "absenting," of the historical subject, and this in the name of freedom from historical determination, which is subjectivity too. Prophetically, Dussel claims to know the meaning of our Age (the coloniality of which he proposes to transcend via what he calls "pluriversal transmodernity"). But there is nothing more sixteenth century than this form of Marxism, since Dusselian emancipation reflects a desire to bask in the light of the Last Judgment while at the same time withholding that Last Judgment in the name of a politics of subjectivist emancipation. Decolonization for Dussel means the world become Christian katechon, fully contained in the age not

of secularism that Marx announced but in the theological age of the Final Judgment that Marx desymbolized. Dussel proposes a Christian-Marxist political theology, a battle of the sacred versus capital, the representation of a more formidable katechon over and above the global capitalism we already have. Dussel is, in this sense, a Christian theologian rather than a philosopher. For Dussel, the imperial history of Catholicism in the Americas — which imposed identity and difference (the word of God, Logos, reason) in imperial form in the first place — offers a definitive deliverance from the history of Eurocentrism and the coloniality of power. This proposition is implausible because the history of the Catholic Church *is* obviously the history of the coloniality of power. Without its deconstruction there can be absolutely no decolonization. There is a long-standing last-resort accusation in the contemporary university, extended by many humanists, culturalists, hegemony thinkers, decolonials, populists, Marxists, post-Marxists, neocommunists, and antitheory types of all persuasions, who openly or secretly accuse deconstruction and its practitioners of being advocates of a distinguished, aristocratic, or apolitical tone in thinking. This is essentially a battle over the specter of Kant, for whom "the mystagogues maintain a *distinguished* or *aristocratic* tone that is opposed to the *cosmopolitan* designs of reason" (Álvarez Solís, "On a Newly Arisen Infrapolitical Tone," 124). But it is really a battle over an inverted version of Kant, since the contemporary mystagogue "is the policeman of academic correctness: the censor of proper forms who appeals to philology, positive science and the humanistic tradition in order to announce the downfall and inoperability of theory . . . the mystagogue is a type of political agent of an academic practice, who aspires to be an organic or inorganic intellectual, who uses any means to politicize his own ends or to rule out alternatives of intellectual production whenever they are theoretical" (131–32).

40. For example, when the sale of illegal commodities such as cocaine is included in the official accounting of gross domestic product (as it is in the United Kingdom, for example), thereby indicating that drug seizures count *negatively* against the indicators of national economic growth, something fundamental has shifted in the relation between *nomos* and *anomie*. See Angela Monaghan, "Drugs and Prostitution to Be Included in UK National Accounts," *The Guardian*, May 29, 2014, https://www.theguardian.com/society/2014/may/29/drugs-prostitution-uk -national-accounts.

41. See, for example, the international fabrication of Juan Guaidó as the "legitimate" president of Venezuela in 2019 or the precipitous appearance from nowhere of Jeanine Áñez, Bible in hand, to declare herself the interim president of Bolivia in the wake of the military ousting of President Evo Morales in November 2019.

42. Cacciari's reading of the *katechon*, it must be said, does tend to run counter to Giorgio Agamben's messianic Paulism in *The Time That Remains*, in which the latter strives to locate in Christianity's original thinker a notion that renders inoperative the relation between prophecy and representation. Agamben sees in this inoperativity the work of an internal deactivation of the law that functions as

a constitutively "weak ground" for messianism. For Agamben the *katechon* is the force that "clashes with and hides *katargesis*, the state of tendential lawlessness that characterizes the messianic . . . and delays unveiling the 'mystery of lawlessness'" (111). For Agamben the task for thinking is to bring to light the inoperativity of the law in order to highlight the illegitimacy of each and every power in messianic time (111). For this reason, the state of exception in Agamben can indicate both naked sovereign decisionism and the Paulist promise of messianic force. The epoch of global war, however, has rendered inoperative Agamben's messianic Paulist formulation, to the extent that the inoperativity of the law is no longer messianic freedom but the market-state duopoly itself. In the epoch of a lack of distinction between inside and outside, order itself is the work of internal deactivation, or inoperativity. Also see Roberto Esposito in recent reference to the *katechon* (*Two*, 76–82), though his treatment does not advance beyond the insights already developed by Cacciari, since both call for a new political theology. Neither does Giorgio Agamben's more recent return to the *katechon* and his essential restating of *The Time That Remains* in *The Mystery of Evil: Benedict XVI and the End of Days* (2017). I am situating Cacciari, then, at a distance from both Agamben and Esposito. However, his thinking is still very much determined by the political-theological legacy he says is already in a state of collapse.

43. In this regard, also see Moreiras, *The Exhaustion of Difference*.

44. See Bazzicalupo: "The neoliberal imaginary dissolves every modern project and representation via the immanence of its own legislative emergence and direct presencing. For this reason, a point of possible symptomatic torsion disappears, a part of those who have no part that, despite forming part of the system, remains without *value*. This was the 'People' conceived by Rancière or Žižek, which utilizes this excessive element, this phantasm, in the struggle for emancipation. On the contrary, now the system presents itself as if it excluded nothing. It does not even exclude the excess; indeed, it considers it to be its prime mover, shifting constantly its limits. . . . This plane of immanence determines the twilight of the parties, of the organizers of mediation, and of all projects" ("Populismo y liberalismo," 372–73). If the former excess is now the ever-shifting prime mover itself, then it is incumbent upon us to think in the direction of the "infra-excess of the political" (Moreiras, "Infrapolítica y política de la infrapolítica," 56).

45. This is precisely why the legacies of deconstruction—and in particular the relation of deconstruction to the thinking of being—remain central to the project of any thought that claims to be progressive now. In the final pages of *Heidegger: The Question of Being and History*, Derrida observes: "No doubt the thinking of being announces the history of non-metaphor on the basis of which metaphoricity is thought. But it does not announce itself prophetically like a new day (prophets only ever announce other metaphors), as something that will be; it announces itself as the impossible on the basis of which the possible is thought as such. . . . So the thinking of being announces the horizon of non-metaphor. But the gesture whereby it announces this horizon, even though it denounces the entirety of *past* metaphor

(onto-theology), happens in a metaphor about which it does not yet know — because it is irreducibly to-come — what that metaphor is hiding. The thinking of being is even the only respect for the future as such, far from being a sentimental and nostalgic traditionalism. It is that on the basis of which all thoughts that claim to be *progressive* can arise as what they are" (223). *Against* the sociopolitical commandments and reactionary onto-theological metaphors of *decontainment*, the infrapolitical register is the thinking of being sustained out of respect for the future as such, as the ceaseless question of the promise. Such is the labor of infrapolitics' negative realism.

46. A hegemonic fantasm is "a referent that signifies an obligation we have — a ligature, a liaison — with regard to which there is no outside. It signals to us what we have to be" (Schürmann, *Broken Hegemonies*, 10).

47. To date, the most sophisticated approaches to posthegemony and to the relation between infrapolitics and posthegemony can be found in Castro Orellana (*Poshegemonía*) and in the 2015 volume of *Debats* edited by Alberto Moreiras, titled "Infrapolítica y posthegemonía" (3). Given its title, it is perhaps natural that for many readers *posthegemony* is connected primarily to the 2010 publication of Jon Beasley-Murray's *Posthegemony: Political Theory and Latin America*. The concept was first addressed in Alberto Moreiras's *The Exhaustion of Difference* (2001) and my own *The Other Side of the Popular* (2002). These are three very different books, working in distinct ways around a shared set of concerns and issues regarding globalization and the limitations of "hegemony thinking." *The Other Side of the Popular* and *The Exhaustion of Difference* came directly out of the experience of the Latin American Subaltern Studies Group in its 1996–1998 phase, with a more or less common conceptual genealogy and *destructive* register that could be summed up in general terms as an engagement with the genealogies of Marx-Nietzsche-Heidegger-Derrida, the postcolonial legacy of South Asian subaltern studies, and psychoanalysis. On the other hand, in *Posthegemony* Beasley-Murray circumvents these genealogies by stating that he is "not content with deconstruction" (5). He positions deconstruction as the *necessary Other* for his own path into posthegemony, prioritizing *affect*, *habitus*, and the *multitude* as so-called positive figures for posthegemonic thinking, voicing his discomfort with what he calls "the labor of the negative." Rodríguez-Matos ("De lo que agujerea lo Real," 38) has pointed out that since politics itself is the creation of *habitus* there appears to be little distance between hegemony and Beasley-Murray's formulation of posthegemony. In *Posthegemony*, Beasley-Murray assigns value negatively to deconstruction yet provides no evaluation of the place of the negative in any conceptual matrix, including his own. In a more recent work Andrés Guzmán (2019) repeats the same gesture against "the negative," once again situating deconstruction as the *necessary Other* for a so-called positive, or affirmative, politics, which is ultimately that of more subjectification. Derrida always posited *deconstruction* as the *necessary Other* of every metaphysics. What anthropocentric, and therefore metaphysical, thinking does is inevitably misconstrue this in order to assign to *deconstruction* the value of the negative, thereby once again reconfirming

the need for a never-ending return to Derrida's entire philosophical trajectory, in the name of responsibility and freedom.

48. The material conditions of posthegemony are still ultimately, though not exclusively, those summed up by Jacques Derrida in *Specters of Marx* (85).

49. For the question of translation and slippage in Gramsci's use of hegemony, that is, as both *direzione* and *dominazione*, see *Selections* (55).

50. For Gramsci on the Resorgimento, see *Notebooks*, vol. 1, NB 1, #151, 231. Buci-Glucksmann (*Gramsci and the State*, 54) notes: "The Resorgimento, as a 'revolution without revolution,' a passive revolution, is the opposite to the French Jacobin model, or the 'accomplished form' of revolutionary process. . . . It is the sign of an absence of Jacobinism . . . i.e., Italy had never known a classical bourgeois revolution."

51. See Gramsci, *Notebooks*, vol. 1, NB 1, #44, 136–67.

52. In contrast to Martínez Marzoa's explanation of the philosophical limitations of "historical materialism," Gramsci is fervent in his fidelity to the notion of hegemony as its fundamental ground: "The value of the concept of hegemony . . . is epistemological. This concept, then, should be regarded as Ilyich's greatest contribution to Marxist philosophy, to historical materialism: an original and creative contribution. In this respect, Ilyich advanced Marxism not only in political theory and economics but also in philosophy (that is, by advancing political theory, he also advanced philosophy)" (*Notebooks*, 2:187–88).

53. The question of "dual power" is clearly central to the Leninist conception of revolution. However, it is not addressed in Budgen, Kouvelakis, and Žižek, *Reloading Lenin*.

54. Whether there is a way of accounting for what Thomas refers to as "the path along which the subaltern classes must learn to travel in a very different way in order to found their own 'non-state state'" is no trivial matter, because as the theory of hegemony itself explains, hegemony can curtail at any point, and for any reason depending on the reigning configuration of forces and class interests, any possible subaltern reconfiguration of what it might mean to travel, learn, and reinvent. Hegemony can stand in, according to whose interests it represents, for an array of signifiers from revolution to conformity and domination.

55. For more on the appetites in the Aristotelian dispositif, see Alvarez Yágüez, "La forma 'política' y el populismo," 204.

56. It should be noted that Laclau and Mouffe's understanding of hegemony as political alliance building — as the formation of chains of equivalence across the social sphere — is incompatible with Gramsci's formulations regarding the historical, strategic, and tactical role of the communist factory councils, cells, and party cadres in the 1920s. For Gramsci, hegemony was the purview of the factory floor, industrial production, and the discipline and uniformity of the proletariat. For this section I refer the reader once again to Jaime Rodríguez-Matos's critique of postfoundational thinking in *Writing of the Formless* (99–122), in particular reference to the Schmittian orientation of Laclau and Mouffe's thinking. Along these same

lines, also see Williams ("Los límites de la hegemonía," 49–65), which is the basis for this section.

57. For the question of unfixity, see Levinson, *Market and Thought*, 152; and Beasley-Murray, *Posthegemony*, 41. While Laclau and Mouffe might consider themselves to be "anti-Hegelian," we encounter in their work not a significant confrontation with Hegel but an attempted evasion of Hegel that haunts the entire theorization of both hegemony and populism. As we will see, their recognition of the historical unmooring of the proletariat does nothing to unhinge the order of decisionism that underlies modern political thought.

58. This claim provides a conceptual line of continuity between Laclau and Mouffe's thinking in 1985 and Laclau's *On Populist Reason* two decades later.

59. It is not by chance, in other words, that since 1985 Chantal Mouffe has become a faithful follower of Schmitt. See *The Return of the Political, On the Political (Thinking in Action)*, her edited volume *The Challenge of Carl Schmitt*, and her recent *For a Left Populism*.

60. "Hegemony arises from the contingent articulation of discursive elements (both linguistic and nonlinguistic) according to the twin principles of equivalence and difference. Specifically, a successful hegemonic project presents a variety of different elements as equivalent in their mutual antagonism toward some other element or elements. A hegemonic formation consists in the articulation of a historical bloc whose unity is not pregiven but constituted in and through the very process of its articulation on an 'antagonistic terrain'" (Beasley-Murray, *Posthegemony*, 44).

61. For a neo-Hegelian reading of Hegel highlighting a constitutive impasse at the heart of Hegel's thinking of the political, see Ruda, *Hegel's Rabble*. The book's argument can be summed up as follows: In Hegel's *Philosophy of Right* the "rabble" is the "constitutive outside" of the state and, as such, of the political. For Ruda, the rabble problem indicates that "Hegel was not Hegelian enough" (168). The problem is not only that Hegel was not Hegelian enough but that he was too Hobbesian for his own good, to the extent that the *rabble* is clearly a reinstantiation of the metaphor of the *state of nature*, as the *lack* upon which, and against which, "real" or "true" political reason — the master's discourse — constructs itself. Ruda does nothing to unsettle the metaphoricity of the inside-outside relation. The master's discourse remains intact for Ruda. As such, *Hegel's Rabble* provides a conventional, myopic approach to the question of the political and to its limitations in times of globalization. Its area of concern has already been superseded by the questions raised around the notion of *posthegemony* over the last two decades, which mark a creative distance for thinking from the limitations of the internal formalities of the Hegelian dialectic and of the ethicality of the modern state as the sole ground for questioning the political (as *nomos*, or as the sole site for the gathering of all political signifiers and subjectivities worthy of the name).

62. As already noted in the Introduction, Alberto Moreiras in *Línea de sombra*

refers to the infinite remove as the exodus from the biopolitical of the "non-subject of the political."

63. Similarly, something in José Luis Villacañas's more recent approach to populism does not add up. In *Populismo* Villacañas affirms categorically, in reference to Antonio Rivera García's "De la hegemonía al populismo," that "in populism there is no trace of the Christian tradition of the *katechon*. There is no will to detain or contain disorder, nor to work in the service of a final eschatology" ("Gramsci"). However, in Villacañas's own formulations we cannot dismiss the fact that (1) populism needs a Hobbesian charismatic leader as the singular and transcendent ("magical," Rivera and Villacañas affirm ["Líder carismático"] unifier of the group); (2) populism depends for its existence on the construction and ontological grounding of an enemy ("Gramsci"); (3) populism wants to "orient its potential in the direction of order" ("Gramsci"); (4) populism perpetuates institutional crisis by "generating via the notion of the 'people' a container wall against a disorder that it itself helps to maintain" ("La cuestión del poder"), thereby indicating with utmost clarity that populism is no stranger to clashing with and concealing a certain mystery of lawlessness within society; and (5) "in populism there is a certain fear of a true social implosion, which is what grounds its decision" ("La cuestión del poder"). These brief enumerations highlight the fact that populism is a specific political form that has developed in modernity along the lines of the history of the onto-theological representation of the subject and of the politics of restraint and salvation in modern secular form. It is conceptually and politically naïve to liberate populism from the question of the modern history of sovereign commandment and the authority of the mortal God. It is of no importance whether the latter is understood in Catholic or Protestant terms, which seems to be of particular interest to Villacañas, since the Vatican is always the object-cause of desire for both the proximity of one as much as for the distance of the other.

64. It might appear that Sumic is uncomfortably close to signaling the definitive demise of the Other. However, this is something that cannot be upheld, since the Other "is always there in its full reality" (Lacan, *Anxiety*, 325). The *actual* inexistence of the Other would be accompanied by the inexistence of its remainder and, as such, by the inexistence of the object *a*, the object-cause of desire, the inexistence of the subject, and of all processes of subjectification. It should be noted, however, that Sumic insists on signaling, on a sociological level, that conditions of legibility and therefore of "readability," which were conceivable under previously given determinations (such as classic sovereignty), are shifting now beyond recognition. In other words, if globalized capitalism "is articulated to the non-existence of the Other," it does not necessarily presuppose the actual death of the Other but a seismic shift in the order of identification with the production of signifiers and their limits, such as the state, sovereignty, "We," community, gathering, etc. Rather than merely throwing out the Other with the bathwater, Sumic places under question the very status of the object itself, and with it the signifying operations of the contemporary as

a result of the historical shift toward global capitalism and biopolitical governance. It might be said, in other words, that in these formulations Sumic is striving to raise the question of the contemporaneity of the contemporary itself, along with the challenges it poses to the very notion of transformative thinking.

65. It could be said that Donald Trump allows us to bear witness, on the rhetorical level at least, to the Schmittian undercurrent of Laclau and Mouffe's theory of hegemony and of a populism gone haywire. The Right is increasingly capable of staking a claim on "the People" in ways that the Left is not because the Right has always loved a good symbolization of the enemy. Trump's faithful consider themselves to be the true "People" *against* any minority population and *against* an abstract caste called "the globalists," of which Hillary Clinton, who should be expelled from society ("Lock Her Up!"), will always be the evil monarch. This vulgar logic has already caught on, and in new ways, across Europe and Latin America (Brazil, Chile, Bolivia, etc.).

66. For the fundamental differentiation between the affirmative biopolitics of the impolitical and the existential analytic of the infrapolitical, see Moreiras, *Manual de infrapolítica*.

67. See Derrida, *Aporias*, 84–5 (n10), in which philosophy is addressed as the secret guardian protecting against war, while the world of public law and politics is its active occlusion in the name of legislative power. Peace is predicated on giving language to the secret possibility of the secret. War is the outcome of this not occurring, and, as we know, in the legislative order of the law the secret is never allowed to express its possibility. Such a thing is dismissed without further ado as mere infrapolitics.

68. "*Humanitas*, explicitly so called, was first considered and striven for in the age of the Roman Republic. *Homo humanus* was opposed to *homo barbarus*" (Heidegger, "Letter on Humanism, 244–45).

69. Axelos's fundamental and largely ignored critical reading of Marx can also be considered in relation to Jason W. Moore's recent work *Capitalism in the Web of Life: Ecology and the Accumulation of Capital*, in which the author's overriding sociological fidelity to Hegelianism trips him up in his critique of the history of a humanism that can only be countered with more humanism and therefore with the advancement of another *world picture* extended once again in the name of freedom. Without an alternative understanding of *world*—and of the *worldhood of the world* via facticity—there can be no new perception of a world ecology devoid of a fully principled, value-defined *world picture*, or preexisting representation.

## Passage II. Narco-Accumulation: Of Contemporary Force and Facticity

1. In contemporary narco-accumulation labor power can in fact be powerless. See, for example, Correa-Cabrera, *Los Zetas Inc.*, 80. Migration is a phenomenon internal to narco-accumulation because the same corporate structures and organizations shape the movement of products and bodies devoid of labor power

while charging for their transportation services and reaping the benefits of value extraction.

2. Decades before the infamous Ayotzinapa murders in Mexico in 2014, it was already widely known and documented that the state and narco-accumulation were deeply intertwined in the workings of a market-state duopoly.

3. By narco-accumulation we refer, then, to the existence and circulation of a $300 billion global commercial enterprise. It is widely recognized that the laundered proceeds of organized crime were the only liquid investment capital available and absorbed into the global banking system during the 2008–2009 world economic collapse (Syal, "Drug Money Saved Banks in Global Crisis"; Wainwright, *Narco-Nomics*, 254). Narco-accumulation, in other words, props up the entire global banking system. In the cocaine supply chain from Colombia to the United States the greatest commodity price hikes occur on the Mexican-US border and in the relation between the point of origin in Colombia and the products' arrival in the Central American isthmus. However, in terms of the products' movement northward, by far the largest price hike for a kilo of cocaine occurs in the territory between the Mexican border cities and the large US urban centers nearby, such as Dallas or Los Angeles. For example, the price of a kilo of cocaine can increase by $8,000 in the 630-mile drive between Ciudad Juárez and Dallas, while its value between Honduras and the Mexico-US border rises by a mere $6,000 (Stewart, "From Columbia to New York"). The military border complex, and in particular the limited number of border crossings, structures both the profits and the violence of the narco-accumulation industry in the Americas. Evidence shows that commodity demand in the United States is essentially inelastic, thereby indicating that a border wall would be excellent news for the industry's overall bottom line. Product dilution, or "cutting," is also central to the value extracted from a kilo of cocaine in its movement from origin to final destination, to such an extent that "the price of a pure kilogram of cocaine at the retail end is in fact about $122,000" (Wainwright, *Narco-Nomics*, 25). Recently one scholar (Zavala, *Los cárteles no existen*) has opined that cartels do not exist and that it is erroneous to frame narco-accumulation within the context of global capital, since the state is solely responsible. Discussion of whether cartels (a term first utilized by the DEA in the 1990s) are actually cartels or not has always been spurious, and the idea of "the state" without any consideration of *state form* remains essentially meaningless. On the other hand, it has been common knowledge that state actors and institutions have been, and remain, involved directly in the development and extension of narco-accumulation for decades. It is equally documented that the US security apparatus has played and continues to play a central role in the institutionalization of narco-accumulation (see Webb, *Dark Alliance*; and the fictionalization of his journalistic account via the "Mexican Trampoline" in Don Winslow's *The Power of the Dog*). The argument against evaluating narco-accumulation in the framework of global capital is fallacious because it reproduces Adam Smith's already disproven separation between the state and the economy (or, in this case, between the nation-state and the global

economy), a separation that was a central tenet of classical political economy first invalidated by Karl Marx's development of the *base-superstructure* relation in the 1860s. Moreover, the argument in question is misguided on a second level because it installs Carl Schmitt's reductive friend-enemy relation as the only basis for understanding the political, a conceptual reduction that was invalidated entirely by Jacques Derrida in *The Politics of Friendship* (88–94) in the late 1990s. For these reasons the arguments therein are more an impediment to our understanding of the complexities of narco-accumulation than an elucidation. For an effective response to some of these injudicious opinions, see Guzmán ("Natalia Almada's *El velador*," 116–17). In contrast, the post-sovereign "market-state duopoly" I reference in these pages attests to the unresolvable aporias of a contemporary state form in which the modern state is both subordinated to the market and militarized; that is, the state does not wither away but shifts in form, in part by relinquishing its historical relation to its rural citizenry, in the name of private interest (in this regard, see Maldonado Aranda, "Stories of Drug Trafficking in Rural Mexico").

4. For a working definition of paramilitary conflict, see Correa-Cabrera, *Los Zetas Inc.*, 92.

5. We can veil the true complexity of this state of affairs with essentially hollow charges of the ideological melancholy and political defeatism of the Left. Such charges are usually accompanied by the promise of a *revamped* consciousness as the definitive solution for the twilight of sovereignty, or as the epochal opening to a form of representation capable of moving beyond the limitations of past subjective forms and prior political failings. It is thought that the "*I represent something*," the *ego cogito* of each and every form of consciousness, and therefore of each and every difference or negativity, can once again be rationalized, mediated, dialecticized, ameliorated, and re-elevated in the direction of the Absolute in the name of a better form, understanding, and experience of the political. The *ego cogito* can have new dialectical life breathed into it ad infinitum, in other words. However, this promises nothing more than the habitual re-presentation of the modern humanist tradition as it is already given at least since Hegel (that is, since the inauguration of the epoch of the integral nation-state), in which, as Heidegger put it in reference to the dialectic, "everything is contained and compensated. Everything is *already unconditionally* secured and accommodated" (Heidegger, *Hegel*, 19). Our current conceptual and practical predicament, which is nothing other than the all-pervasive fulfillment of the closure of metaphysics in all its conceptual and societal forms, including those of the nation-state and the subject—a fulfillment that extends itself in conjunction with the extreme assertiveness of that closure's violent reactionary symptoms on a global scale—is much more than an ideological tight spot for the modern history of consciousness, negativity, subjectivity, humanism, or historicity. It demands taking negativity—the ontological difference between beings and *being* itself—seriously.

6. As seen in the Introduction, this is essentially the question that Alain Badiou seeks to address in *The Rebirth of History* (2012). However, it is also the question that Badiou seeks to occlude via the Promethean demand for "the Idea," which is

NOTES TO PAGES 117–23

designed to restrain, or to contain, the closure of metaphysics in the name of a new ontology of the subject.

7. *Facticity* is articulated with respect to, on the basis of, and with a view to understanding and interpreting the question of *being* at any given moment. By facticity we understand "man's a priori thrownness into the ability to give meaning and thus for man's ability to understand this or that thing. Facticity is an essential component of being-in-meaning (*In-der-Welt-sein*). It is a preliminary name for man's appropriation to the *factum* of meaning-giving" (Sheehan, "Facticity and Ereignis," 60). Facticity is therefore only ever a hermeneutical question of thinking in relation to mortality (that is, of time itself): "The fact that sense-making *can* be taken away from each of us at any moment is what Heidegger means by mortality (*Sein zum Tode*: being ever at the point of death). Mortality and first-order ἑρμηνεία are two sides of the same human coin. Mortality lets us make sense of . . . and in fact *requires* us to do so if we don't want to die. The facticity of thrown-ness into meaning becomes utterly serious when we realize that meaning-making — our very way of staying alive — is possible only because we are mortal; and our mortality is the groundless ground for why we have to make sense" (47).

8. "When we say of somebody that he is 'in power' we actually refer to his being empowered by a certain number of people to act in their name" (Arendt, *Crises of the Republic*, 142).

9. In the 1930s Simone Weil was merciless in her critique of the Marxian conception of history: "There is a contradiction, an obvious, glaring contradiction, between Marx's analytic method and his conclusions. This is not surprising; he worked out the conclusions before the method. Hence Marxism's claim to be a science is rather amusing" (*Oppression and Liberty*, 147). Weil is pointing essentially toward the failure of the tradition of Marxism to comprehend the historicity of capitalism (also see Nancy, *The Creation of the World or Globalization*, 53). Hannah Arendt, of course, was acutely aware not only of the influence of this conceptualization of violence and historicity but also of the limitations of its oversimplification and glorification in the twentieth century. This was the basis for much of her criticism of Marxist humanism at the time of the Vietnam War and of Georges Sorel, Max Weber, Jean Paul Sartre, and Franz Fanon in particular. See Arendt, *Crises of the Republic*, 114, 134. Sartre's preface to Fanon's *The Wretched of the Earth* comes in for particularly sharp criticism by Arendt: "Sartre is unaware of his basic disagreement with Marx on the question of violence, especially when he states that 'irrepressible violence . . . is man creating himself,' that it is through 'mad fury' that 'the wretched of the earth' can 'become men'" (114). Sartre's certainty is clearly nothing more than the glorification of the will to power of subjectivism.

10. See Nancy, "War, Right, Sovereignty — *Techne*," 101–44.

11. *World* and *globalization* are obviously not synonyms. *World* does not presuppose itself and remains without representation and subject, whereas globalization is the absolute presupposition and domination of the principles of *techne* and value on a planetary scale. For this reason, globalization is the reduction

of humanity to means alone and the casting of *world* into oblivion (see Nancy, *The Creation of the World or Globalization*, 42–43), whereas World is the *wherein of being* and therefore the basis upon which factical life can be thought and lived (Heidegger, *Ontology*, 65). As a result, to embrace the category of *world literature* is to embrace the constitutive nihilism of technicity, *against world*, which is by definition without reason and *devoid of metaphysical storytelling*.

12. Overall it remains to be seen how the government of Andrés Manuel López Obrador (AMLO) will, or could possibly, handle the question of post-katechontic force, though it is clear that his support for and creation of a new military entity, the National Guard, with the full support in January 2019 of the Institutional Revolutionary Party (PRI), intensifies militarism. The EZLN has always been clear about its overridingly negative appraisal of AMLO for the future of indigenous society in Mexico.

13. There is a fundamental tension at the heart of Galli's work, which on one hand calls for *deconstruction* in the quest for a previously unrecognized perception while, on the other, suggesting the need for a new planetary order or previously unimaginable world-image (see Galli, *Global War*, 191). Perhaps there is a difficult question herein that Galli fails to address, that is, whether there has ever been a "collective action-image," or a world picture, that is not, or would not become, an image of rationalized subordination or domination. Heidegger would say that technological domination and "world picture" are essentially, and always, synonyms, and this is no trivial matter, as his own relation to Nazism clearly demonstrates. Galli, who is a political realist, might prefer to steer clear of the question of domination, but something would obviously be lost in such a circumvention.

14. It is noteworthy in this regard that Patrick Dove expresses considerable unease with the term *interregnum* in his book *Literature and "Interregnum"* (hence the use of quotation marks in the book's title): "Interregnum is a juridical term that designates either a temporary hiatus between orders (in the Roman tradition) or a crisis of representation in which the authority of the ruling class is no longer legitimated through the universal acceptance and internalization of its ideas (the revolutionary situations of the nineteenth and twentieth centuries). Although interregnum for Lenin and Gramsci names a gap or a crisis that could potentially give rise to revolution, it remains for them a temporal term whose concept presupposes the eventual closing of this gap and the inauguration of a new sovereign order — even if it is one whose configuration will turn out to be radically different from those of its predecessors. . . . Interregnum belongs to the imperial history of sovereignty and serves to guarantee the continuity of political reason despite its momentary interruptions and crises. . . . In view of these complications I have opted for the imperfect solution of leaving 'interregnum' in the title of my book while placing it, as Derrida would say, under erasure" (11). In this gesture, the term *interregnum* is utilized and legitimized yet placed under erasure in the same way *postmodernity* places the grand narratives of *modernity* "under erasure." My sense, however, is that we can no longer refer to the *interregnum* as an extended transitional

period of latency for a new sovereign order. We are approaching a moment in which it is no longer enough to keep the term *interregnum* under erasure in the Derridean sense or in quotation marks. By this I mean that decontainment — the fully unleashed globalizing force of contemporary *techne* — can no longer guarantee even the veneer of the continuity of a political reason grounded in the modern social bond, citizenship, and the time of development. The primacy of futurity inherent in the teleology of progress and development is no more but is still safeguarded by placing it "under erasure" as a transitional time of "interregnum." However, in the generalized, never-ending, warlike postulation that characterizes our times, we are experiencing the demise of the primary regulatory and synthesizing function of *philia*, together with the collapse of all received notions of representation, of the ethical, the political, the developmental, etc. This demands the creation of a previously unheard-of task for contemplating existence at a distance from the history of nihilism that reigns supreme. It is no longer clear to me what work the term *interregnum* does for us, if it is understood as a period of latency in the modern history of representational consciousness. What is clear is that the closure of metaphysics can no longer be cordoned off, placed under erasure, ignored, or resolved. It can only be accepted, allowed to be, and thought through with a view to infrapolitical posthegemony. Dove's *Literature and "Interregnum"* does not move in this direction.

15. "'¿Plata o plomo?' That's all that needed to be said. The meaning was clear — you can get rich or you can get dead. You choose" (Winslow, *The Power of the Dog*, 306). Mexico's mass graves are the abyssal signposts of a national "topography of cruelty" (Balibar, "Outlines of a Topography of Cruelty"), the inert and unresponsive contours of zones of death that bear witness to the economic interactions between *Untermenschen* (subhumans) — or "población chatarra" — and *Übermenschen* (supermen) (25). "This is not," says Balibar, "a contingent phenomenon; it is the result of an irreversible process that imposes on democracy the immediate task of a renewed foundation, in which the essence of the political is at stake" (18). Examples of the lack of distinction between consent, freedom, and annihilation are endless: "Some guys approach a college student, and they ask him to hold something for them. He refuses. They beat him to death" (Bowden, *Murder City*, 158); "They promised safety in exchange for his participation or death in exchange for his refusal. If he refused he received three bullets: chest, abdomen, head. He refused" (Martínez, *The Beast*, 83–84); "Because when the thugs pronounce their famous motto, when you hear, 'We are Los Zetas,' you either fold or they are going to fold you" (124); "If someone says they're a Zeta, they're a Zeta. If they say they're a Zeta and they're not a Zeta, it won't be too long before they're dead" (112). Here labor power means both absolute domination and absolute submission, with the despotism of capital working on both sides of the constitutive (non)freedom to choose. There can be little doubt that force points to the everyday networks, and indeed to the everydayness, of the narco-economy: "Where do you find Los Zetas? . . . We found them in a group of girls selling sodas, in a police officer, in a journalist, in some

petty delinquent riding the rails. We found them everywhere, in a town riddled
with fear" (109); "Violence is now woven into the very fabric of the community and
has no single cause and no single motive and no on-off button. Violence is not a
part of life, now it is life" (Bowden, *Murder City*, 105). For the relation between this
endemic violence and the burgeoning heroin industry, see Partlow, "In Mexico,
the Price of America's Hunger for Heroin." Also see Epstein, "The Opioid Crisis in
America and Mexico."

16. Rosanna Reguillo notes that "it is difficult to affirm that the violence
unleashed by 'narco-power' and organized crime can be characterized as an illegal
outside. This analysis seems simplistic and insufficient to me. For this reason, I
propose opening a third analytical space: para-legality, which emerges just on
the border zone opened up by a violence that generates not an illegal order, but
a parallel order with its own codes, norms and rituals" ("De las violencias," 44).
Along these same lines, the *a-legal State* for González Rodríguez is "a State that
simulates legality and legitimacy . . . (from the prefix 'an,' from the Greek 'a'):
the privation and negation of itself. . . . In Mexico, as in other nations, we live in
the culture of a-legality" (*Campo de Guerra*, 20–21). The anthropologist Salvador
Maldonado Aranda puts it in the following terms: "If the army and the Federal
police are free to practice violence with exactly the same degree of illegality as the
drug lords, then what arises is a network of impunities in which justice ceases to
be a concrete reference, and [leads to] the view that drug-trafficking is actually
redrawing the formal limits between State and nation" ("Stories of Drug Trafficking
in Rural Mexico," 62). It could be conjectured that the traditional political
party system itself is collapsing. The year 2017 was the most violent to date. That
same year there was extensive evidence of vote buying in Coahuila and Mexico
State; the Mexican government was caught using Pegasus software to spy on the
opposition; it was widely recognized that the state investigation of the Ayotzinapa
massacre of 2014 had been a cover-up; the state passed the Law of Internal Security,
granting police duties to the army; four state governors were arrested on corruption
charges; and Transparency International placed Mexico at the bottom of their
ranking for public sector corruption (https://www.transparency.org/). Everyone
knows how paralegality, the second state, and a-legality play themselves out on
a daily basis. In Shaul Schwarz's 2013 documentary *Narco Cultura*, neighbors in
Ciudad Juárez sweep the blood down the storm drains from a Christmas drive-by
shooting (33:06–33:07). Neighbors gather on the street corner and comment on the
way the passing of a police car on two occasions signifies not the arrival of help or
of the law but institutional complicity in the killing: "Son de lo mismo, lo mismo"
("They're the same, the same"), comments a young man. Others nod in agreement
and provide additional information about the unusual police presence in the
wake of a street killing, given the usual state of abandonment in which they live.
"Bonita Navidad," a woman concludes, melancholically. The effects on freedom
of expression have been catastrophic in Mexico. The state of Veracruz, for example,
is currently the most dangerous place to be a journalist in the Western Hemisphere.

Globally, only Afghanistan and Somalia are more perilous than Mexico in terms of the use of violence against journalists. See Ahmed, "In Mexico, It's Easy to Kill a Journalist."

17. Also Williams, "Decontainment, Stasis, and Narco-Accumulation."

18. With this logic, the Spanish Civil War could not have been considered either a civil war or a war between sovereigns, precisely because it was a war conducted along the fault lines of a geopolitical *stasis-polemos* relation characterized, on one hand, by the political factionalism of the citizenry and, on the other, by the international participation of General Franco's Moroccan "Regulares," the pro-Republic Abraham Lincoln Brigade, and the direct involvement of Soviet, German, and Italian intelligence and military apparatuses. The same can be said of the Vietnam War, which was a conventional and unconventional guerrilla and counterinsurgency war, an ideological and religious civil war, an anticolonial and anti-imperial war of national liberation, a war for nationalism, and a proxy war between external imperial powers in the context of the Cold War, all at the same time. It is clear that in contemporary narco-accumulation the regime of silence and fear that this conflict often imposes on public language is more characteristic of the long-lasting effects of a civil war than it is of either a revolution or a war between distinct sovereign domains.

19. For the legacies of the sovereign exception in Mexico prior to 1994, see Williams, *The Mexican Exception*.

20. Toward a definition of "excess": Jean Franco writes of "the scaffolding of government — state assembly, governor, judges and police — [as] a colossal trompe l'oeil" (*Cruel Modernity*, 217); "extreme rage against the female" (219); "a state of perpetual mourning without reprieve" (220); "the changes that the world is experiencing in our time" (221); quoting Rita Laura Segato, Franco observes that "'micro-fascisms' have come to exercise totalitarian control" (222–23); "what remains unexplained is the fury and sadism of the killers" (224); "the killing of women confirms grotesque forms of masculinity, beheadings are acts of sovereignty in the shadow state of drug cartels" (225); "the executioners describe themselves as God's enforcers. Evil has now become good; to kill is a divine right" (226); citing Sergio González Rodríguez, Franco notes that beheading is "an act of fundamentalist fury" (227), the beheader is "the messenger of the dark side of humanity, the restorer of the kingdom of death and the vast savagery that imposes destruction and imposes a negative meaning on the world" (227); "beheading goes right to the question of sovereignty, making it a dramatic statement of the mutilation of the sovereign state" (227); "what religion sanctifies is this absolute indifference to the life of another" (229); "the global immensity of crime" (234), "the desert of boredom" (238). Rage, mourning, micro-fascism, beheading, the dark side, evil, divine right, mutilation, savagery, indifference, sovereignty, boredom. Franco's writing presents us with a passional, at times almost orgiastic, vocabulary of indifference, behind which stand, no doubt, some of the most imperious questions regarding the perishing of modern political theology today.

21. Correa-Cabrera cites the work of Aaron Daugherty and Steven Dudley: "The Zetas are not just violent because their leaders have a penchant for aggression — they follow an economic model that relies on controlling territory in a violent way. Within that territory, they extract rents from other criminal actors and move only a limited number of illicit goods via some of their networks. . . . Without that territory, they have no rent (known in Mexican as 'piso'). The Zetas are, in essence, parasites. Their model depends on their ability to be more powerful and violent than their counterparts, so they can extract this rent" (Correa-Cabrera, *Los Zetas Inc.*, 54; see also 64).

22. It is in the same vein that Alberto Moreiras comments on the aforementioned book by Jean Franco, *Cruel Modernity*, in such a way as to exemplify the relation between excessive violence and the everyday existence of the infrapolitical: "Franco reviews atrocious stories of violence in recent Latin American history, and she does it to such an extent that, towards the end of the book, one hesitates to continue to conceptualize them in terms of stories, as cumulatively they become something else. Take the last chapter, for instance, on narco violence, the cult of Santa Muerte, religion gone over to the dark side, or the reference to Bolaño's (and Baudelaire's) 'an oasis of horror in a desert of boredom.'" Moreiras closes with the following questions, together with an example: "Could we not make the claim that the uncanny surplus of violence in all the histories reviewed by Franco constitutes, precisely, infrapolitical violence? We know that violence is constitutive of politics. But how do you still retain a political dimension in the very excess of violence? There is no political valence to that excess; in fact, it makes a mockery of politics, whatever the latter is. So this is the example: the excessive, post-catechontic violence deployed endemically in Latin American contemporary life, from Guatemala to the US-Mexico border, from the favelas of Rio de Janeiro to the Atacama desert, and from the Colombian jungles to the Devil's Mouth is infrapolitical violence. Which does not mean that infrapolitics refers only to violence" (Moreiras, "An Example of Infrapolitics").

23. For companion evaluations of Agamben's approach to stasis, see Beasley Murray, "Stasis"; and Moreiras, "Comentario a *Stasis* de Giorgio Agamben."

24. For a significant examination of stasis in the modern context of Latin American border wars, see Dowd, "Stasis."

25. The inconsistencies in Agamben's essay on *stasis* are consonant with the overall conceptual trajectory and critical apparatus by which he strives to restate, and indeed to re*instate*, the notion of *life* (*bios* versus *zoe*) as the sole relation and means through which to rethink "from scratch" the foundations of Western metaphysics. Ultimately what Agamben's repeated engagement with *life* presents is, on one hand, a revisitation and empirical rethematization of the very beginning of Western metaphysics (namely, Aristotle's *Metaphysics*) and, on the other, the reconversion of Hegel's speculative consciousness (*Phenomenology of Spirit*, or life as the actualization of spirit) into the *bios-zoe* dialectic. Through Agamben, then, the beginning and spirit of Western metaphysics speaks via empirical re-

presentation and reconversion. It remains unclear, however, to what extent "the foundation of Western politics" can be "rethought from scratch" via Agamben's approach to the modern actuality of spirit, which, in Hegel, is *life* as the experience of the appearance to itself of consciousness, and therefore of subjectivity as the sole placeholder and object of representation (Heidegger, *Hegel*, 101). Since the repoliticization of *bare life* is not beyond, or an *other to*, the order of technicity but remains at all times internal and coextensive to it, it cannot provide for a turn within the history of Western metaphysics but only to its reinstatement. Perhaps it could be said that my own writing partakes of a similar (inevitable) empirical rethematization of the very beginning of Western metaphysics (via its approach to force). The difference is that I make no claim to rethink the foundation of Western politics from scratch but rather to move in the direction of the infraexcess of the political (Moreiras, "A Conversation").

26. The dialectical image between development and underdevelopment can no longer be reduced to the metaphoric comparison between two cities or geopolitical areas (for example, Mexico City versus New York City, as in the opening images of Luis Buñuel's *Los olvidados/The Young and the Damned*). What is now lacking at both ends of such a metaphorical relation is the very idea of the city ( *polis*) itself. Obviously, I am not suggesting that extreme inequality no longer exists or is unimportant, just that we are undergoing the collapse of an entire inherited spatial, political, and cultural imaginary.

27. For the fundamental work of *polemos* in Heidegger, see Fried, *Heidegger's Polemos*.

28. See Jacques Derrida in reference to Plato's understanding of war (*Politics of Friendship*, 92): "Even when Greeks fight and wage war among themselves, we should say that they are no less naturally friends ( *phúsei phílous einai*). Sickness is what then emerges, an equally natural sickness, an evil naturally affecting nature. It is divided, separated from itself. When such an event occurs, one must speak of a pathology of the community. In question here is a clinic of the city. In this respect the Republic develops a nosological discourse; its diagnostic is one of ill health and dissension, a faction inside Greece (*nosein d'en to iouto ten 'Helláda kai stasiásein*). Stasis, the name that should apply to this hatred or to this enmity (*ékhthra*), is also a category of political nosography. In following a certain logic staged by *Menexenus*, this accident, evil or sickness that internal dissension (*stásis*) could not be explained, even, in the last instance, by hatred, enmity (*ekhthra*) or malice. One would have to spot in this *stásis* a fatal disorder, a stroke of bad luck, misfortune (*dustukhía*) (244a)."

29. Derrida references Loraux's essay "Cratyle a l'epreuve de Stasis," *Revue de philosophie ancienne* 1 (1987): 56–57.

30. I am aware that the term *publicness* is fraught with question marks regarding the meaning and overall milieu of *being-with, being-in common*, or *Mitsein* in Heidegger's thinking.

31. We are now in *polemos*'s death throes and, as Jean-Luc Nancy puts it, "what is taking shape . . . is the possibility of a religious or hyperreligious upheaval

or surrection. Where modes of rationality are stuck in understanding, where institutional religions poorly prolong their traditions (in fundamentalist rigidity or humanistic compromise), and where, consequently, the void in question was hollowed out . . . in the eye of the hurricane of globalization, grows inexorably an expectation, still almost silent, which surreptitiously builds toward the point of igniting" (*Dis-Enclosure*, 3).

32. Beyond the conceptual and dramatic preeminence of *The Wire* and *Breaking Bad* (in this regard see, in particular, Kraniauskas, "The Reflux of Money" and "Elasticity of Demand"), perhaps the only works (that I am aware of at this time, at least) that do not fall either in the category of moralizing complacency or of anthropological costumbrism are Víctor Hugo Rascón Banda's *Contrabando*, Juan Villoro's *El testigo*, Sara Uribe's *Antígona González*, and Antonio Ortuño's *La fila india*. For the work of costumbrist complacency, see, for example, Netflix's stable of narco-productions, *Narcos*, *Narcos Mexico*, *Sicario*, *Inside the Real Narcos*, *El Chapo*, *Pablo Escobar: El patrón del mal*, *Drug Lords*, *Surviving Escobar*, *Loving Pablo*, and *Pablo Escobar: Countdown to Death*, all of which are different variations of *Law and Order*, in which the narco-ontotheological battle between good and evil assigns the latter to the south of the US-Mexico border and the former to the north. The Galician-Spanish *Fariña* (*Cocaine Coast*) offers a respite from such contrived self-righteousness. The condition of the DEA agent Art Keller's lapsed Catholicism in Don Winslow's *The Power of the Dog* and *The Cartel* allows for a certain engagement with moral complexity and, at least, with the development and exploration of shared responsibility between north and south, even though the entire moral-legal matrix that underlies and structures US narco-*noir* can never stop preassigning guilt in a southward direction. Otherwise, the cultural representation of narco-accumulation has become largely an exploration of regional and national anthro-/necrocostumbrism (see the novels of Elmer Mendoza, Yuri Herrera's *Trabajos del reino*, Shaul Schwarz's documentary film *Narco Cultura*, Gianfranco Rosi's *Sicario Room 164*, Mathew Heineman's *Cartel Land*, or Natalia Almada's *El velador*).

33. I do not share, for example, the positive value that Rebecca Biron ("It's a Living") assigns to "death-giving" in her interpretation of Luis Estrada's 2010 film *El infierno*. Biron establishes a comparison between Molloy and Bowden's testimonial *El Sicario: The Autobiography of a Mexican Assassin* (2011) and the fiction film *El infierno*, with the conviction that the latter offers a political alternative to the former's loyalty to domination. The figuration of freedom, in other words, is what is at stake in Biron's reading. *El infierno* is the story of the protagonist Benny's immersion into his home town's drug trade after being ejected as an undocumented worker from the United States. Biron's reading is precise in terms of her thematization of the labor process represented in the works she analyzes. The film ends, however, with a desperate Benny attending the local Mexican independence bicentenary celebrations and massacring each and every one of the corrupt political, military, and ecclesiastical public officials gathered on the dais. The film's final gesture is

interpreted by Biron as the protagonist declaring "full ownership of his own labor . . . speaking back (in a hail of gunfire) to an economy based on death" (832). At this moment, Biron says, the film's protagonist "transcends the logic of work and enters the realm of being" (831), as "perhaps the only way in which the fully human — understood as radical freedom and creative performance — comes alive . . . when the *sicario* kills his capitalist bosses" (832). The ending of the film for Biron, in other words, is productive; it reinstates a humanist economy of freedom and redemption. But I find this to be a bewildering conclusion, since in the massacre the main protagonist neither transcends the logic of work nor enters the realm of being. The only thing that the final massacre guarantees is the reproduction and deepening of the technicity of the relation between the male exercise of extreme violence and the subjectivist will to power, with no inclination whatsoever toward social transgression, freedom, autonomy, or political representation. There is nothing creative or radically free in the film's final act, since the massacre merely reinstates what it purports to overthrow. The supposed supersession of self-estrangement that Biron's reading attempts to highlight occupies in fact precisely the same ground as the self-estrangement the film portrays throughout, thereby also indicating the ways in which so-called modern revolutionary thinking is never really revolutionary enough, to the extent that it reproduces the determinations of its negated object. The film is titled *El infierno* but could well have been called *El nihilismo*. Indeed, I would conjecture that it is as a result of its overriding nihilism that the film is titled *El infierno* in the first place. Though stylistically and cinematically more sophisticated than Estrada's production, exactly the same can be said of Amat Escalante's equally nihilistic film *Heli* (2013).

34. In contrast to the character of the Counselor, Art Keller, Don Winslow's DEA agent protagonist in *The Power of the Dog*, understands narco-accumulation as a fallen monotheism, but, almost as a precursor to Cormac McCarthy's analysis via the figure of "Jefe," Keller understands his complicity only in Christian terms. For this reason, while "Jefe" acts like God, Keller, in the wake of a vicious massacre, can only perform the absolution of a fake priest: "He forces himself to look at the bodies again. It's my fault, Art thinks. I brought this on these people. I'm sorry, Art thinks. I'm so so sorry. Bending over the mother and child, Art makes the sign of the cross and whispers: '*In nomine Patris et Filii et Spiritus Sancti.*' '*El poder del perro,*' he heard one of the Mexican cops murmur" (5). *The Power of the Dog* provides one of the most sophisticated interpretations of the history of narco-accumulation to date, framing it as a hemispheric upheaval in the order of war, metaphor, and state form. The "power of the dog" refers not only to the deliverance from evil petitioned in Psalms 22:20 but also to the exhaustion of the Greek-Latinic myth of Cerberus, the monstrous hound charged with guarding the gates of Hades to prevent the dead from crossing its boundary. In Winslow's novel (99–232), this metaphor of the power of the *container* succumbs to post-katechontic decontainment. In the context of the "Mexican Trampoline," in which the CIA organizes and chaperones shipments of cocaine into the United States as part of the war against communism in Central

America in the 1980s (also see Webb, *Dark Alliance*), the US state becomes an active participant in transnational narco-accumulation and the killing industry it produces: "Then Art understands —Cerberus isn't a guard, he's an usher. A panting, grinning, tongue-lolling doorman who eagerly invites you into the underworld. And you can't resist" (178). In *The Power of the Dog* Cerberus refers not to containment but to its emptying out. It is the demetaphorization of the modern Hobbesian state form. It is decontainment, the post-katechontic order.

35. As Heidegger tells us: "*Technikon* means that which belongs to *techne*. . . . *Techne* is the name not only for the activities and skills of the craftsman, but also for the arts of the mind and the fine arts. *Techne* belongs to bringing-forth, to *poiesis*; it is something poietic. . . . Technology comes to presence in the realm where revealing and unconcealment take place, where *aletheia*, truth, happens" ("The Question concerning Technology," 12–13).

36. Herein lies the distinction between the politics of *hegemony*, which places repetition on the side of the sufficiency of the signifier to represent (thereby striving to conceal the problem of the signifier itself), and *posthegemony*, which inhabits and strives to think from within the split of the signifier from the real and the unconcealment of the insufficiency of the signifier to represent. Hegemony closes off the real in the name of a specific politics, or circumscription of "freedom," or law of subjectivity, whereas posthegemony is fearless before the horrors of the law's inherent inability to conceal or circumscribe —to contain — its split from the real, which is namelessness.

37. Once again, I refer the reader to Derrida: "No doubt the thinking of being announces the history of non-metaphor on the basis of which metaphoricity is thought. But it does not announce itself prophetically like a new day (prophets only ever announce other metaphors), as something that will be; it announces itself as the impossible on the basis of which the possible is thought as such. . . . So the thinking of being announces the horizon of non-metaphor. But the gesture whereby it announces this horizon, even though it denounces the entirety of *past* metaphor (onto-theology), happens in a metaphor about which it does not yet know — because it is irreducibly to-come —what that metaphor is hiding. The thinking of being is even the only respect for the future as such, far from being a sentimental and nostalgic traditionalism. It is that on the basis of which all thoughts that claim to be *progressive* can arise as what they are" (*Heidegger*, 223).

38. It remains unclear at the end of *2666* what precisely Bolaño understood by "taking care" or "safekeeping." It has to be clear, however, given the writing itself, that it is related intimately to the question of mortality, including his own. Caring in Heidegger refers to the "authentic mode of being in a world," for, he continues, "in its caring, life approaches itself and addresses itself in a worldly manner" (*Ontology*, 79). In *Being and Time* caring is reckoning with time and temporality, for "temporality reveals itself as the meaning of authentic care" (374). Caring "occurs and runs its course in time" and reckons with it from therein. As such, care is Being-toward-death (378) as "coming-towards-oneself," understood in factical terms as

temporalization. Care and facticity, or reckoning in order to come to understanding by circumventing "all those significations of 'future,' 'past,' and 'Present' which thrust themselves upon us from the ordinary conception of time" (374), is constitutive for "Being-in-the-world" (382). In "Letter on Humanism" Heidegger observes that "the greatest care must be fostered on the ethical bond" (268). Here Heidegger does not understand ethics as a collective accommodation to a common (Christian, for example) law, which would be a moralist, sociological gesture. On the contrary, he considers the ethical bond to be one's reckoning with the perceiving, thinking, and hearing of the thrownness of *ek-sistence*, or Being-toward-death, from within the ontological difference, that is, from within the difference between *beings* and *Being*. *2666* is not entirely un-Heideggerian in its concern for caring or in its opening to the possibility of reckoning with the limitations and clearing of a way toward understanding and meaningfulness, or facticity. Having said that, neither is *2666* entirely Heideggerian (which is of little importance to me), since it does not reckon with the "significations of 'future,' 'past,' and 'Present' which thrust themselves upon us from the ordinary conception of time" (Heidegger, *Being and Time*, 374). It is certainly significant — though at the same time utterly fortuitous, since Bolaño apparently did not conceive of *2666* as a single novel (at least according to his calculations in the face of death) — that the writing should have reached its outer limit, its finality, on the basis of the question for caring in the context of limitless death-giving and mortality.

39. The 2019 meeting of the Latin American Studies Association, the official professional arm of the field of Latin Americanism in general, was titled "Nuestra América: Justice and Inclusion," which is symptomatic of the occlusion of the real question handed down in globalization.

40. See Hernández, *La verdadera noche de Iguala*. The uncovering of mass graves in Mexico will be ongoing for decades to come. See, for example, Grillo, "The Paradox of Mexico's Mass Graves."

41. See Castillo, "The Mexican Government's Frontera Sur Program."

42. It is not by chance that at the time of writing Central American asylum seekers in the United States are now returned to Mexican territory in order to await the result of their legal petition for protection and state recognition by the US government. Indeed, even El Salvador has agreed to take asylum seekers sent from the United States. The agreement, which is similar to one signed with Guatemala in July 2019, indicates that any asylum seeker who does not hail from El Salvador can be deported and forced to seek asylum there. Although US officials have said the agreements would apply to people who passed through El Salvador or Guatemala on their way to the United States, the agreement does not actually make that clear. Such agreements essentially strip asylum seekers of all rights in the United States.

43. I find Rita Segato's use of the term "second state" (*La escritura en el cuerpo*), her embrace more recently of the notion of "Second Reality," and her understanding of social violence as a specular reality in relation to the social sphere controlled by the State to be overly simplistic, since the post-sovereign market-state duopoly

exhausts specular, and therefore potentially dialectical, relations between state and society.

44. In this regard also see Villalobos Ruminott, "Las edades del cadáver."

45. *La jaula de oro* (lit. "the golden cage") takes its title from the *corrido* of the same name by Los Tigres del Norte, in which the American Dream is portrayed as a fallacy. Ironically, the title of Quemada Díez's film was retitled *The Golden Dream* for an English-speaking audience, presumably echoing a moment in the film in which its Guatemalan main characters are asked by the Mexican *migra* where they are from. One of the characters, Juan, responds that they are from a place called "*Sueño de oro*" but that they have no documentation to prove it. They are immediately deported back to Guatemala. In the pages that follow I refer to the film as *The Golden Cage*, presumably reflecting the original intention of the filmmaker.

46. See Solórzano, "La jaula de oro de Diego Quemada-Díez." Solórzano is correct to point out a distinction between Quemada Díez's production and other films of migration such as *Sin nombre* (Cary Fukunaga, 2009) and *La vida precoz y breve de Sabina Rivas* (Luis Mandoki, 2012), which tend to emphasize, in their subordination to anthropological costumbrism, depthless victimization over narrative and filmic complexity. My sojourn into *The Golden Cage* is, of course, determined by the fact that I am not a film scholar and am uninterested in the overriding subordination to technicity, encyclopedic descriptivism, and subjectivism of that field.

47. At this moment we encounter an echo and inversion of the final frames of Sergei Eisenstein's 1925 *Strike*, a film that provides us with one of the very first examples of cinematic montage, understood as the cutting, disorientation, and re-setting of the image itself. In this classic, the final sequences, titled "The Carnage," depict a massacre of striking workers by tsarist government forces. These images of antilabor violence are interspersed with the gruesome butchery of a cow in a slaughterhouse, the obvious analogy being that striking labor is treated no better than cattle by the tsarist class structure (https://www.youtube.com /watch?v=uLiNKaUpoAA). In *The Golden Cage* we merely witness the solitude of a collective form of migrant labor that is subordinated fully to the industrialized technicity of death-giving as a living, and as a way of life. At the end of *The Golden Cage* humanity is merely held fast as a laboring animal, as value producing itself by producing via its equipment the meat of dead animal objects. Herein there is literally no room for freedom, sexual difference, or the animal.

48. For this reason, it is not farfetched to suggest that Chauk marks the staging of the voice of the friend and, in particular, the representation of the foreignness of voice. Through Chauk the film *thematizes*, on the ontic level alone, the voice of the friend and the voice of the alien. It stages the foreignness of voice as the friend-alien itself. Sara "hears" and is hospitable to the relation. Juan refuses to lend an ear. At one point, Chauk addresses Juan in Spanish as "Hermano" (Brother). Juan rejects the gesture of fraternity by responding "Fucking Chauk. You think you can speak Spanish now?" The figure of Chauk points the story in the direction of the

question of being itself, to the extent that his trajectory throughout the film can be placed closer to the voice of ontological difference than any other figure or presence therein. As David Farrell Krell puts it in *Phantoms of the Other*, in reference to Heidegger's notion of *Geschlecht* (sex, race, species, genus, gender, stock, family, generation or genealogy, community): "If the voice of the friend speaks words we cannot understand, even though we can hear them, would we not be opened up in a very special way to the fragility of our being and its ownmost possibility? Furthermore, would not the struggle *against* such a foreign friend, turning a deaf ear to his or her wants and needs, indicate not open resolve but an attempted yet futile flight from one's ownmost ability to be?" (112–13). What Farrell Krell points to here could be considered to be precisely the historical movement of Juan in *The Golden Cage*, who slowly passes from deafness to hearing in the face of being-toward-death.

49. Here the term *ex-scription* is taken from Jean-Luc Nancy's essay "Decision of Existence" (107). In a recent work, Alberto Moreiras observes that via the use of such a term Nancy offers "a parergonal possibility of infrapolitics—an infrapolitical parergon, or an infrapolitics as a practice of the parergon. The infrapolitical *Durchbruch* [breakthrough], to the precise extent that it does not go anywhere (else), is always and only ever parergonal rupture, or ex-scription" (*Diferencia absoluta*, 25). *Parergon* refers to the ornamental accessory or embellishment of a work (of art, for example), a subordinate activity or work simultaneously in and beyond the work that unworks the work of the work, liberating it from the centering of its own symbolic order (in this regard see Derrida, *The Truth in Painting*). In the case of *The Golden Cage*, *teiv* and its images mark a movement in the direction of parergonal rupture with, or ex-scription from, the industrialized screening of positive anthropology.

50. I am referring to spaciousness here in a sense that should not be equated with the notion of space as *extensio*, or as "political space." Akin to the German *Erstreckung* referenced in Heidegger, I am referring to spaciousness as a "spacing which, 'before' the determination of space as *extensio*, comes to extend or stretch out being-there, the *there* of Being, *between* birth and death. Essential dimension of *Dasein*, the *Erstreckung* opens up the *between* that links it at once to its birth and to its death, the movement of suspense by which it is *tended* out and extended of itself *between* birth and death, these two receiving meaning only from that intervallic movement. *Dasein* affects itself, and that auto-affection belongs to the ontological structure of its historicity" (Derrida, "Geschlecht," 77). There is nothing pessimistic here. For the Hegelian Alexandre Kojève, space is quite simply "the place where things are stopped" (*Introduction to the Reading of Hegel*, 136–37), and man is the servant of the power of representation. In contrast, there is an affirmation in Heidegger, for instrumentalism, calculation, and representation succumb before the previously unavailable unconcealment of what was previously concealed, now presencing forth from itself: "Space spatializes. It makes room. Space frees up, namely, nearness and farness. . . . In the spatializing of space, clearing plays. . . . In the temporalizing of time, clearing plays" ("On the Question concerning the Determination of the Matter for Thinking," 221).

51. Note also in relation to the end of storytelling, that "being-in-the-world is always fallen. *Dasein's 'average everydayness' can be defined as 'Being-in-the-world which is falling and disclosed, thrown and projecting, and for which its ownmost potentiality-for-Being is an issue, both in its Being alongside the 'world' and in its Being-with Others*" (Heidegger, *Being and Time*, 225). Also see Derrida, *Heidegger*, 223.

52. "Experiencing the groundlessness of sense-making returns you to the meaningful in its meaningfulness, with an awareness that mortality — being ever at the point of mortality — underlies the entire meaning-process" (Sheehan, "Facticity and Ereignis," 65).

53. It is precisely in this regard that the film's numerous sequences of migrants just being with each other atop the Beast, a momentary shelter from the violence below, before, and behind them, take on particular significance.

54. "The problematic of the Being of space . . . must be turned in such a direction as to clarify the possibilities of Being in general. . . . Unless we go back to the world, space cannot be conceived . . . spatiality is not discoverable at all except on the basis of the world" (Heidegger, *Being and Time*, 148).

55. This is also the basis for Jorge Alemán's syntagm "Solitude:Common," which refers to that which constitutes an experience of radical solitude that is, nevertheless, most common to all. Solitude here is understood in Heideggerian terms as thrownness in its relation to death. See Alemán, *En la frontera*.

# Works Cited

Aeschylus. *Prometheus Bound*. Trans. James Scully and C. J. Herington. New York: Oxford University Press, 1989.

Agamben, Giorgio. *The Time That Remains: A Commentary on the Letter to the Romans*. Trans. Patricia Dailey. Stanford, CA: Stanford University Press, 2005.

———. *Homo Sacer: Sovereign Power and Bare Life*. Trans. Daniel Heller-Roazen. Stanford, CA: Stanford University Press, 1998.

———. *Stasis: Civil War as a Political Paradigm*. Trans. Nicholas Heron. Stanford, CA: Stanford University Press, 2015.

———. *The Mystery of Evil: Benedict XVI and the End of Days*. Trans. Adam Kotsko. Stanford, CA: Stanford University Press, 2017.

Ahmed, Azam. "In Mexico, It's Easy to Kill a Journalist." *New York Times*. April 29, 2017. https://www.nytimes.com/2017/04/29/world/americas/veracruz-mexico -reporters-killed.html.

Alemán, Jorge. *En la frontera: Sujeto y capitalismo (Conversaciones con María Victoria Gimbel)*. Barcelona: Gedisa Editorial, 2014.

Althusser, Louis. *Philosophy of the Encounter: Later Writings, 1978–1987*. New York: Verso, 2006.

Álvarez Solís, Ángel Octavio. "On a Newly Arisen Infrapolitical Tone in Theory." *Transmodernity: Journal of Peripheral Cultural Production of the Luso-Hispanic World* 5, no. 1, special issue on "Infrapolitics and Posthegemony," ed. Jaime Rodríguez-Matos (2015): 123–41.

Álvarez Yágüez, Jorge. "Crisis epocal: La política en el límite." *Debats* 128, no. 3, special issue on "Infrapolítica y posthegemonía," ed. Alberto Moreiras (2015): 9–28.

———. "La forma 'política' y el populismo." In *Populismo versus Republicanismo: Genealogía, historia, crítica*, ed. José Luis Villacañas Berlanga and César Ruiz Sanjuán, 191–209. Madrid: Biblioteca Nueva, 2018.

Anderson, Perry. "The Antinomies of Antonio Gramsci." *New Left Review* 1, no. 100 (1976): 5–78.

Arendt, Hannah. *Crises of the Republic.* New York: Harcourt Brace & Co., 1972.

———. *The Origins of Totalitarianism.* New York: Harcourt, 1976.

Arrighi, Giovanni. *The Long Twentieth Century: Money, Power, and the Origins of Our Times.* New York: Verso, 1994.

———. *Adam Smith in Beijing: Lineages of the 21st Century.* New York: Verso, 2010.

Axelos, Kostas. *Alienation, Praxis, and Techne in the Thought of Karl Marx.* Trans. Ronald Bruzina. Austin: University of Texas Press, 1976.

———. *Introduction to a Future Way of Thought: On Marx and Heidegger.* Ed. Stuart Elden. Lüneburg: Meson Press, Leuphana University of Lüneburg, 2015.

Badiou, Alain. *The Communist Hypothesis.* Trans. David Macey and Steve Corcoran. New York: Verso, 2010.

———. *Saint Paul: The Foundation of Universalism.* Trans. Ray Brassier. Stanford, CA: Stanford University Press, 2003.

———. *The Rebirth of History: Time of Riots and Uprisings.* Trans. Gregory Elliott. New York: Verso, 2012.

———. *The True Life.* Trans. Susan Spitzer. Malden: Polity, 2017.

Balibar, Etienne. "Outlines of a Topography of Cruelty." *Constellations* 8, no. 1 (2001): 15–29.

———. "Towards a New Critique of Political Economy: From Generalized Surplus Value to Total Subsumption." In *Capitalism: Concept, Idea, Image, Aspects of Marx's Capital Today*, ed. Peter Osborne, Éric Alliez, and Eric-John Russell, 36–57. London: CRMEP, 2019.

Balibar, Etienne, and Immanuel Wallerstein. *Race, Nation, Class: Ambiguous Identities.* Trans. Chris Turner. New York: Verso, 1991.

Bazzicalupo, Laura. "Populismo y liberalismo: La pretensión de la inmanencia." In *Populismo versus Republicanismo: Genealogía, historia, crítica*, ed. José Luis Villacañas Berlanga and César Ruiz Sanjuán, 365–77. Madrid: Biblioteca Nueva, 2018.

Beasley-Murray, Jon. *Posthegemony: Political Theory and Latin America.* Minneapolis: University of Minnesota Press, 2010.

———. "Stasis: Civil War as Threshold between Infrapolitics and Politics." 2016. https://infrapolitica.com/2016/05/25/stasis-civil-war-as-threshold-between-infrapolitics-and-politics/.

Benjamin, Walter. "Critique of Violence." In *Selected Writings*, vol. 1: *1913–1926*, ed. Marcus Bullock and Michael W. Jennings, 236–52. Cambridge, MA: Harvard University Press, 1996.

———. "The Destructive Character." In *Selected Writings*, vol. 2: *1927–1934*, ed. Marcus Bullock and Michael W. Jennings, 541–42. Cambridge, MA: Harvard University Press, 1999.

Biron, Rebecca E. "It's a Living: Hit Men in the Mexican Narco War." *PMLA* 127, no. 4 (2012): 820–34.

Bolaño, Roberto. *2666*. New York: Vintage Español, 2009.

Bowden, Charles. *Murder City: Ciudad Juárez and the Global Economy's New Killing Fields*. New York: Nation Books, 2011.

Braunstein, Néstor. *El inconsciente, la técnica y el discurso capitalista*. México: Siglo XXI Editores, 2011.

Brown, Wendy. *Walled States, Waning Sovereignty*. New York: Zone, 2010.

Buci-Glucksmann, Christine. *Gramsci and the State*. London: Lawrence & Wishart, 1980.

Budgen, Sebastian, Stathis Kouvelakis, and Slavoj Žižek, eds. *Lenin Reloaded: Toward a Politics of Truth*. Durham, NC: Duke University Press, 2007.

Buñuel, Luis, dir. *Los olvidados*. 1950. DVD.

Cabezas, Óscar. *Postsoberanía: Literatura, política y trabajo*. Lanús: Ediciones La Cebra, 2013.

Cacciari, Massimo. *Europe and Empire: On the Political Forms of Globalization*. Ed. Alessandro Carrera. Trans. Massimo Verdicchio. New York: Fordham University Press, 2016.

———. *The Withholding Power: An Essay on Political Theology*. Trans. Edi Pucci. Intro. Howard Caygill. New York: Bloomsbury Academic, 2018.

Castillo, Alejandra. "The Mexican Government's Frontera Sur Program: An Inconsistent Immigration Policy." Council on Hemispheric Affairs, October 25, 2016. http://www.coha.org/wp-content/uploads/2016/10/The-Mexican -Government%E2%80%99s-Frontera-Sur-Program-An-Inconsistent-Immigration -Policy.pdf.

Castro Orellana, Rodrigo, ed. *Poshegemonía: El final de un paradigma de la filosofía política en América Latina*. Madrid: Biblioteca Nueva, 2015.

Cerrato, Maddalena. "Infrapolitics and Shibumi: Infrapolitical Practice Between and Beyond Metaphysical Closure and End of History." *Transmodernity: Journal of Peripheral Cultural Production of the Luso-Hispanic World* 5, no. 1, special issue on "Infrapolitics and Posthegemony," ed. Jaime Rodríguez-Matos (2015): 81–105.

Copjec, Joan. *Read My Desire: Lacan against the Historicists*. New York: Verso, 2015.

Correa-Cabrera, Guadalupe. *Los Zetas Inc.: Criminal Corporations, Energy, and Civil War in Mexico*. Austin: University of Texas Press, 2017.

Davidson, Neil. *How Revolutionary Were the Bourgeois Revolutions?* Chicago: Haymarket, 2012.

Deleuze, Gilles. "Postscript on the Societies of Control." *October* 59 (1992): 3–7.

Derrida, Jacques. *Aporias*. Stanford, CA: Stanford University Press, 1993.

———. "Cogito and the History of Madness." In *Writing and Difference*, trans. Alan Bass, 31–63. Chicago: University of Chicago Press, 1978.

———. "Faith and Knowledge: The Two Sources of 'Religion' at the Limits of Reason Alone." In *Acts of Religion*, ed. Gil Anidjar, 40–101. New York: Routledge, 2001.

——. "Geschlecht II: Heidegger's Hand." In *Deconstruction and Philosophy: The Texts of Jacques Derrida*, ed. John Sallis, trans. John P. Leavey, 161–96. Chicago: University of Chicago Press, 1987.

——. *The Gift of Death.* Trans. David Wills. Chicago: University of Chicago Press, 1995.

——. *Heidegger: The Question of Being and History.* Ed. Thomas Dutoit. Trans. Geoffrey Bennington. Chicago: University of Chicago Press, 2016.

——. *The Politics of Friendship.* Trans. George Collins. New York: Verso, 1997.

——. *Rogues: Two Essays on Reason.* Trans. Pascale-Anne Brault and Michael Naas. Stanford, CA: Stanford University Press, 2005.

——. *Specters of Marx: The State of the Debt, the Work of Mourning, and the New International.* Trans. Peggy Kamuf. New York: Routledge, 1994.

——. *Of Spirit: Heidegger and the Question.* Trans. Geoffrey Bennington and Rachel Bowlby. Chicago: University of Chicago Press, 1989.

——. *The Truth in Painting.* Trans. Geoffrey Bennington and Ian McLeod. Chicago: University of Chicago Press, 1987.

Derrida, Jacques, Hans-Georg Gadamer, and Phillipe Lacoue-Labarthe. *Heidegger, Philosophy, and Politics: The Heidelberg Conference.* New York: Fordham University Press, 2016.

Dove, Patrick. *Literature and "Interregnum": Globalization, War, and the Crisis of Sovereignty in Latin America.* Albany: SUNY Press, 2016.

Dowd, Shannon E. "Stasis: Border Wars in Twentieth- and Twenty-First-Century Latin American Literature and Film." PhD diss., University of Michigan, 2017.

Eisenstein, Sergei, dir. *Strike.* 1925. https://www.youtube.com/watch?v=u8lLty-jW7g.

Epstein, Louis. "The Opioid Crisis in America and Mexico." Council on Hemispheric Affairs, August 1, 2017. http://www.coha.org/the-opioid-crisis -in-america-and-mexico/.

Esposito, Roberto. *The Origin of the Political: Hannah Arendt or Simone Weil?* Trans. Vincenzo Binetti and Gareth Williams. New York: Fordham University Press, 2017.

——. *Two: The Machine of Political Theology and the Place of Thought.* Trans. Zakiya Hanafi. New York: Fordham University Press, 2015.

Farrell Krell, David. *Phantoms of the Other: Four Generations of Derrida's Geschlecht.* Albany: SUNY Press, 2015.

Foucault, Michel. *The Birth of Biopolitics: Lectures at the Collège de France, 1978– 1979.* New York: Picador, 2004.

——. *The Courage of Truth (The Government of Self and Others II): Lectures at the Collège de France, 1983–1984.* Trans. Graham Burchill. New York: Picador, 2011.

——. *"Society Must Be Defended": Lectures at the Collège de France, 1975–1976.* New York: Picador, 2003.

Franco, Jean. *Cruel Modernity.* Durham, NC: Duke University Press, 2013.

Freud, Sigmund. *Group Psychology and the Analysis of the Ego.* Trans. James Strachey. London: International Psychoanalytical Press, 1922.

Fried, Gregory. *Heidegger's Polemos: From Being to Politics.* New Haven, CT: Yale University Press, 2000.

———. "A Letter to Emmanuel Faye." *Philosophy Today* (Fall 2011): 219–52.

Galli, Carlo. *Janus's Gaze: Essays on Carl Schmitt.* Ed. Adam Sitze. Trans. Amanda Minervini. Durham, NC: Duke University Press, 2015.

———. "Left and Right: Why They Still Make Sense." In *Sovereignty in Ruins: A Politics of Crisis,* ed. George Edmondson and Klaus Mladek. Durham, NC: Duke University Press, 2017.

———. *Political Spaces and Global War.* Ed. Adam Sitze. Trans. Elisabeth Fay. Minneapolis: University of Minnesota Press, 2010.

González Rodríguez, Sergio. *Campo de Guerra.* México: Anagrama, 2014.

Gramsci, Antonio. *Prison Notebooks.* Vols. 1–3. Ed. and trans. Joseph A. Buttigieg. New York: Columbia University Press, 2007.

———. *Selections from the Prison Notebooks.* Ed. and trans. Quintin Hoare and Geoffrey Nowell Smith. New York: International Publishers, 1971.

Grillo, Ioan. "The Paradox of Mexico's Mass Graves." *New York Times,* July 19, 2017. https://www.nytimes.com/2017/07/19/opinion/mexico-mass-grave-drug-cartel.html.

Guzmán, R. Andrés. "Natalia Almada's *El velador* and the Violence of Narco-Capitalism." *Journal of Latin American Cultural Studies* 26, no. 1 (2017): 109–29.

———. *Universal Citizenship: Latina/o Studies at the Limits of Identity.* Austin: University of Texas Press, 2019.

Harcourt, Bernard E. *Exposed: Desire and Disobedience in the Digital Age.* Cambridge, MA: Harvard University Press, 2015.

Hardt, Michael, and Antonio Negri. *Empire.* Cambridge, MA: Harvard University Press, 2001.

———. *Multitude: War and Democracy in the Age of Empire.* New York: Penguin, 2004.

Harney, Stefano, and Fred Moten. *The Undercommons: Fugitive Planning and Black Study.* New York: Minor Compositions, 2013.

Harvey, David. *A Brief History of Neoliberalism.* New York: Oxford University Press, 2005.

———. *The New Imperialism.* Oxford: Oxford University Press, 2003.

Heidegger, Martin. "The Age of the World Picture." In *The Question concerning Technology and Other Essays,* 115–54. New York: Harper & Row, 1977.

———. *Being and Time.* Trans. John Macquarrie and Edward Robinson. Oxford: Basil Blackwell, 1978.

———. *Hegel.* Trans. Joseph Arel and Niels Feuerhahn. Bloomington: Indiana University Press, 2015.

———. *The History of Beyng.* Trans. William McNeill and Jeffrey Powell. Bloomington: Indiana University Press, 2015.

———. *Hölderlin's Hymn "Remembrance."* Trans. William McNeill and Julia Ireland. Bloomington: Indiana University Press, 2018.

——. "Letter on Humanism." In *Pathmarks*, ed. William McNeill, 239–76. Cambridge: Cambridge University Press, 1998.

——. *Nietzsche*. Vol. 4: *Nihilism*. Ed. David Farrell Krell. Trans. Joan Stambaugh, David Farrell Krell, and Frank A. Capuzzi. San Francisco: Harper Collins, 1982.

——. "On the Essence of Ground." In *Pathmarks*, ed. William McNeill, 97–135. Cambridge: Cambridge University Press, 1998.

——. "The Origin of the Work of Art." In *Poetry, Language, Thought*, 15–87. New York: Harper & Row, 1971.

——. *Parmenides*. Trans. André Schuwer and Richard Rojcewicz. Bloomington: University of Indiana Press, 1998.

——. "The Question concerning Technology." In *The Question concerning Technology and Other Essays*, 3–35. New York: Harper & Row, 1977.

——. "The Word of Nietzsche: 'God Is Dead.'" In *The Question concerning Technology and Other Essays*, 53–114. New York: Harper & Row, 1977.

——. "On the Grammar and Etymology of the Word 'Being.'" In *Introduction to Metaphysics*, translated Gregory Fried and Richard Polt, 57–81. New Haven, CT: Yale University Press, 2014.

——. "On the Question concerning the Determination of the Matter for Thinking." *Epoché* 14, no. 2 (2010): 213–23.

——. *Ontology: The Hermeneutics of Facticity*. Bloomington: Indiana University Press, 1999.

Hell, Julia. *The Conquest of Ruins: The Third Reich and the Fall of Rome*. Chicago: University of Chicago Press, 2019.

——. "Katechon: Carl Schmitt's Imperial Theology and the Ruins of the Future." *The Germanic Review* 84, no. 4 (2009): 283–356.

Hernández, Anabel. *La verdadera noche de Iguala: La historia que el gobierno trató de ocultar*. México: Vintage Español, 2016.

Hileman, Garrick, and Michel Rauchs. "Global Cryptocurrency Benchmarking Study." Cambridge Centre for Alternative Finance, University of Cambridge Judge Business School, 2017. https://www.jbs.cam.ac.uk/fileadmin/user_upload /research/centres/alternative-finance/downloads/2017-global-cryptocurrency -benchmarking-study.pdf.

Hobbes, Thomas. *Leviathan*. Ed. J. C. A. Gaskin. Oxford: Oxford University Press, 1998.

Hoelzl, Michael. "Before the Anti-Christ Is Revealed: On the Katechontic Structure of Messianic Time." In *The Politics to Come: Power, Modernity, and the Messianic*, ed. Arthur Bradley and Paul Fletcher, 98–110. New York: Bloomsbury Academic, 2010.

Hoyos, Héctor. *Beyond Bolaño: The Global Latin American Novel*. New York: Columbia University Press, 2015.

Huntington, Samuel. *The Clash of Civilizations and the Remaking of World Order*. New York: Simon and Schuster, 1996.

———. *Who Are We? The Challenges to America's National Identity*. New York: Simon and Schuster, 2005.

Infrapolitical Deconstruction Collective. https://infrapolitica.com/.

Jameson, Fredric. "Future City." *New Left Review* 21 (May/June 2003): 65–79.

———. *The Seeds of Time*. New York: Columbia University Press, 1994.

Kalimtzis, Kostas. *Aristotle on Political Enmity and Disease: An Inquiry into Stasis*. Albany, SUNY Press, 2000.

Kennan, George. "Long Telegram to George Marshall." February 22, 1946. Harry S. Truman Administration File, Elsey Papers. https://digitalarchive.wilsoncenter.org /document/116178.pdf.

Kierkegaard, Soren. *The Concept of Anxiety: A Simple Psychologically Oriented Deliberation in View of the Dogmatic Problem of Hereditary Sin*. Trans. Alastair Hannay. New York: Norton, 2015.

Kissinger, Henry. *World Order*. New York: Penguin, 2014.

Kojève, Alexandre. *Introduction to the Reading of Hegel: Lectures on "The Phenomenology of Spirit."* Ed. Allan Bloom. Trans. James H. Nichols Jr. Ithaca, NY: Cornell University Press, 1980.

Kraniauskas, John. "Elasticity of Demand: Reflections on *The Wire*." *Radical Philosophy* 154 (March/April 2009): 25–34.

———. "The Reflux of Money: Outlaw Accumulation and Territorialization in *Breaking Bad*." In *Capitalism: Concept, Idea, Image. Aspects of Marx's Capital Today*, ed. Peter Osborne, Éric Alliez, and Eric-John Russell, 219–45. Kingston upon Thames: CRMEP, 2019.

Lacan, Jacques. *Anxiety: The Seminar of Jacques Lacan, Book X*. Ed. Jacques-Alain Miller. Trans. A. R. Price. Malden: Polity, 2014.

———. "Discours de Jacques Lacan à l'Université de Milan le 12 mai 1972." In *Lacan in Italia 1953–1978*, 32–55. Milan: La Salamandra, 1978.

———. *The Other Side of Psychoanalysis: The Seminar of Jacques Lacan, Book XVII*. Trans. Russell Grigg. New York: Norton, 2007.

Laclau, Ernesto, and Chantal Mouffe. *Hegemony and Socialist Strategy: Towards a Radical Democratic Politics*. New York: Verso, 1985/2001.

———. *On Populist Reason*. New York: Verso, 2005.

Lacoue-Labarthe, Phillipe. *Heidegger, Art, and Politics*. Oxford: Basil Blackwell, 1990.

Lenin, Vladimir. "The Dual Power." *Pravda*, April 1917. https://www.marxists.org /archive/lenin/works/1917/apr/09.htm.

Levinson, Brett. "Case Closed: Madness and Dissociation in *2666*." *Journal of Latin American Cultural Studies* 18, nos. 2–3 (December 2009): 177–91.

———. *Market and Thought: Meditations on the Political and Biopolitical*. New York: Fordham University Press, 2004.

Loraux, Nicole. "Cratyle a l'epreuve de Stasis." *Revue de Philosophie Ancienne* 1 (1987): 56–57.

————. *The Divided City: On Memory and Forgetting in Ancient Athens*. New York: Zone, 2006.

Lupher, David A. *Romans in a New World: Classical Models in Sixteenth-Century Spanish America*. Ann Arbor: University of Michigan Press, 2006.

Lyotard, Francois. *The Postmodern Condition: A Report on Knowledge*. Trans. Geoffrey Bennington and Brian Massumi. Minneapolis: University of Minnesota Press, 1984.

Maldonado Aranda, Salvador. "Stories of Drug Trafficking in Rural Mexico: Territories, Drugs, and Cartels in Michoacán." *European Review of Latin American and Caribbean Studies* 94 (2013): 43–64.

————. "'You Don't See Any Violence but Here It Leads to Ugly Things': Forced Solidarity and State Violence in Michoacán, Mexico." *Dialectical Anthropology* 38, no. 2 (2014): 153–71.

Marchart, Oliver. *Post-Foundational Political Thought: Political Difference in Nancy, Lefort, Badiou, and Laclau*. Edinburgh: Edinburgh University Press, 2007.

Marramao, Giacomo. *The Passage West: Philosophy after the Age of the Nation State*. Trans. Matteo Mandarini. New York: Verso, 2012.

Martínez, Oscar. *The Beast: Riding the Rails and Dodging Narcos on the Migrant Trail*. New York: Verso, 2014.

Martínez Marzoa, Felipe. *La filosofía de El Capital*. Madrid: Abada Editores, 2018.

Marx, Karl. *Capital: A Critique of Political Economy*. Vol. 1. Trans. Ben Fowkes. London: Penguin, 1990.

————. *The Eighteenth Brumaire of Louis Bonaparte*. New York: International Publishers, 1994.

Mbembe, Achille. "Necropolitics." *Public Culture* 15, no. 1 (2003): 11–40.

McCarthy, Cormac. *The Counselor: A Screenplay*. New York: Vintage, 2013.

Mendoza de Jesús, Ronald. "Sovereignty: An Infrapolitical Question." *Transmodernity: Journal of Peripheral Cultural Production of the Luso-Hispanic World* 5, no .1, special issue on "Infrapolitics and Posthegemony," ed. Jaime Rodríguez-Matos (2015): 52–80.

Monaghan, Angela. "Drugs and Prostitution to Be Included in UK National Accounts." *The Guardian*, May 29, 2014.

Moore, Jason W. *Capitalism in the Web of Life: Ecology and the Accumulation of Capital*. New York: Verso, 2015.

Moreiras, Alberto. "Comentario a *Stasis* de Giorgio Agamben." 2016. https://infrapolitica.com/2015/09/10/comentario-a-stasis-de-giorgio-agamben-por-alberto-moreiras/.

————. "A Conversation with Alberto Moreiras Regarding the Notion of Infrapolitics." With Alejandra Castillo, Jorge Álvarez Yágüez, Maddalena Cerrato, Sam Steinberg, and Ángel Octavio Álvarez Solís. *Transmodernity: Journal of Peripheral Cultural Production of the Luso-Hispanic World* 5, no. 1, special issue on "Infrapolitics and Posthegemony," ed. Jaime Rodríguez-Matos (2015): 142–58.

———. "An Example of Infrapolitics." 2014. https://infrapolitica.com/2014/09/18/an-example-of-infrapolitics-by-alberto-moreiras/.

———. *The Exhaustion of Difference: The Politics of Latin American Cultural Studies*. Durham, NC: Duke University Press, 2001.

———. *Infrapolítica: La diferencia absoluta (entre vida y política) de la que ningún experto puede hablar*. Santiago de Chile: Palinodia Editores, 2019.

———. "Infrapolítica y política de la infrapolítica." *Debats* 128, no. 3, special issue on "Infrapolítica y posthegemonía," ed. Alberto Moreiras (2015): 53–73.

———. "Infrapolitics: The Project and Its Politics: Allegory and Denarrativization; A Note on Posthegemony." *Transmodernity: Journal of Peripheral Cultural Production of the Luso-Hispanic World* 5, no. 1, special issue on "Infrapolitics and Posthegemony," ed. Jaime Rodríguez-Matos (2015): 9–35.

———. "Keynes y el Katechon." *Anales del Seminario de Historia de la Filosofía* 30, no. 1 (2013): 157–68.

———. *Línea de sombra: El no sujeto de lo político*. Santiago de Chile: Palinodia Editores, 2006.

———. *Manual de infrapolítica*. Unpublished manuscript. 2019.

———. *Marranismo e inscripción, o el abandono de una conciencia desdichada*. Madrid: Escolar y mayo, 2016.

———. *Tercer espacio: Literatura y duelo en América Latina*. Santiago de Chile: LOM Ediciones, 1999.

Mouffe, Chantal, ed. *The Challenge of Carl Schmitt*. New York: Verso, 1999.

———. *For a Left Populism*. New York: Verso, 2018.

———. *On the Political (Thinking in Action)*. New York: Routledge, 2005.

———. *The Return of the Political*. New York: Verso, 2005.

Nancy, Jean-Luc. *The Creation of the World or Globalization*. Trans. François Raffoul and David Pettigrew. Albany: SUNY Press, 2007.

———. "The Decision of Existence." In *The Birth to Presence*, 82–109. Stanford, CA: Stanford University Press, 1993.

———. *Dis-enclosure: The Deconstruction of Christianity*. Trans. Bettina Bergo, Gabriel Malenfant, and Michael B. Smith. New York: Fordham University Press, 2008.

———. *The Gravity of Thought: Philosophy and Literary Theory*. Trans. François Raffoul and Gregory Recco. Toronto: Humanity Books, 1997.

———. "War, Right, Sovereignty—Techne." In *Being Singular Plural*, 101–44. Stanford, CA: Stanford University Press, 2000.

Nietzsche, Friedrich. *Twilight of the Idols/The Anti-Christ*. London: Penguin, 1990.

Paley, Dawn. *Drug War Capitalism*. Oakland, CA: AK Press, 2014.

Partlow, Joshua. "In Mexico, the Price of America's Hunger for Heroin." *Washington Post*, May 30, 2017. https://www.washingtonpost.com/graphics/2017/world/violence-is-soaring-in-the-mexican-towns-that-feed-americas-heroin-habit/?utm_term=.97648db48b7b.

Pullella, Philip. "Pope Rails against Dictatorship of the Economy, Urges Reform."
    *Reuters*, May 16, 2013. https://www.reuters.com/article/pope-economy/pope-rails
    -against-dictatorship-of-the-economy-urges-reform-idUSL6N0DX27N20130516.

Quemada Díez, Diego, dir. *La jaula de oro*. 2013. DVD.

Reguillo, Rosanna. "De las violencias: caligrafía y gramática del horror." *Desacatos*
    40 (September–December 2012): 33–46.

Rivera García, Antonio. "De la hegemonía al populismo: Ernesto Laclau, la
    evolución de un 'Schmittiano antischmittiano.'" In *Poshegemonía: El final de un
    paradigma de la filosofía política en América Latina*, ed. Rodrigo Castro Orellana,
    29–48. Madrid: Biblioteca Nueva, 2015.

Robinson, William I. *Global Capitalism and the Crisis of Humanity*. New York:
    Cambridge University Press, 2014.

Rodríguez-Matos, Jaime. "De lo que agujerea lo Real: Lacan, crítico de la (pos)
    hegemonía." *Debats* 128, no. 3, special issue on "Infrapolítica y posthegemonía,"
    ed. Alberto Moreiras (2015): 29–40.

———. "Introduction. After the Ruin of Thinking: From Locationism to
    Infrapolitics." *Transmodernity: Journal of Peripheral Cultural Production of the
    Luso-Hispanic World* 5, no. 1, special issue on "Infrapolitics and Posthegemony,"
    ed. Jaime Rodríguez-Matos (2015): 1–8.

———. "Nihilism and the Deconstruction of Time: Notes Toward Infrapolitics."
    *Transmodernity: Journal of Peripheral Cultural Production of the Luso-Hispanic
    World* 5, no. 1, special issue on "Infrapolitics and Posthegemony," ed. Jaime
    Rodríguez-Matos (2015): 36–51.

———. *Writing of the Formless: José Lezama Lima and the End of Time*. New York:
    Fordham University Press, 2017.

Ruda, Frank. *Hegel's Rabble: An Investigation into Hegel's Philosophy of Right*.
    New York: Bloomsbury Studies in Philosophy, 2011.

Schmitt, Carl. *The Concept of the Political*. Trans. George Schwab. Chicago:
    University of Chicago Press, 1996.

———. *The Nomos of the Earth in the International Law of the Jus Publicum
    Europaeum*. Trans. G. L. Ulmen. New York: Telos, 2003.

———. *Political Theology: Four Chapters on the Concept of Sovereignty*. Trans.
    George Schwab. Chicago: University of Chicago Press, 2005.

———. *Theory of the Partisan*. New York: Telos, 2007.

Schürmann, Reiner. *Broken Hegemonies*. Trans. Reginald Lilly. Bloomington:
    Indiana University Press, 2003.

Schwarz, Shaul, dir. *Narco Cultura*. 2013. DVD.

Segato, Rita. *La escritura en el cuerpo de las mujeres asesinadas en Ciudad Juárez:
    Territorio, soberanía y crímenes de segundo estado*. Mexico: Ediciones de la
    Universidad del Claustro de Sor Juana, 2006.

Sheehan, Thomas. "Facticity and Ereignis." In *Interpreting Heidegger: Critical
    Essays*, ed. Daniel O. Dahlstrom, 42–68. Cambridge: Cambridge University
    Press, 2011.

Shelley, Percy Bysshe. "The Daemon of the World." In *The Complete Works*, ed. Thomas Hutchinson. Oxford, 1914.

———. "Prometheus Unbound: A Lyrical Drama in Four Acts." In *The Major Works Including Poetry, Prose, and Drama*, ed. Zachary Leader and Michael O'Neill, 229–313. Oxford: Oxford University Press, 2009.

Sloterdijk, Peter. *Not Saved: Essays after Heidegger*. Malden: Polity, 2017.

Solórzano, Fernanda. "La jaula de oro de Diego Quemada-Díez." *Letras libres*, July 15, 2013. https://www.letraslibres.com/mexico-espana/cinetv/la-jaula-oro -diego-quemada-diez.

Spivak, Gayatri. "Subaltern Studies: Deconstructing Historiography." In *Selected Subaltern Studies*, ed. Ranajit Guha and Gayatri Chakravorty Spivak. 3–32. New York: Oxford University Press, 1988.

Stewart, Scott. "From Colombia to New York: The Narconomics of Cocaine." *Business Insider*, June 27, 2016. https://www.businessinsider.com/from-colombia- to-new-york-city-the-economics-of-cocaine-2015-7.

Stiegler, Bernard. *Technics and Time I: The Fault of Epimetheus*. Trans. Richard Beardsworth and George Collins. Stanford: Stanford University Press, 1998.

Sumic, Jelica. "Is There a Politics in Psychoanalysis?" *Política común* 9 (2016). https://quod.lib.umich.edu/p/pc/12322227.0009.007?view=text;rgn=main.

———. "Politics in the Era of the Inexistent Other." *Política común* 2 (2012). https:// quod.lib.umich.edu/p/pc/12322227.0002.004?view=text;rgn=main.

Syal, Rajeev. "Drug Money Saved Banks in Global Crisis, Claims UN Advisor." *The Guardian*, December 12, 2009. https://www.theguardian.com/global/2009/dec/13 /drug-money-banks-saved-un-cfief-claims.

Szendy, Peter. "Katechon." In *Political Concepts: A Critical Lexicon*. https://www .politicalconcepts.org/katechon-peter-szendy/.

Taylor, Astra, dir. *Žižek!* 2005. DVD.

Thayer, Willy. "Raúl Ruiz: Imagen Estilema." *Política común* 12 (2017). https://quod .lib.umich.edu/p/pc/12322227.0012.013?view=text;rgn=main.

Thomas, Peter. *The Gramscian Moment: Philosophy, Hegemony, and Marxism*. Chicago: Haymarket, 2011.

Thunberg, Greta. "I Want You to Panic." https://womenintheworld.com/2019/01/29 /i-want-you-to-panic-climate-activist-greta-thunberg-16-lays-it-on-the-line-for -world-leaders/.

———. "You Did Not Act in Time." *The Guardian*, April 23, 2019. https://www .theguardian.com/environment/2019/apr/23/greta-thunberg-full-speech-to-mps -you-did-not-act-in-time.

Tiqqun. *Introduction to Civil War*. Los Angeles: Semiotext(e), 2010.

Villacañas, José Luis. *Populismo*. Madrid: La Huerta Grande Editorial, 2015.

Villalobos-Ruminott, Sergio. "Las edades del cadáver: dictadura, guerra, desaparición." In *Heterografías de la violencia: Historia, nihilismo, destrucción*, 199–214. Santiago de Chile: La Cebra, 2016.

———. "El poema de la universidad: nihilismo e infrapolítica." *Transmodernity:*

*Journal of Peripheral Cultural Production of the Luso-Hispanic World* 5, no. 1, special issue on "Infrapolitics and Posthegemony," ed. Jaime Rodríguez-Matos (2015): 106–22.

———. "¿En qué se reconoce el pensamiento? Poshegemonía e infrapolítica en la época de la realización de la metafísica." *Debats* 128, no. 3, special issue on "Infrapolítica y posthegemonía," ed. Alberto Moreiras (2015): 41–52.

———. *Soberanías en suspenso: Imaginación y violencia en América Latina.* Lanús: Ediciones La Cebra, 2013.

Virno, Paolo. *Multitude: Between Innovation and Negation.* Los Angeles: Semiotext(e), 2008.

Wainwright, Tom. *Narco-Nomics: How to Run a Drug Cartel.* New York: PublicAffairs, 2016.

Webb, Gary. *Dark Alliance: The CIA, the Contras, and the Crack Cocaine Explosion.* New York: Seven Stories, 1998.

Weil, Simone. "The Iliad, or the Poem of Force." *Chicago Review* 18, no. 2 (1965): 5–30.

———. *Oppression and Liberty.* Amherst: University of Massachusetts Press, 1978.

Whitener, Brian. *Crisis Cultures: The Rise of Finance in Mexico and Brazil.* Pittsburgh, PA: University of Pittsburgh Press, 2019.

Williams, Gareth. "Decontainment, Stasis, and Narco-Accumulation." *The Global South* 12, no. 2, special issue, "Men with Guns: The Poetics of Paramilitarism," ed. Joshua Lund and Anne Garland Mahler (2018): 90–108.

———. "Los límites de la hegemonía: Algunas reflexiones sobre *El momento Gramsciano* de Peter Thomas y *Hegemonía y estrategia socialista* de Ernesto Laclau y Chantal Mouffe." In *Poshegemonía: El final de un paradigma de la filosofía política en América Latina,* ed. Rodrigo Castro Orellana, 49–66. Madrid: Biblioteca Nueva, 2015.

———. *The Mexican Exception: Sovereignty, Police, and Democracy.* New York: Palgrave Macmillan, 2011.

———. *The Other Side of the Popular: Neoliberalism and Subalternity in Latin America.* Durham, NC: Duke University Press, 2002.

———. "The Subalternist Turn in Latin American Postcolonial Studies, or, Thinking in the Wake of What Went Down Yesterday (November 8, 2016)." *Política común* 10 (2016). https://quod.lib.umich.edu/p/pc/12322227.0010.016?view=text;rgn=main.

Winslow, Don. *The Cartel: A Novel.* New York: Random House, 2015.

———. *The Power of the Dog.* New York: Vintage, 2005.

Zavala, Oswaldo. *Los cárteles no existen: Narcotráfico y cultura en México.* Mexico: Malpaso, 2018.

# Index

GARETH WILLIAMS is Professor of Spanish and Latin American & Caribbean Studies at the University of Michigan, where he is Chair of the Department of Romance Languages and Literatures.

CPSIA information can be obtained
at www.ICGtesting.com
Printed in the USA
LVHW090007241120
672548LV00006B/479